STEVENSON • WATTERS • NOWAK • LAIHO

LUMBERJANES™

A TERRIBLE PLAN

BOOM!
BOX™

BOOM! BOX™

LUMBERJANES Volume Three, February 2016. Published by BOOM! Box, a division of Boom Entertainment, Inc. Lumberjanes is ™ & © 2016 Shannon Watters, Grace Ellis, Noelle Stevenson & Brooke Allen. Originally published in single magazine form as LUMBERJANES No. 9-12. ™ & © 2015 Shannon Watters, Grace Ellis, Noelle Stevenson & Brooke Allen. All rights reserved. BOOM! Box™ and the BOOM! Box logo are trademarks of Boom Entertainment, Inc., registered in various countries and categories. All characters, events, and institutions depicted herein are fictional. Any similarity between any of the names, characters, persons, events, and/or institutions in this publication to actual names, characters, and persons, whether living or dead, events, and/or institutions is unintended and purely coincidental. BOOM! Box does not read or accept unsolicited submissions of ideas, stories, or artwork.

A catalog record of this book is available from OCLC and from the BOOM! Studios website, www.boom-studios.com, on the Librarians Page.

BOOM! Studios, 5670 Wilshire Boulevard, Suite 450, Los Angeles, CA 90036-5679. Printed in China. First Printing.

ISBN: 978-1-60886-803-2, eISBN: 978-1-61398-474-1

THIS LUMBERJANES FIELD MANUAL BELONGS TO:

NAME:_____

TROOP:_____

DATE INVESTED:_____

FIELD MANUAL TABLE OF CONTENTS

LUMBERJANES
FIELD MANUAL

For the Intermediate Program

Tenth Edition • March 1984

Prepared for the

**Miss Qiunzella Thiskwin
Penniquiqul Thistle Crumpet's**

CAMP FOR ~~BOYS~~ HARDCORE LADY-TYPES

"Friendship to the Max!"

A MESSAGE FROM THE LUMBERJANES HIGH COUNCIL

miss Quinzella Thiskwin
Penniquiqul Thistle Crumpet's
Camp for
HARDCORE LADY TYPES
FRIENDSHIP to the MAX!

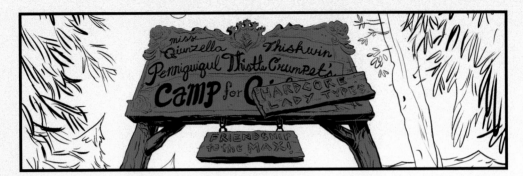

Catch and release is an essential part of learning how to fish and it also teaches us how to deal with many things that we might come across throughout our long-lived lives. In most cases anglers can keep their catch as a trophy or for their table. This is no different than when you pass a course and get to move forward in your education, you are essentially taking your trophy with you to move to the next step. Some trophies in life might be actual physical trophies but most will not be, they will be something that you will take you with and you with share with others, whether you realize it or not. When it comes to catch and release, there are cases when fish are released by state fishing rules and regulations or by choice. In the case of fishing rules and regulations, the fish may be under-sized, or the species may be regulated, or the waters themselves may be regulated. In other cases, it may be the intent of the angler from the outset. In all cases, every effort should be made to release fish quickly and unharmed. The rules are there for a reason, and just as any young scout will learn as they prepare for their first catch, these rules are meant to keep us safe and everything around us safe.

Rules are important. The rules are there for a reason. Rules give us a way to regulate ourselves, they give us a chance to enter worlds that we once only dreamed of as little girls. Think about the benefits of proper catch and release and how with those rules, it has proven vital to the future of a number of important fisheries around the country as it is a means of preserving and enhancing fish populations. By following the rules anglers contribute to fishing's long-standing commitment to conservation and preservation of our natural resources, a commitment that we share as a Lumberjane.

At this camp we look forward to showing you the world through our eyes, and we look forward to teaching you the practices and rules that will not only make your time with us enjoyable, but also unforgettable.

THE LUMBERJANES PLEDGE

I solemly swear to do my best
Every day, and in all that I do,
To be brave and strong,
To be truthful and compassionate,
To be interesting and interested,
To pay attention and question
The world around me,
To think of others first,
To always help and protect my friends,
[redacted]
And to make the world a better place
For Lumberjane scouts
And for everyone else.

THEN THERE'S A LINE ABOUT GOD, OR WHATEVER

LUMBERJANES™

A TERRIBLE PLAN

Written by
Noelle Stevenson
& Shannon Watters

"If You Got It Haunt It"
Illustrated by
Brittney Williams

"Wrong Number"
Illustrated by
Aimee Fleck

"Ghost Girl"
Written and Illustrated by
Faith Erin Hicks
with colors by **Maarta Laiho**

"Bad Candy"
Illustrated by
Rebecca Tobin

"Lonely Road"
Illustrated by
Carolyn Nowak

"Tailypo"
Illustrated by
Felicia Choo

"Old Betty"
Illustrated by
T. Zysk

Illustrated by
Carolyn Nowak
(Chapters Ten through Twelve)

Colors by
Maarta Laiho
(Chapters Ten through Twelve)

Letters by
Aubrey Aiese

Cover by
Noelle Stevenson

Badge Designs
Kate Leth and Scott Newman

Designer
Scott Newman

Associate Editor
Whitney Leopard

Editor
Dafna Pleban

*Special thanks to **Kelsey Pate**
for giving the Lumberjanes their name.*

Created by **Shannon Watters, Grace Ellis, Noelle Stevenson & Brooke Allen**

LUMBERJANES FIELD MANUAL
CHAPTER NINE

Lumberjanes "Out-of-Doors" Program Field

IF YOU GOT IT, HAUNT IT BADGE

"Because you weren't going to sleep anyway."

Things go bump in the night, it's basically the best time to go bump if one had to choose a timeframe. This is a lesson that every Lumberjane will learn as she continues on her path. Every Lumberjane should leave camp with the basic understanding of what is out there, how it could get you, and why it won't. She will encounter many problems through life and it will be this knowledge that will help her through. Scary stories are more than just a chance to give your neighbor goosebumps, they are also a chance for you to share your knowledge in a way that is not only fun, but entertaining. After all, aren't the best scary tales the ones that have a little truth to them? It should come as no surprise that both friendship and scary story telling are combined in the *If You Got It, Haunt It* badge.

Haunting is just a fact of life. Spirits are everywhere. Both living and long past, they often want to reach out to

us in the only ways they know how. A Lumberjane will want to not only help these spirits, but with her friends, she'll be able to go above and beyond the call of a scout. And if she is unable to connect with the spirits as so many before her have, well then hopefully she'll at least be able to come up with a good story or two around the camp fire.

To obtain the *If You Got It, Haunt It* badge, a Lumberjane must have already received her *Up All Night* badge, and should have shown great promise in her creative thinking skills. A good picture might be worth a thousand words, but in the same amount of words, a good story is only the beginning. There are many things we can learn from the great storytellers before us. The women who put pen to paper and wove such intricate drama that their stories still stick with us to this very day. It is important for a Lumberjane to

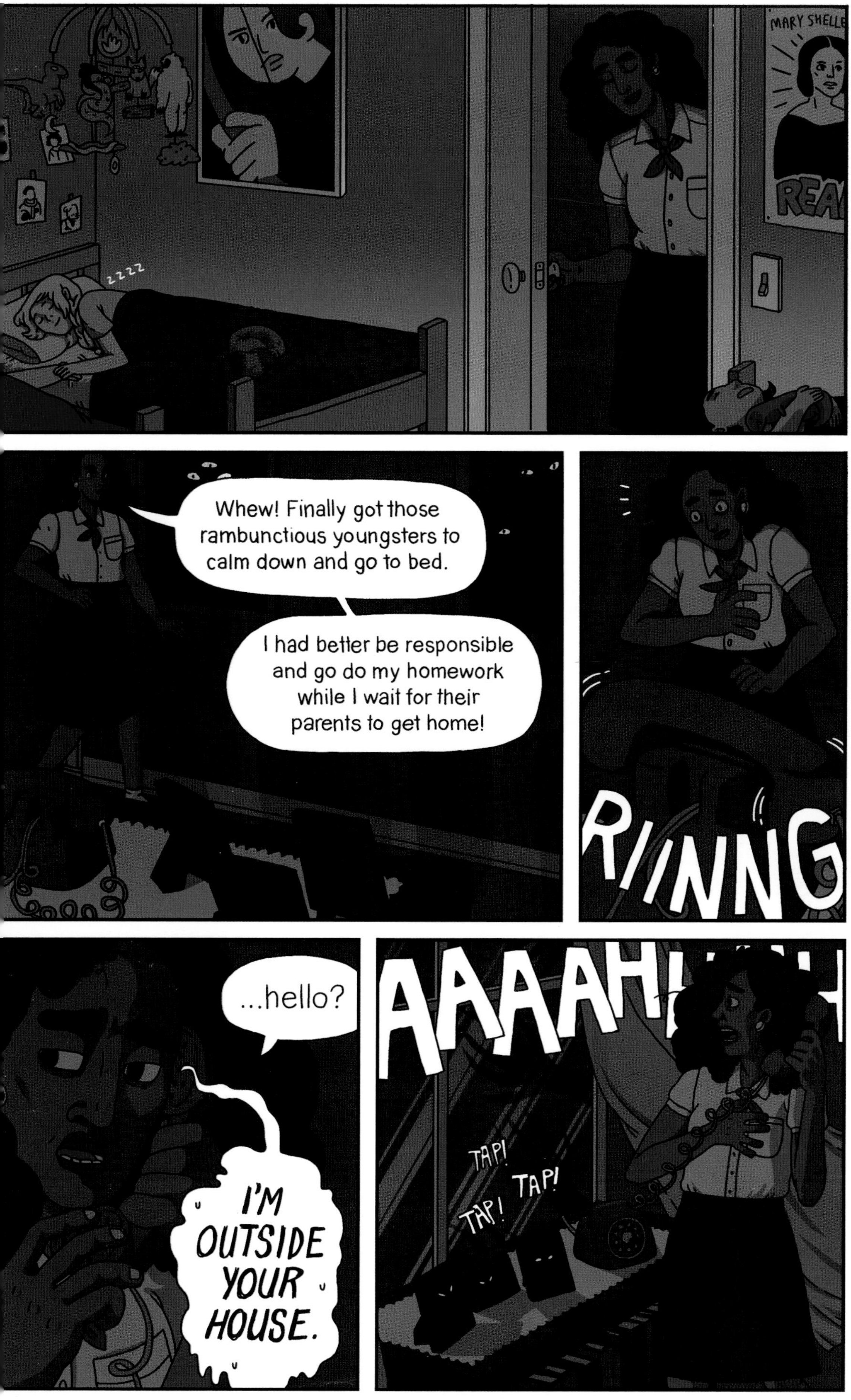
MARY SHELLE
REA
ZZZZ
Whew! Finally got those rambunctious youngsters to calm down and go to bed.
I had better be responsible and go do my homework while I wait for their parents to get home!
RIINNG
...hello?
I'M OUTSIDE YOUR HOUSE.
AAAAH
TAP! TAP! TAP!

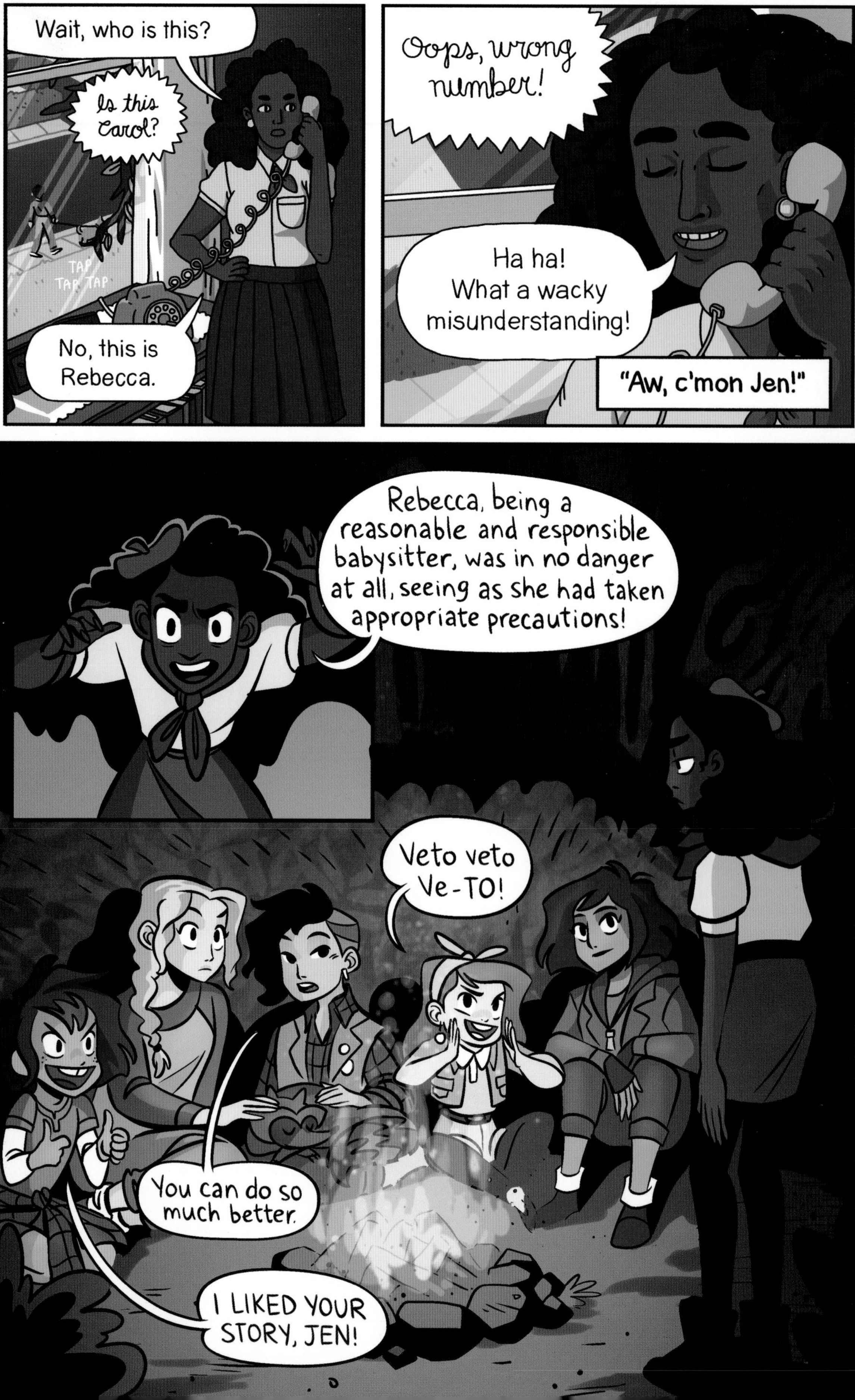

Wait, who is this?
Is this Carol?
TAP TAP TAP
No, this is Rebecca.
Oops, wrong number!
Ha ha! What a wacky misunderstanding!
"Aw, c'mon Jen!"
Rebecca, being a reasonable and responsible babysitter, was in no danger at all, seeing as she had taken appropriate precautions!
Veto veto Ve-TO!
You can do so much better.
I LIKED YOUR STORY, JEN!

for one, think it's RIDICULOUS that a badge like IF YOU'VE GOT IT, HAUNT IT is even REQUIRED for getting your silver axe pin.

Heh, yeah, those gals in the badge division of the Lumberjanes Grand Lodge are always up for a chuckle.

Remember when April had to get her NANCY DRAW badge in forensic sketching before she could earn her ILLUSTRIOUS ILLUSTRATION pin?

Luckily we were all so good at describing the suspect...

Who knew that in the end, the culprit in "The Case of My Absconded Ascot" was really...

YOU!

Mher?

Jo, Jo! Tell the one about the **Ghost Girl!**

Ha, you got it!

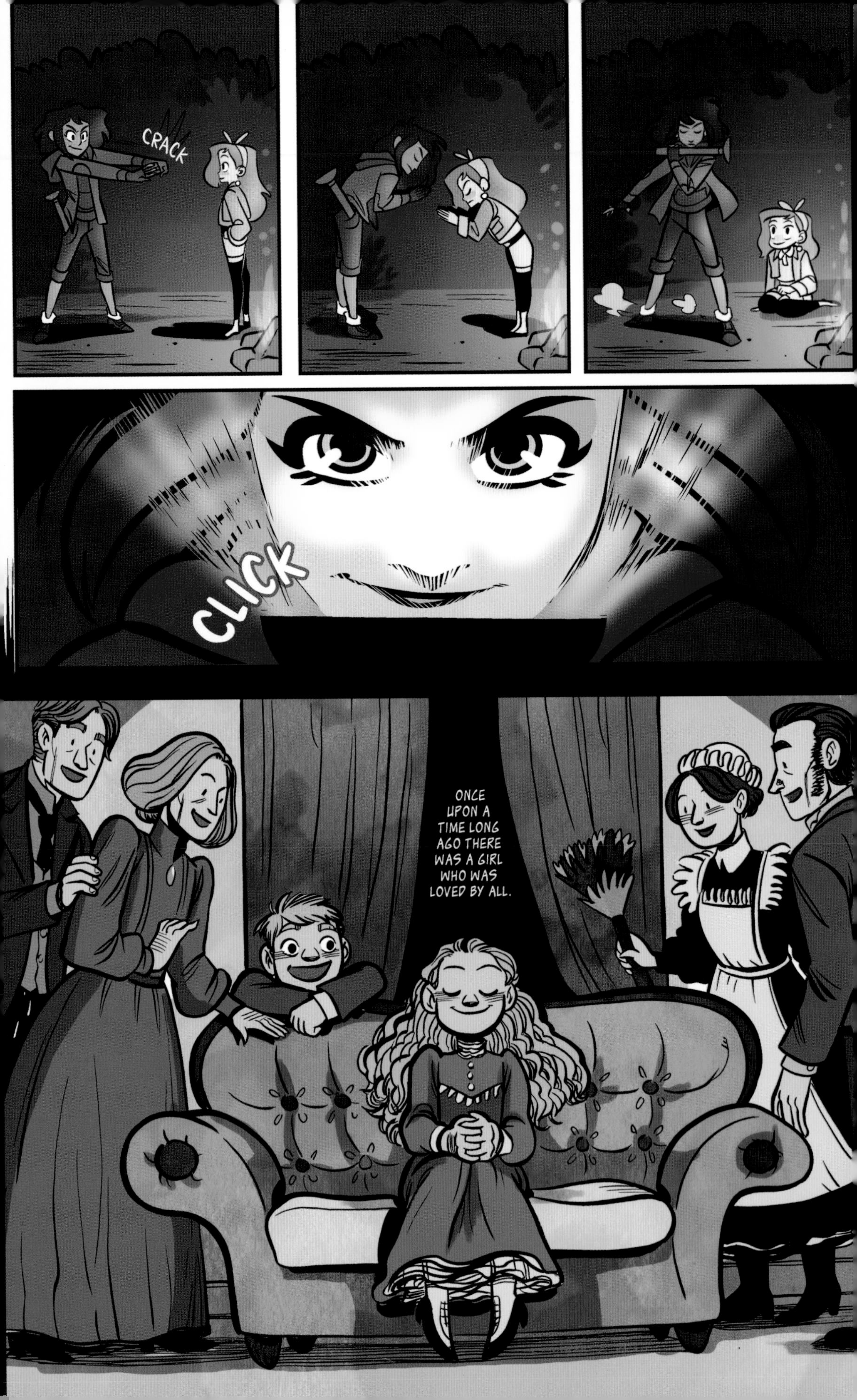
CRACK
CLICK
ONCE UPON A TIME LONG AGO THERE WAS A GIRL WHO WAS LOVED BY ALL.

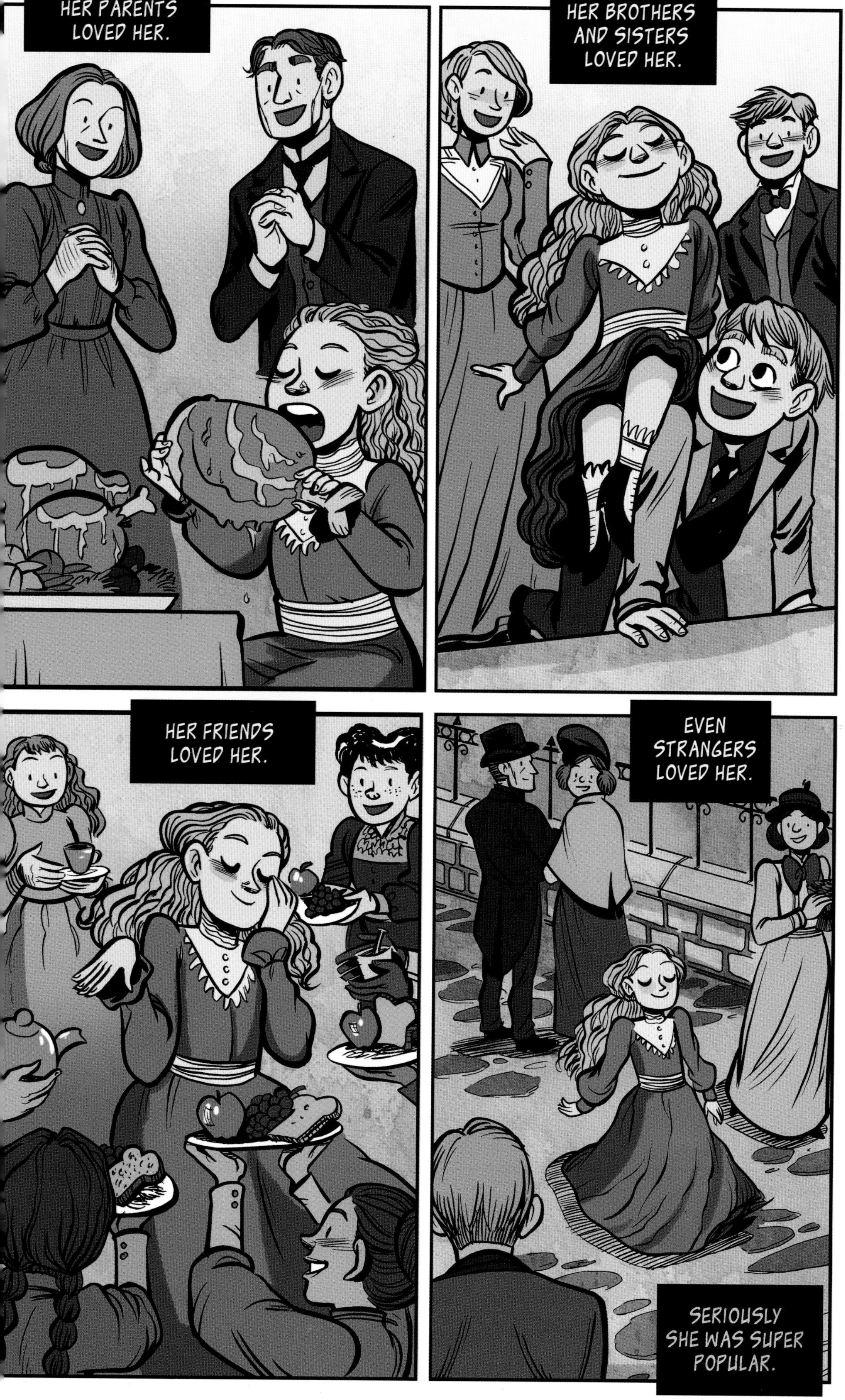
HER PARENTS LOVED HER.
HER BROTHERS AND SISTERS LOVED HER.
HER FRIENDS LOVED HER.
EVEN STRANGERS LOVED HER.
SERIOUSLY SHE WAS SUPER POPULAR.

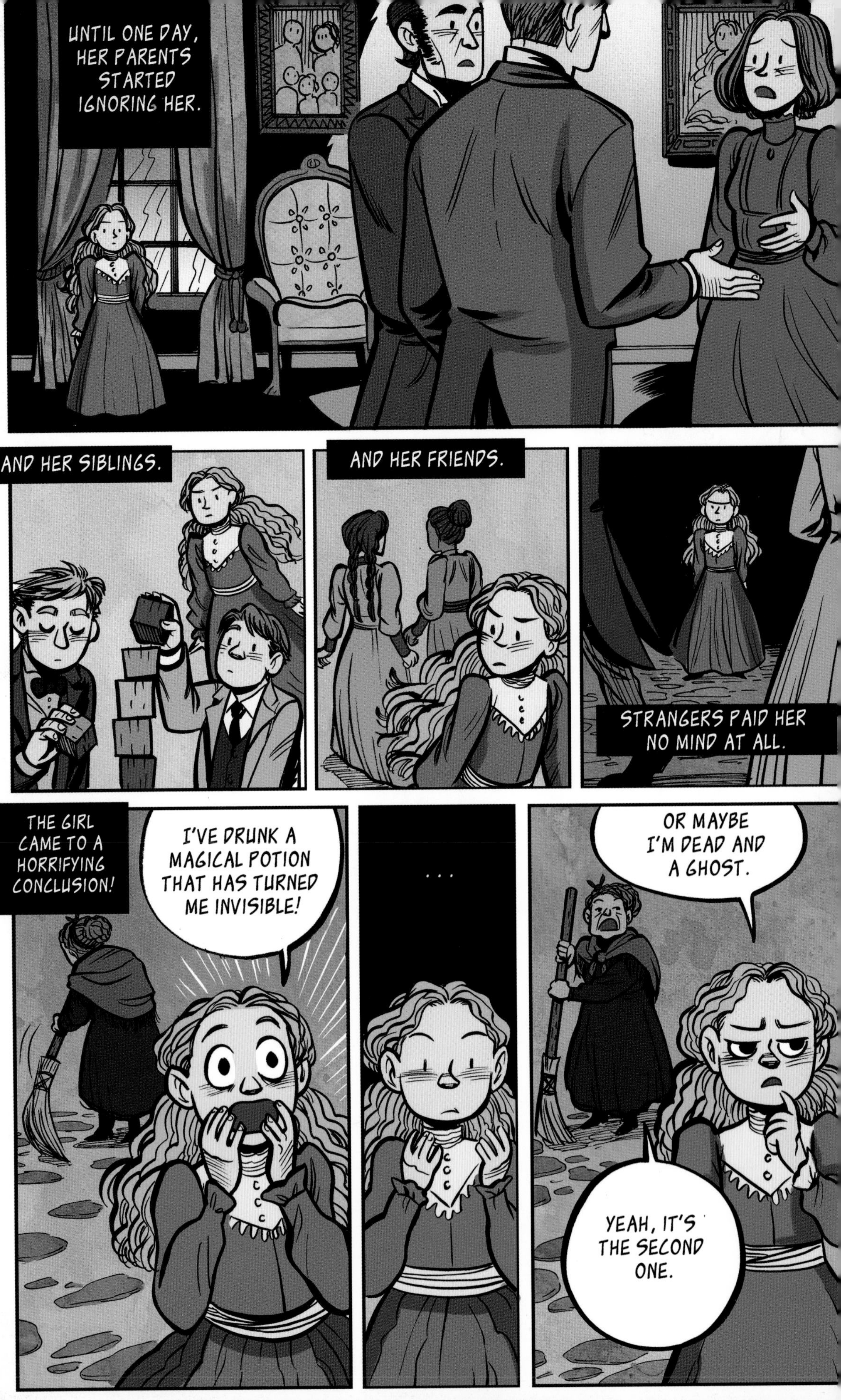
UNTIL ONE DAY, HER PARENTS STARTED IGNORING HER.
AND HER SIBLINGS.
AND HER FRIENDS.
STRANGERS PAID HER NO MIND AT ALL.
THE GIRL CAME TO A HORRIFYING CONCLUSION!
I'VE DRUNK A MAGICAL POTION THAT HAS TURNED ME INVISIBLE!
. . .
OR MAYBE I'M DEAD AND A GHOST.
YEAH, IT'S THE SECOND ONE.

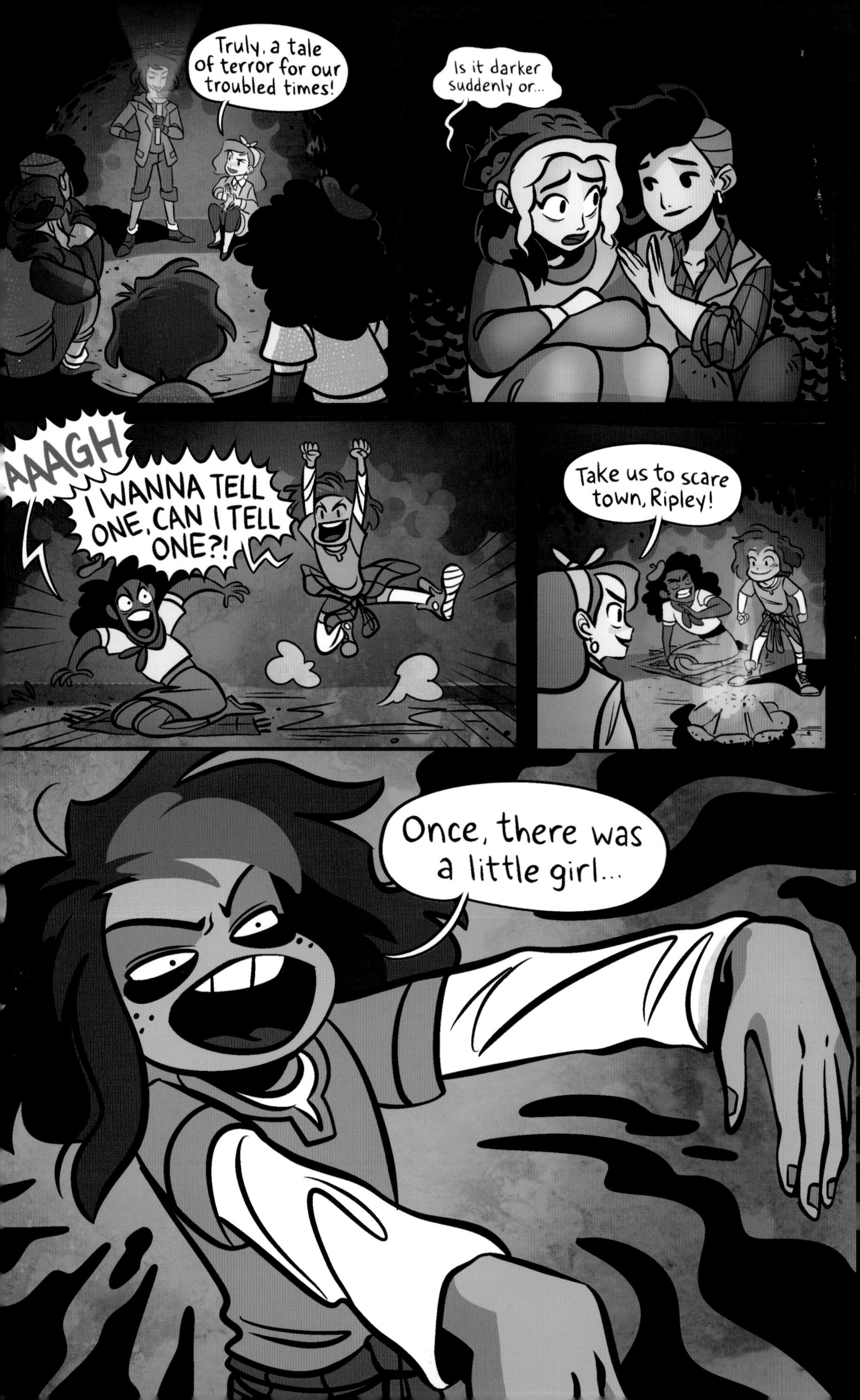
Truly, a tale of terror for our troubled times!
Is it darker suddenly or...
AAAGH
I WANNA TELL ONE, CAN I TELL ONE?!
Take us to scare town, Ripley!
Once, there was a little girl...

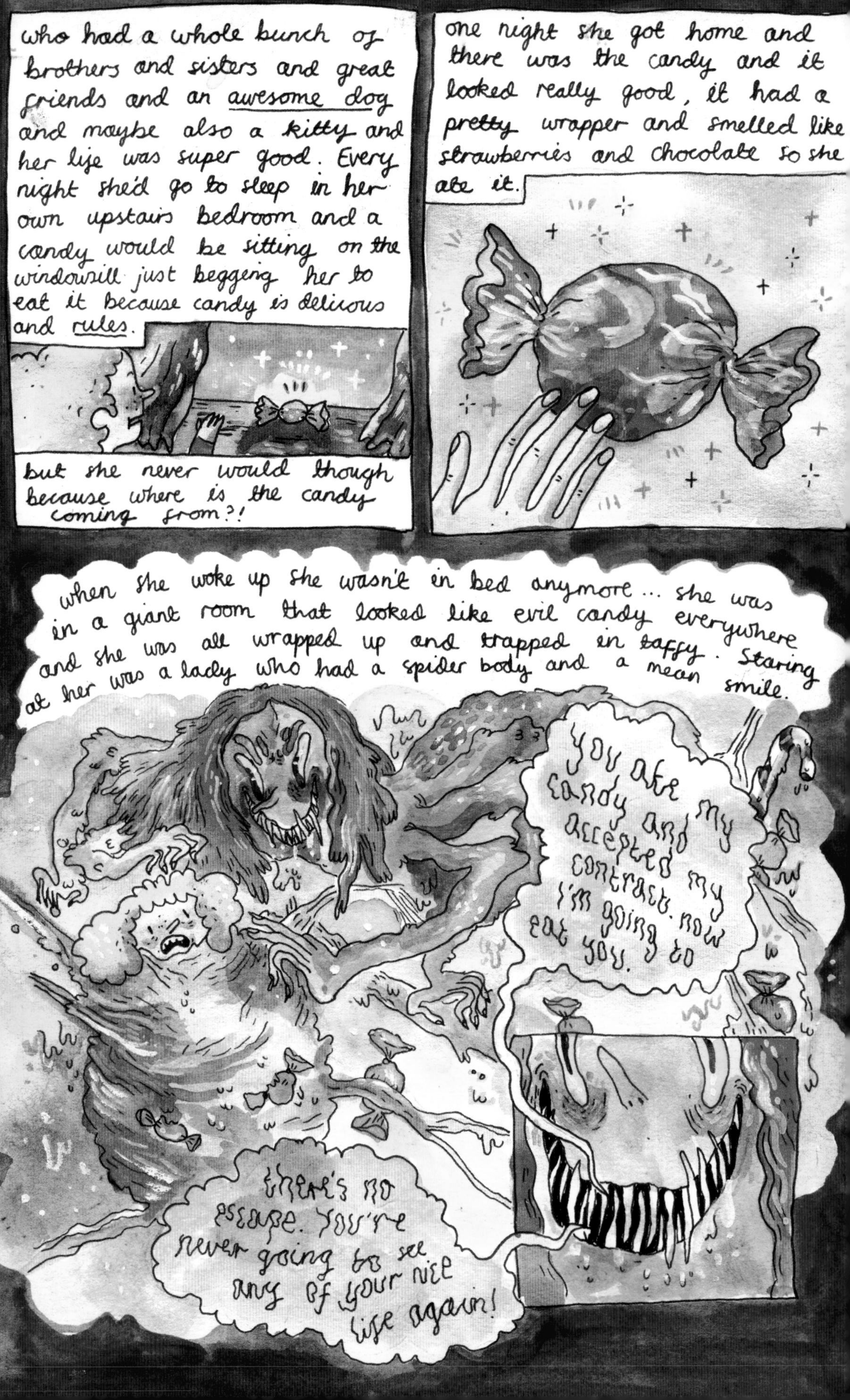
who had a whole bunch of brothers and sisters and great friends and an awesome dog and maybe also a kitty and her life was super good. Every night she'd go to sleep in her own upstairs bedroom and a candy would be sitting on the windowsill just begging her to eat it because candy is delicious and rules.
but she never would though because where is the candy coming from?!
one night she got home and there was the candy and it looked really good, it had a pretty wrapper and smelled like strawberries and chocolate so she ate it.
when she woke up she wasn't in bed anymore... she was in a giant room that looked like evil candy everywhere and she was all wrapped up and trapped in taffy. Staring at her was a lady who had a spider body and a mean smile.
You ate my candy and accepted my contract. Now I'm going to eat you.
There's no escape. You're never going to see any of your nice life again!

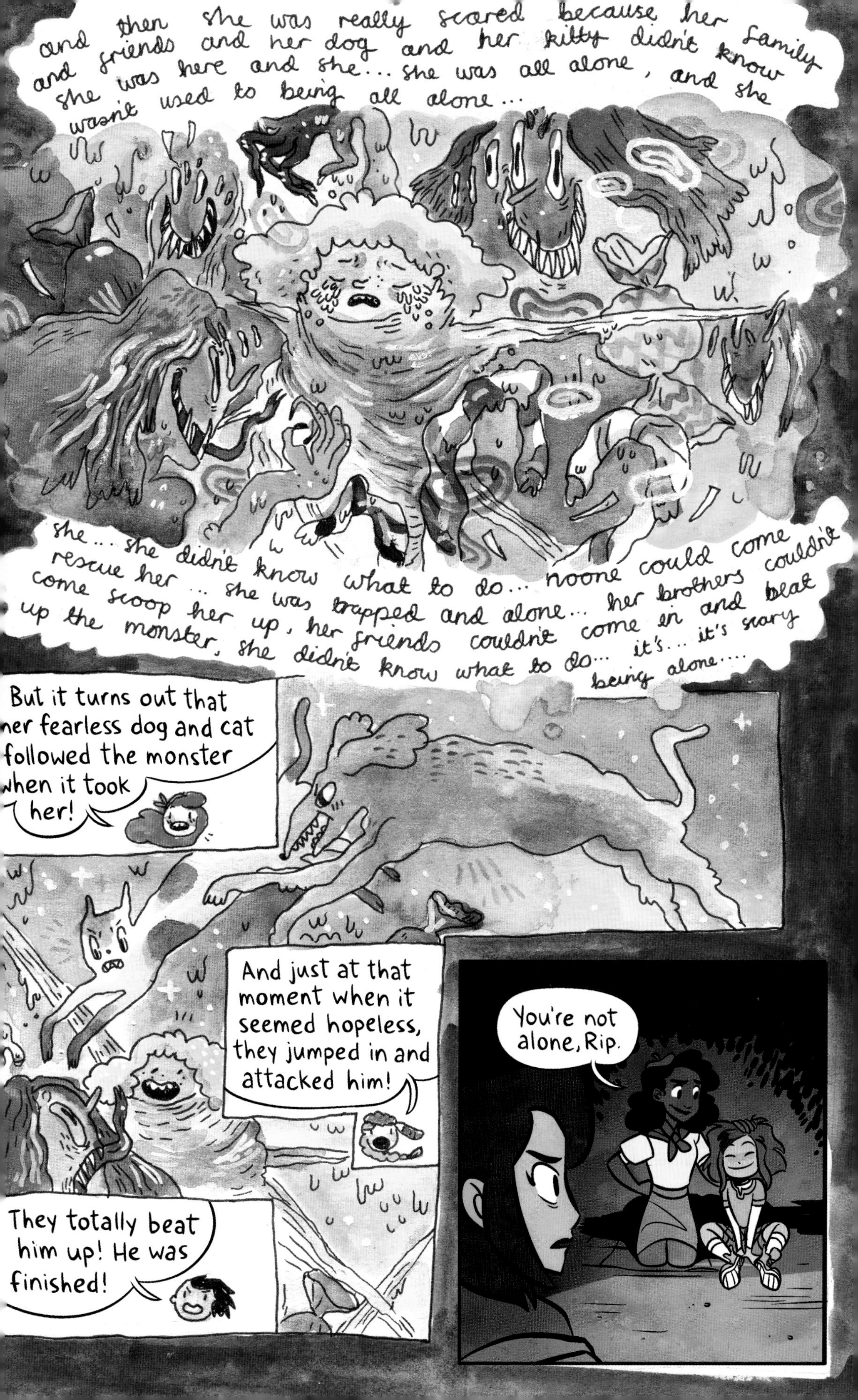
and then she was really scared because her family and friends and her dog and her kitty didn't know she was here and she... she was all alone, and she wasn't used to being all alone...
she... she didn't know what to do... noone could come rescue her ... she was trapped and alone... her brothers couldn't come scoop her up, her friends couldn't come in and beat up the monster, she didn't know what to do... it's... it's scary being alone....
But it turns out that her fearless dog and cat followed the monster when it took her!
And just at that moment when it seemed hopeless, they jumped in and attacked him!
They totally beat him up! He was finished!
You're not alone, Rip.

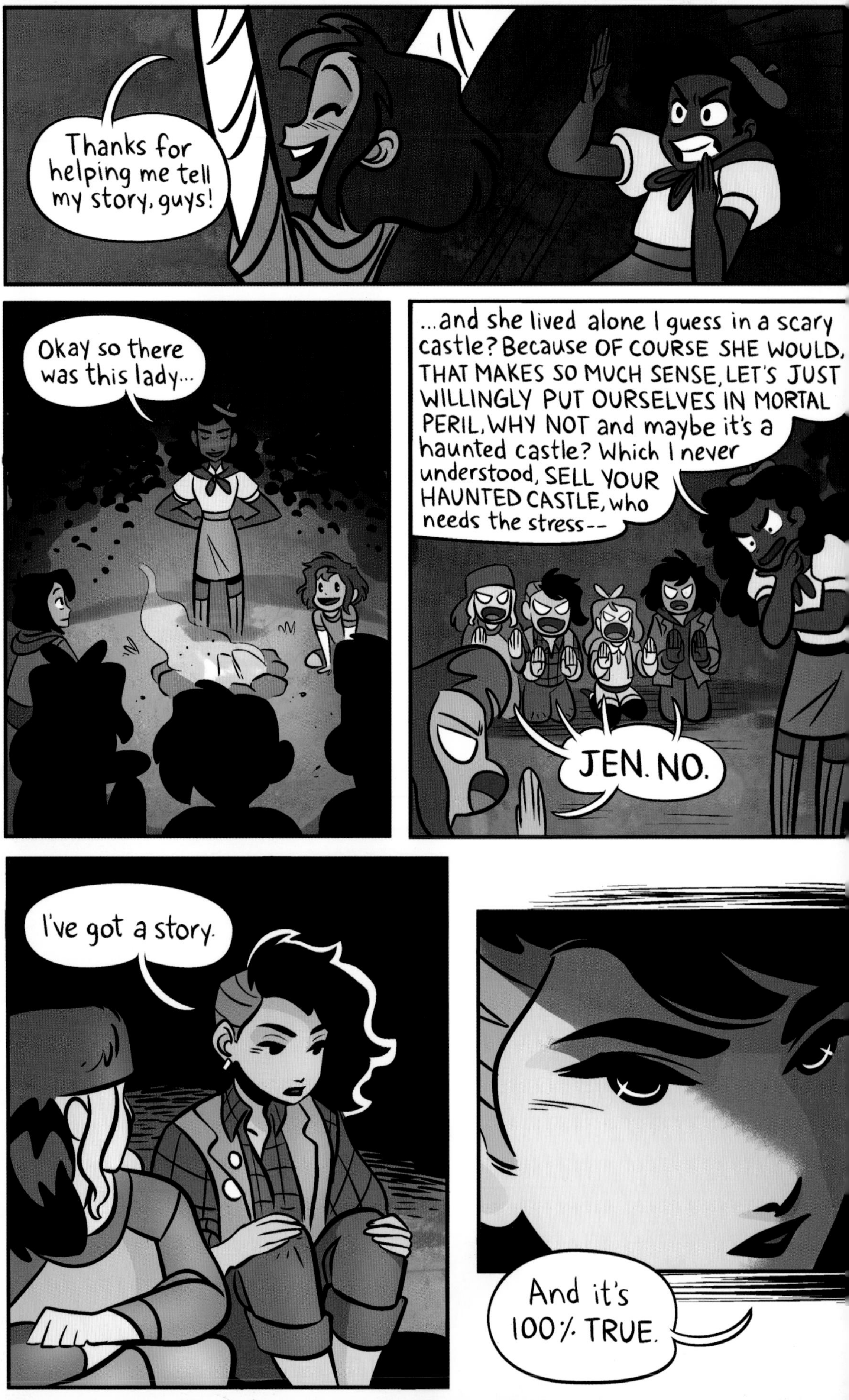
Thanks for helping me tell my story, guys!
Okay so there was this lady...
...and she lived alone I guess in a scary castle? Because OF COURSE SHE WOULD, THAT MAKES SO MUCH SENSE, LET'S JUST WILLINGLY PUT OURSELVES IN MORTAL PERIL, WHY NOT and maybe it's a haunted castle? Which I never understood, SELL YOUR HAUNTED CASTLE, who needs the stress--
JEN. NO.
I've got a story.
And it's 100% TRUE.

ONCE, THERE WAS A YOUNG COUPLE, DRIVING HOME AT NIGHT IN THE WINTER. IT WAS ALREADY LATE, SO THE MAN DECIDED TO TAKE A SHORTCUT.

WITHIN MINUTES, OF COURSE, THEY WERE LOST.

BEFORE THEY COULD MANAGE TO FIND THEIR WAY, THEIR TIRE BLEW OUT...

POP!

...SENDING THEM CAREENING INTO A SHALLOW DITCH JUST OFF THE ROAD.

IT WAS MUCH TOO COLD FOR THEM TO WALK ANYWHERE, AND THEY WERE LOST TOO REMOTELY TO CALL FOR HELP. ALL THE COUPLE COULD DO WAS SIT IN THE WARMTH OF THE RUNNING CAR AND WAIT UNTIL MORNING.

THE WOMAN SOON FELL ASLEEP AND IT WAS THEN THAT THE MAN BEGAN TO HEAR LONG, DISQUIETING SCRATCHES PULLING ALONG THE TOP OF THE CAR.

SKRRRRRRTCHHHH SKRRRRRRTCHHH SKRRITCH

AT FIRST HE THOUGHT IT WAS THE WIND, BUT THE SCRATCHES CONTINUED TO GET LOUDER...AND LOUDER...

EVENTUALLY IT WAS ALL THE MAN COULD HEAR!! SCRATCHES COMING FROM EVERY DIRECTION, SOMEONE... SOMETHING TRYING TO GET INTO THE CAR, THE SOURCE OBSCURED BY THE THICK SNOW SWIRLING OUTSIDE.

SKRRRR RRRRITCH SKRRRITCHHHH SKRITCHHHH SKRITCH SKRITCHHHH SSSSSSSKRRR

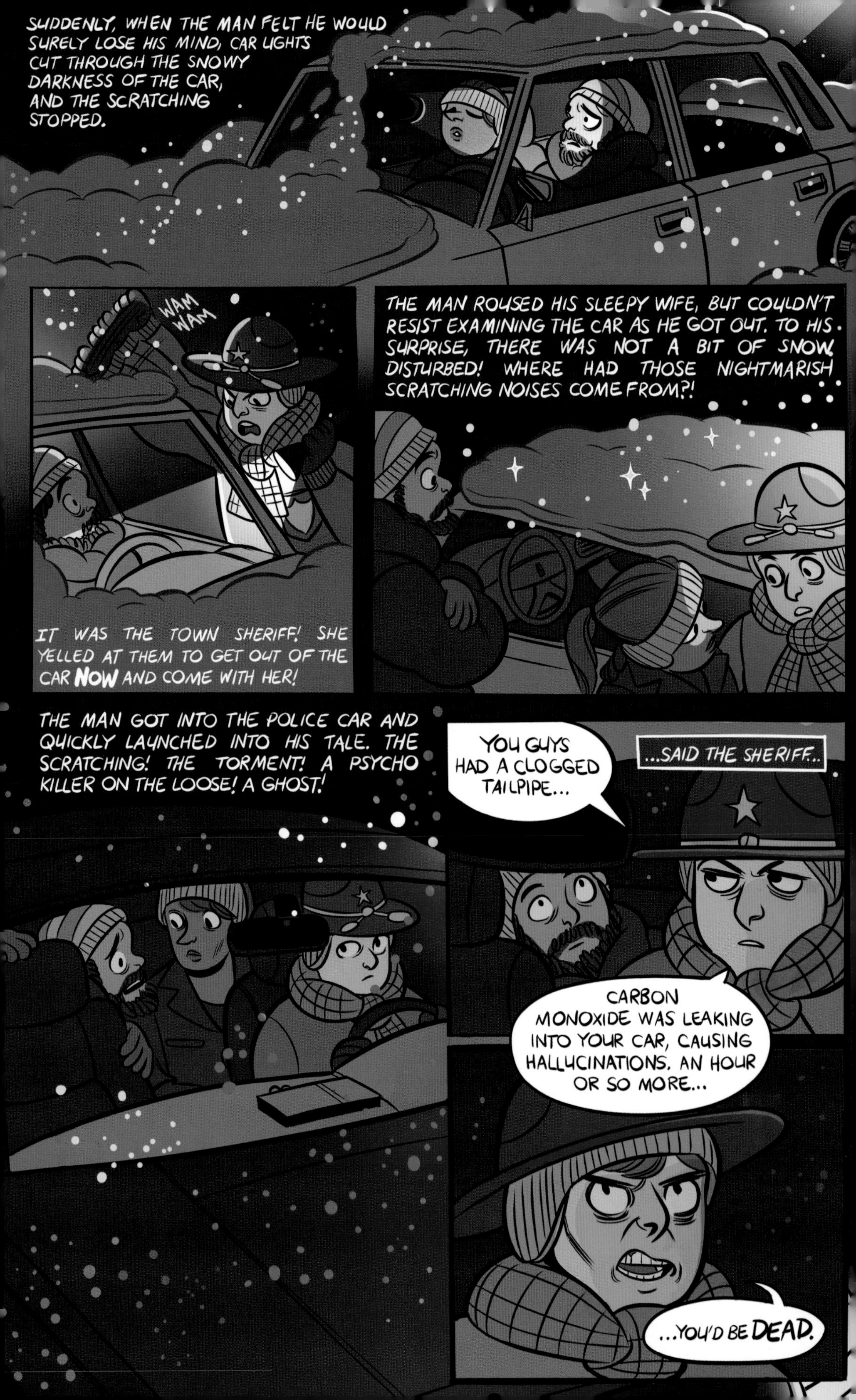
SUDDENLY, WHEN THE MAN FELT HE WOULD SURELY LOSE HIS MIND, CAR LIGHTS CUT THROUGH THE SNOWY DARKNESS OF THE CAR, AND THE SCRATCHING STOPPED.
WAM WAM
IT WAS THE TOWN SHERIFF! SHE YELLED AT THEM TO GET OUT OF THE CAR NOW AND COME WITH HER!
THE MAN ROUSED HIS SLEEPY WIFE, BUT COULDN'T RESIST EXAMINING THE CAR AS HE GOT OUT. TO HIS SURPRISE, THERE WAS NOT A BIT OF SNOW DISTURBED! WHERE HAD THOSE NIGHTMARISH SCRATCHING NOISES COME FROM?!
THE MAN GOT INTO THE POLICE CAR AND QUICKLY LAUNCHED INTO HIS TALE. THE SCRATCHING! THE TORMENT! A PSYCHO KILLER ON THE LOOSE! A GHOST!
YOU GUYS HAD A CLOGGED TAILPIPE...
...SAID THE SHERIFF...
CARBON MONOXIDE WAS LEAKING INTO YOUR CAR, CAUSING HALLUCINATIONS. AN HOUR OR SO MORE...
...YOU'D BE DEAD.

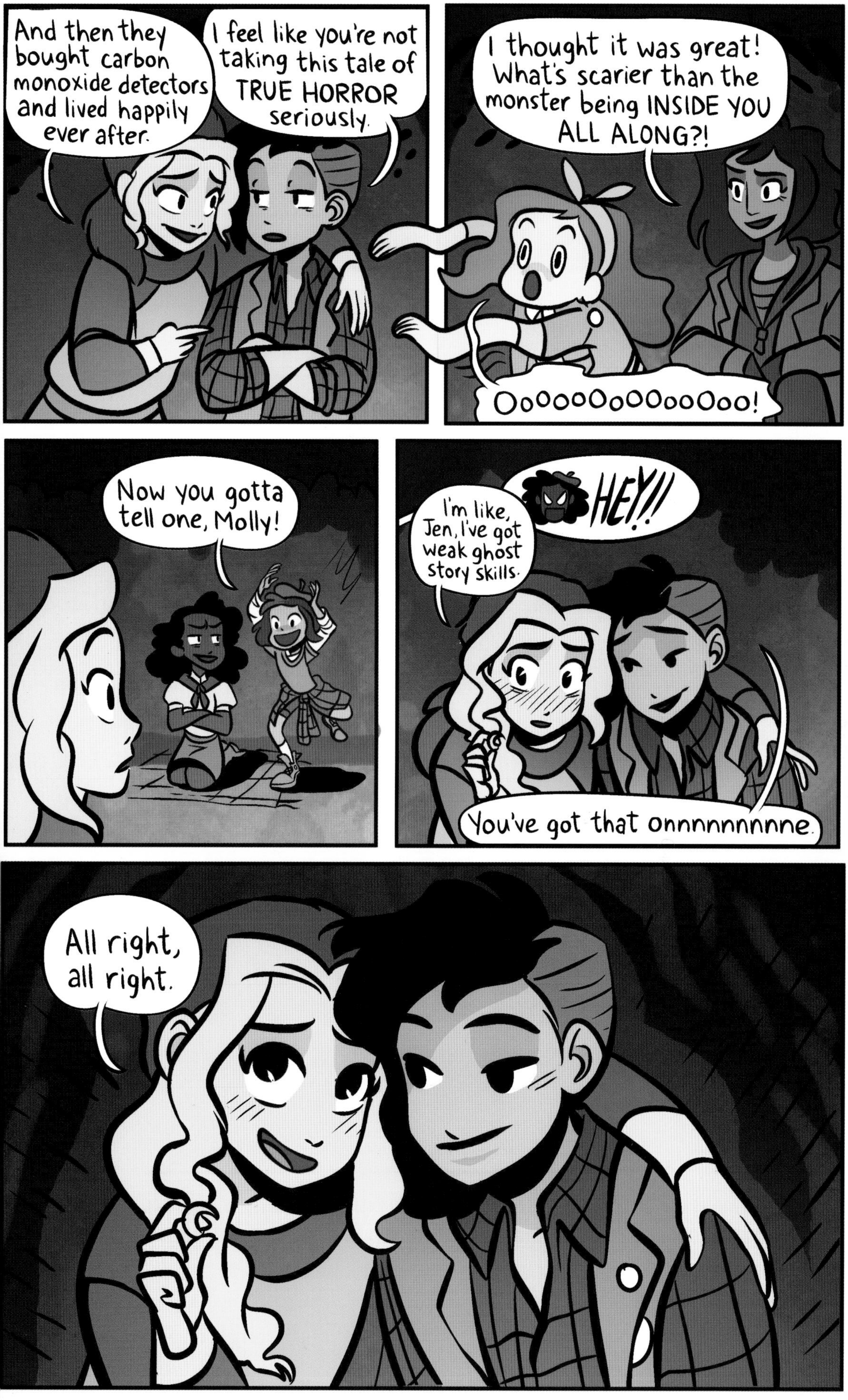
And then they bought carbon monoxide detectors and lived happily ever after.
I feel like you're not taking this tale of TRUE HORROR seriously.
I thought it was great! What's scarier than the monster being INSIDE YOU ALL ALONG?!
OoOoOOoOOooOoo!
Now you gotta tell one, Molly!
I'm like, Jen, I've got weak ghost story skills.
HEY!!
You've got that onnnnnnnne.
All right, all right.

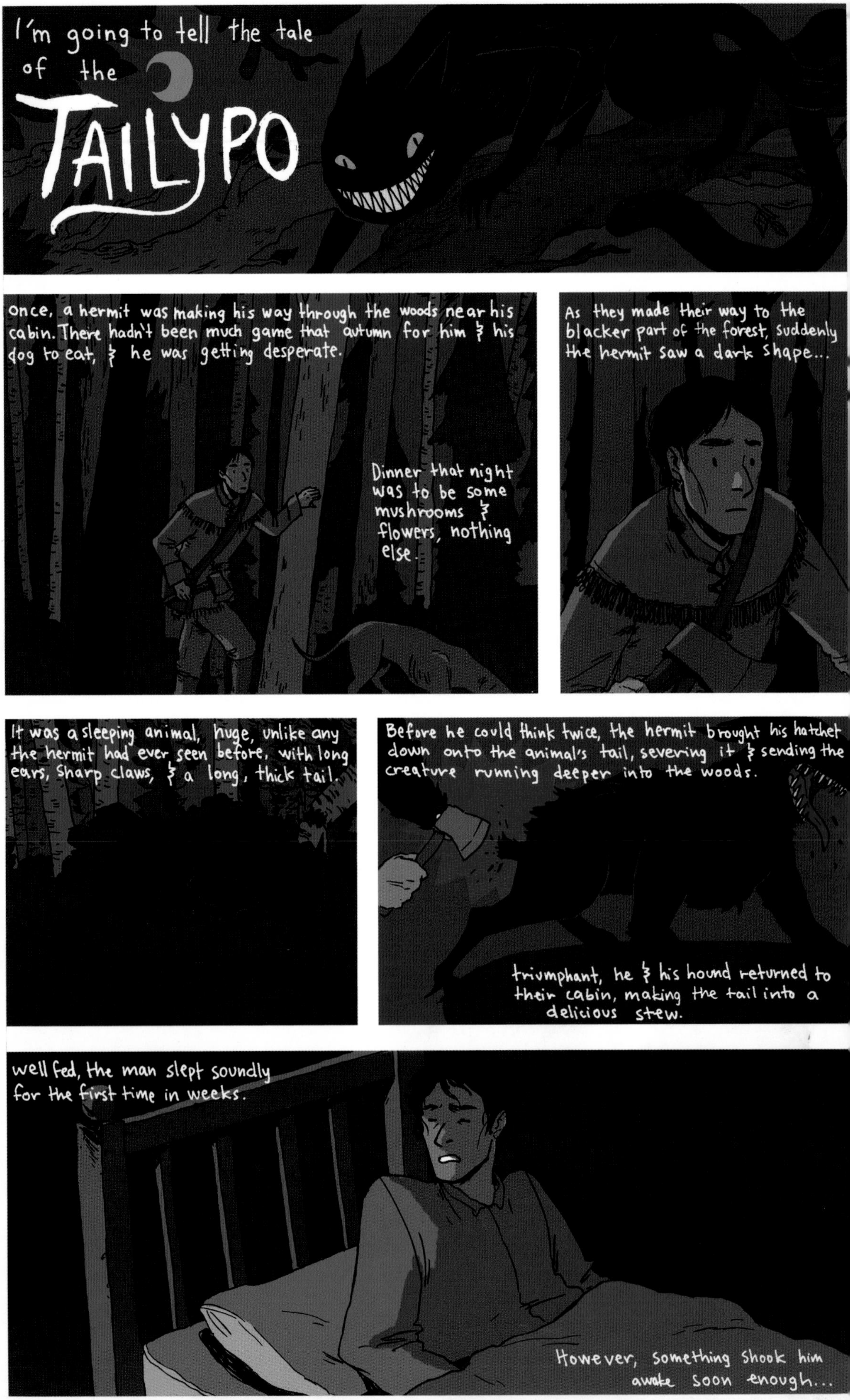
I'm going to tell the tale of the
TAILYPO
Once, a hermit was making his way through the woods near his cabin. There hadn't been much game that autumn for him & his dog to eat, & he was getting desperate.
Dinner that night was to be some mushrooms & flowers, nothing else.
As they made their way to the blacker part of the forest, suddenly the hermit saw a dark shape...
It was a sleeping animal, huge, unlike any the hermit had ever seen before, with long ears, sharp claws, & a long, thick tail.
Before he could think twice, the hermit brought his hatchet down onto the animal's tail, severing it & sending the creature running deeper into the woods.
triumphant, he & his hound returned to their cabin, making the tail into a delicious stew.
well fed, the man slept soundly for the first time in weeks.
However, something shook him awake soon enough...

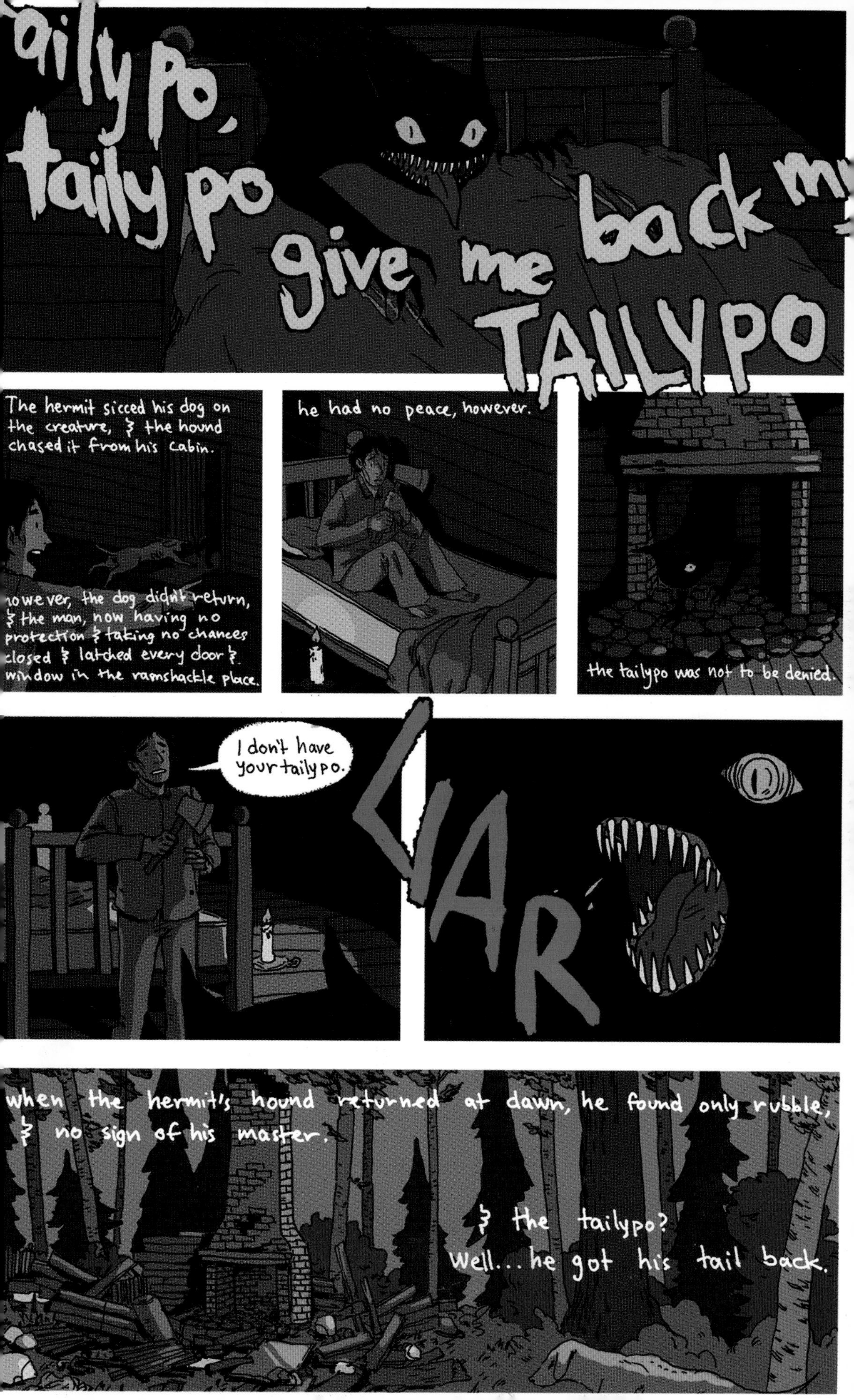

tailypo, tailypo
give me back my TAILYPO
The hermit sicced his dog on the creature, & the hound chased it from his cabin.
however, the dog didn't return, & the man, now having no protection & taking no chances closed & latched every door & window in the ramshackle place.
he had no peace, however.
the tailypo was not to be denied.
I don't have your tailypo.
WAR
when the hermit's hound returned at dawn, he found only rubble, & no sign of his master.
& the tailypo?
Well... he got his tail back.

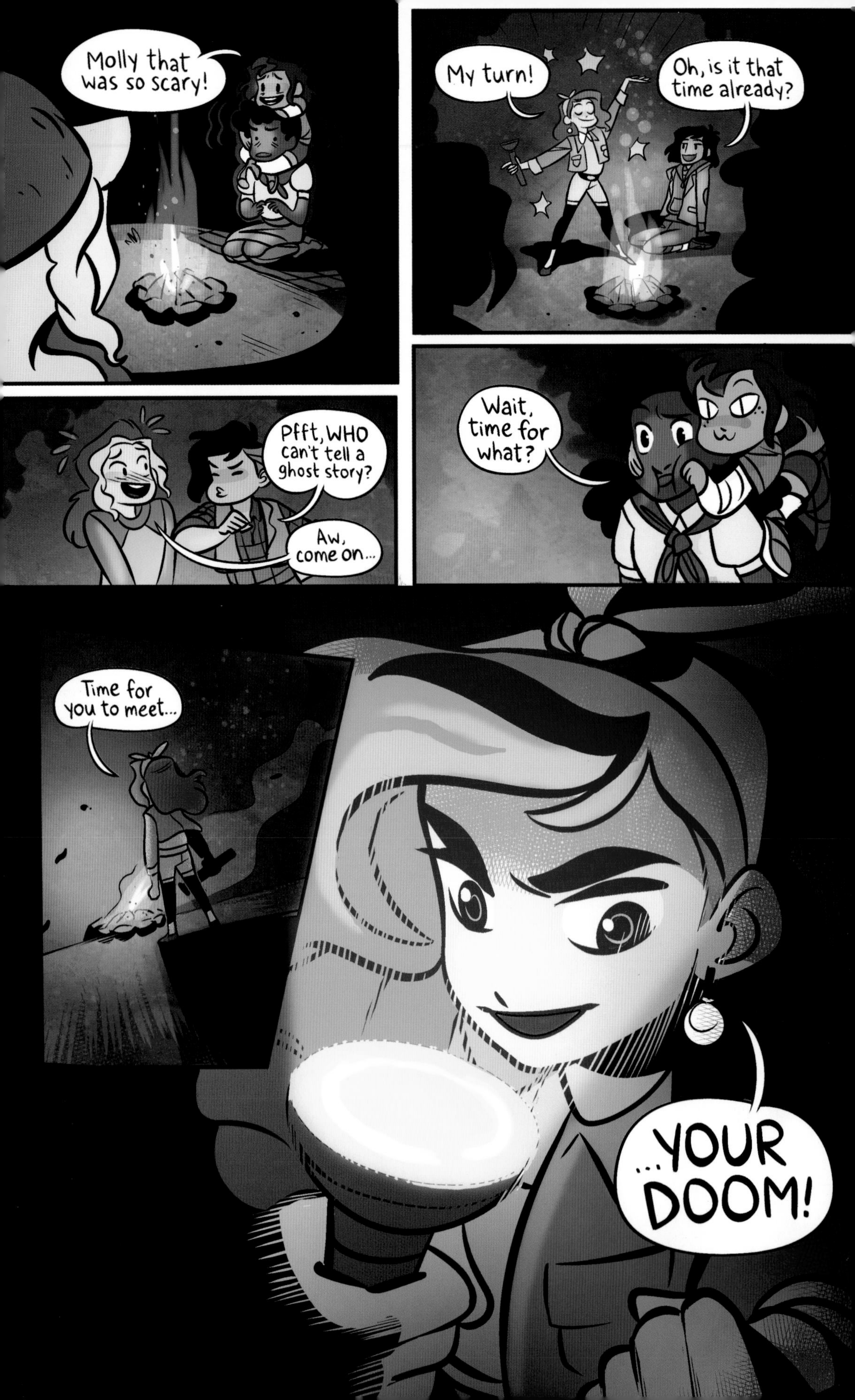
Molly that was so scary!
My turn!
Oh, is it that time already?
Pfft, WHO can't tell a ghost story?
Aw, come on...
Wait, time for what?
Time for you to meet...
...YOUR DOOM!

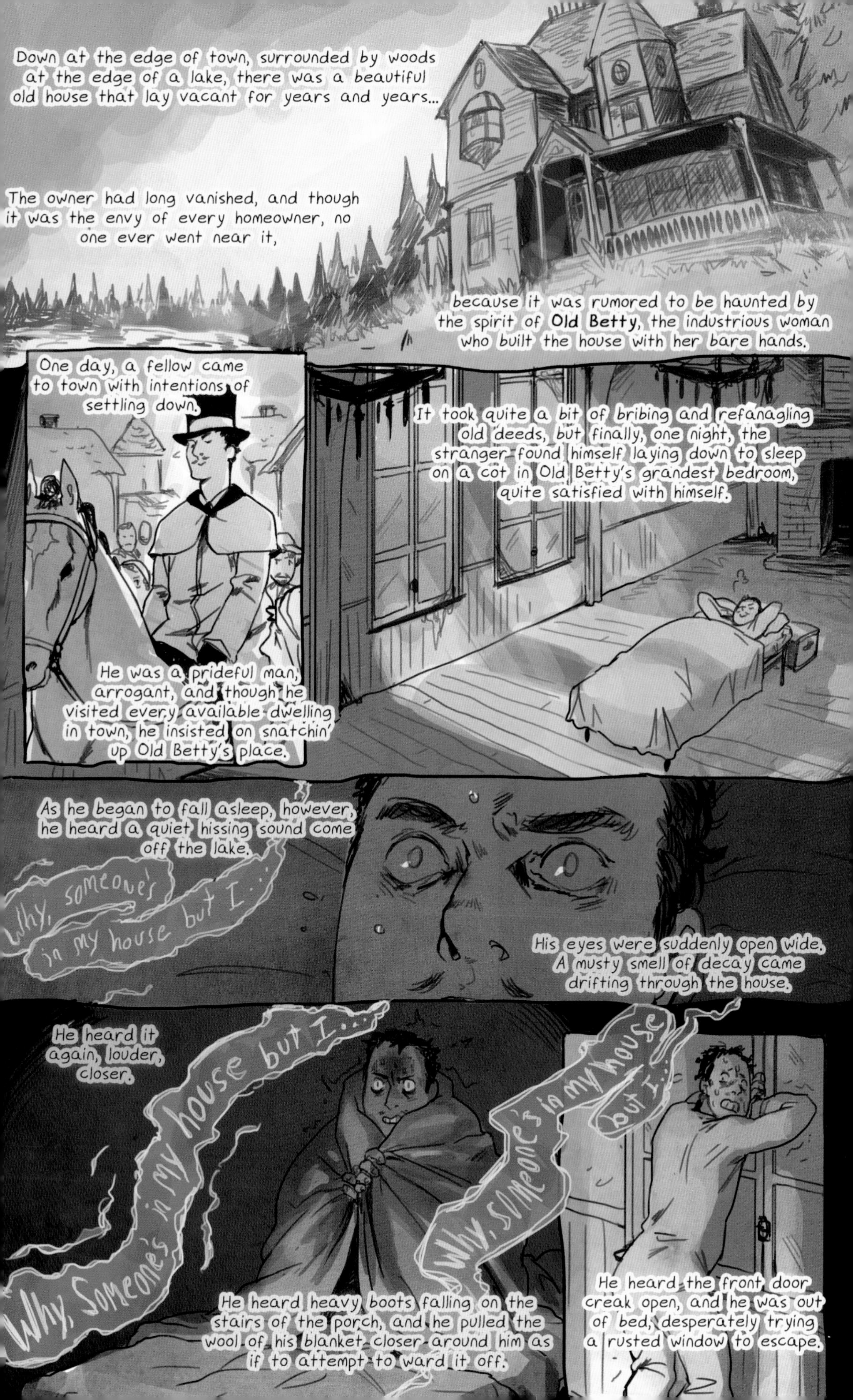
Down at the edge of town, surrounded by woods at the edge of a lake, there was a beautiful old house that lay vacant for years and years...
The owner had long vanished, and though it was the envy of every homeowner, no one ever went near it,
because it was rumored to be haunted by the spirit of Old Betty, the industrious woman who built the house with her bare hands.
One day, a fellow came to town with intentions of settling down.
He was a prideful man, arrogant, and though he visited every available dwelling in town, he insisted on snatchin' up Old Betty's place.
It took quite a bit of bribing and refanagling old deeds, but finally, one night, the stranger found himself laying down to sleep on a cot in Old Betty's grandest bedroom, quite satisfied with himself.
As he began to fall asleep, however, he heard a quiet hissing sound come off the lake.
Why, someone's in my house but I...
His eyes were suddenly open wide. A musty smell of decay came drifting through the house.
He heard it again, louder, closer.
Why, Someone's in my house but I...
He heard heavy boots falling on the stairs of the porch, and he pulled the wool of his blanket closer around him as if to attempt to ward it off.
Why, Someone's in my house but I...
He heard the front door creak open, and he was out of bed, desperately trying a rusted window to escape.

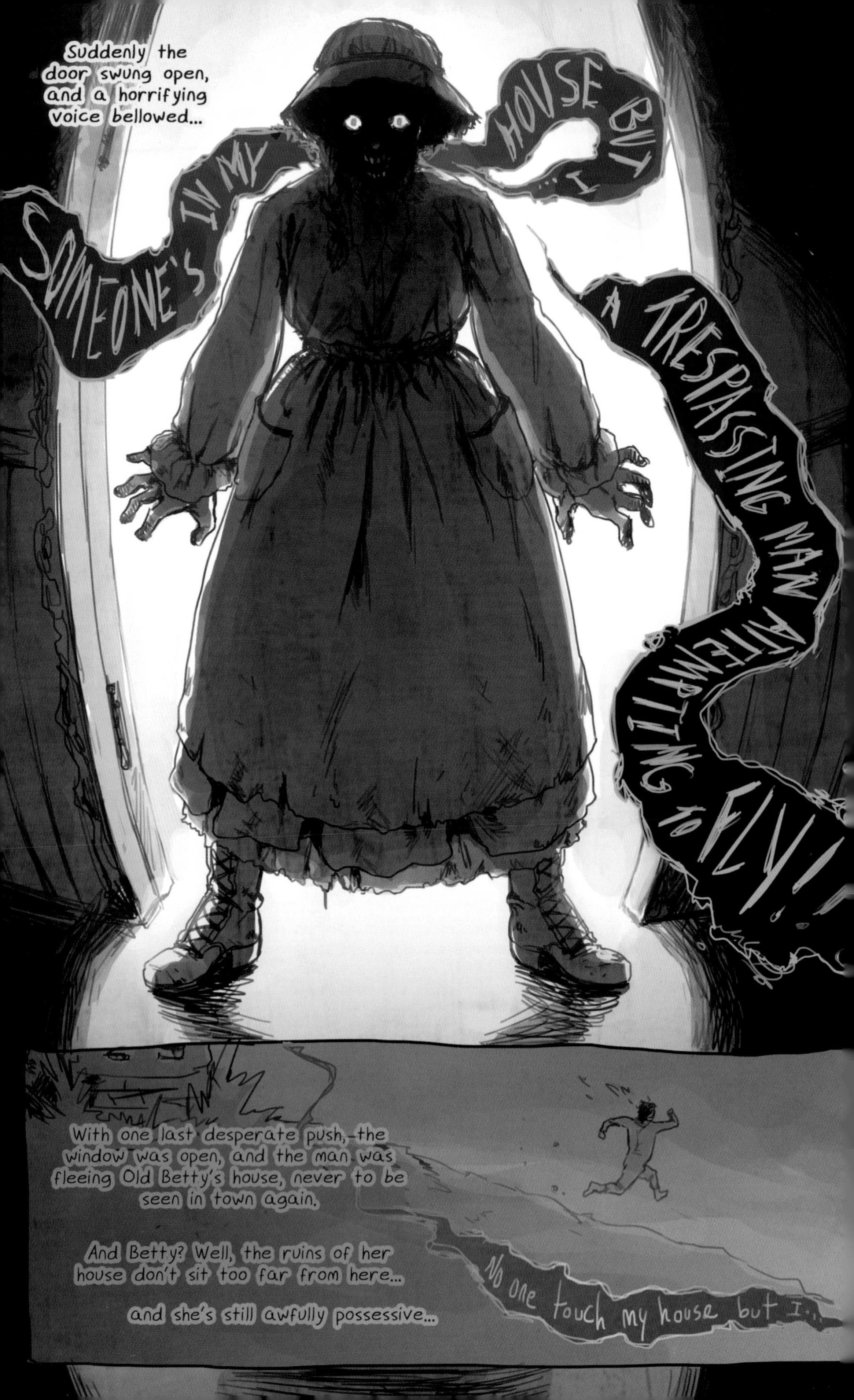
Suddenly the door swung open, and a horrifying voice bellowed...
SOMEONE'S IN MY HOUSE BUT I...
A TRESPASSING MAN ATTEMPTING TO FLY!!
With one last desperate push, the window was open, and the man was fleeing Old Betty's house, never to be seen in town again.
And Betty? Well, the ruins of her house don't sit too far from here...
and she's still awfully possessive...
No one touch my house but I...

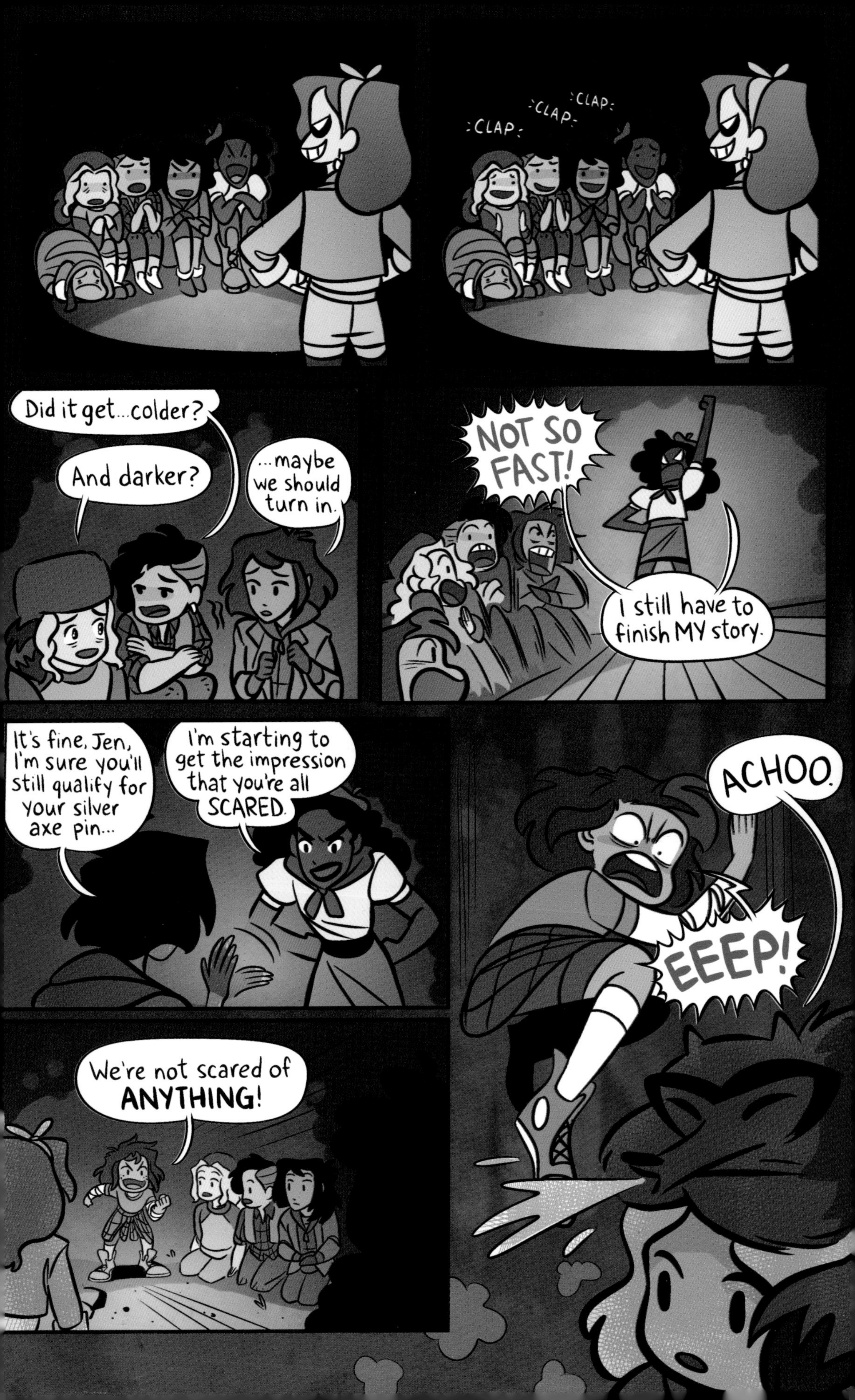

:CLAP:
:CLAP:
:CLAP:
Did it get...colder?
And darker?
...maybe we should turn in.
NOT SO FAST!
I still have to finish MY story.
It's fine, Jen, I'm sure you'll still qualify for your silver axe pin...
I'm starting to get the impression that you're all SCARED.
We're not scared of ANYTHING!
ACHOO.
EEEP!

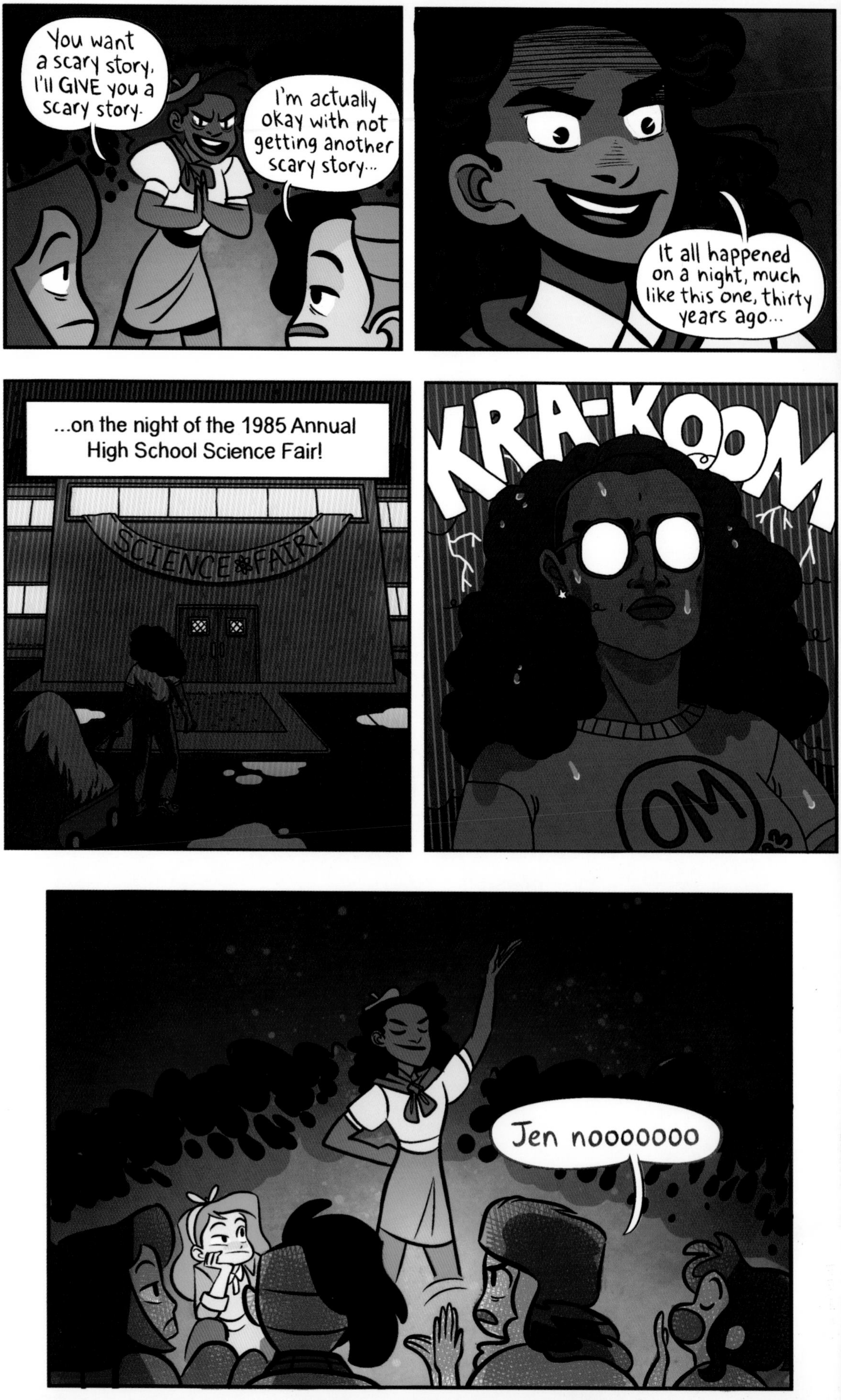
You want a scary story, I'll GIVE you a scary story.
I'm actually okay with not getting another scary story...
It all happened on a night, much like this one, thirty years ago...
...on the night of the 1985 Annual High School Science Fair!
SCIENCE FAIR!
KRA-KOOM
OM
Jen nooooooo

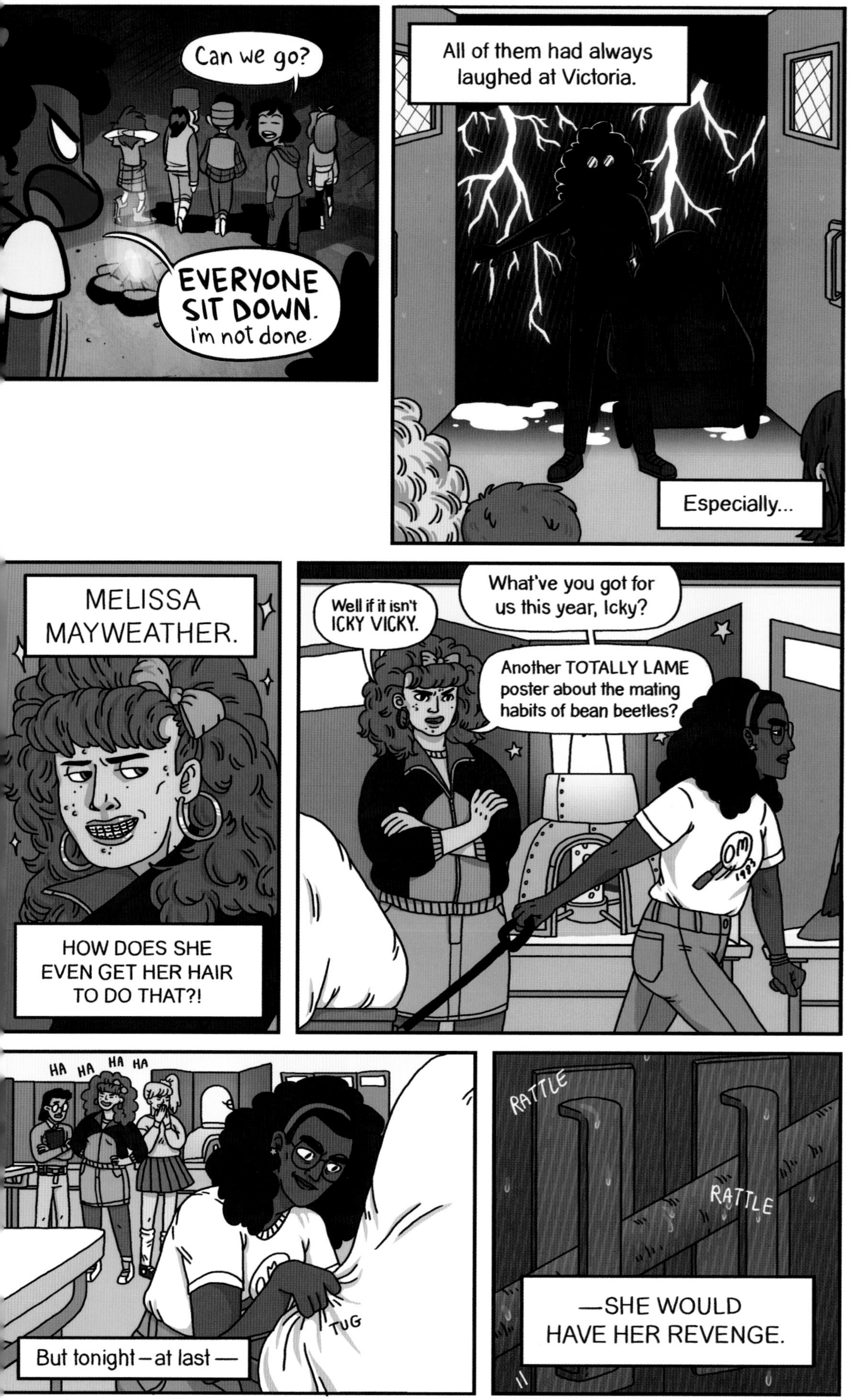
Can we go?
EVERYONE SIT DOWN. I'm not done.
All of them had always laughed at Victoria.
Especially...
MELISSA MAYWEATHER.
HOW DOES SHE EVEN GET HER HAIR TO DO THAT?!
Well if it isn't ICKY VICKY.
What've you got for us this year, Icky?
Another TOTALLY LAME poster about the mating habits of bean beetles?
HA HA HA HA
But tonight—at last—
TUG
RATTLE
RATTLE
—SHE WOULD HAVE HER REVENGE.

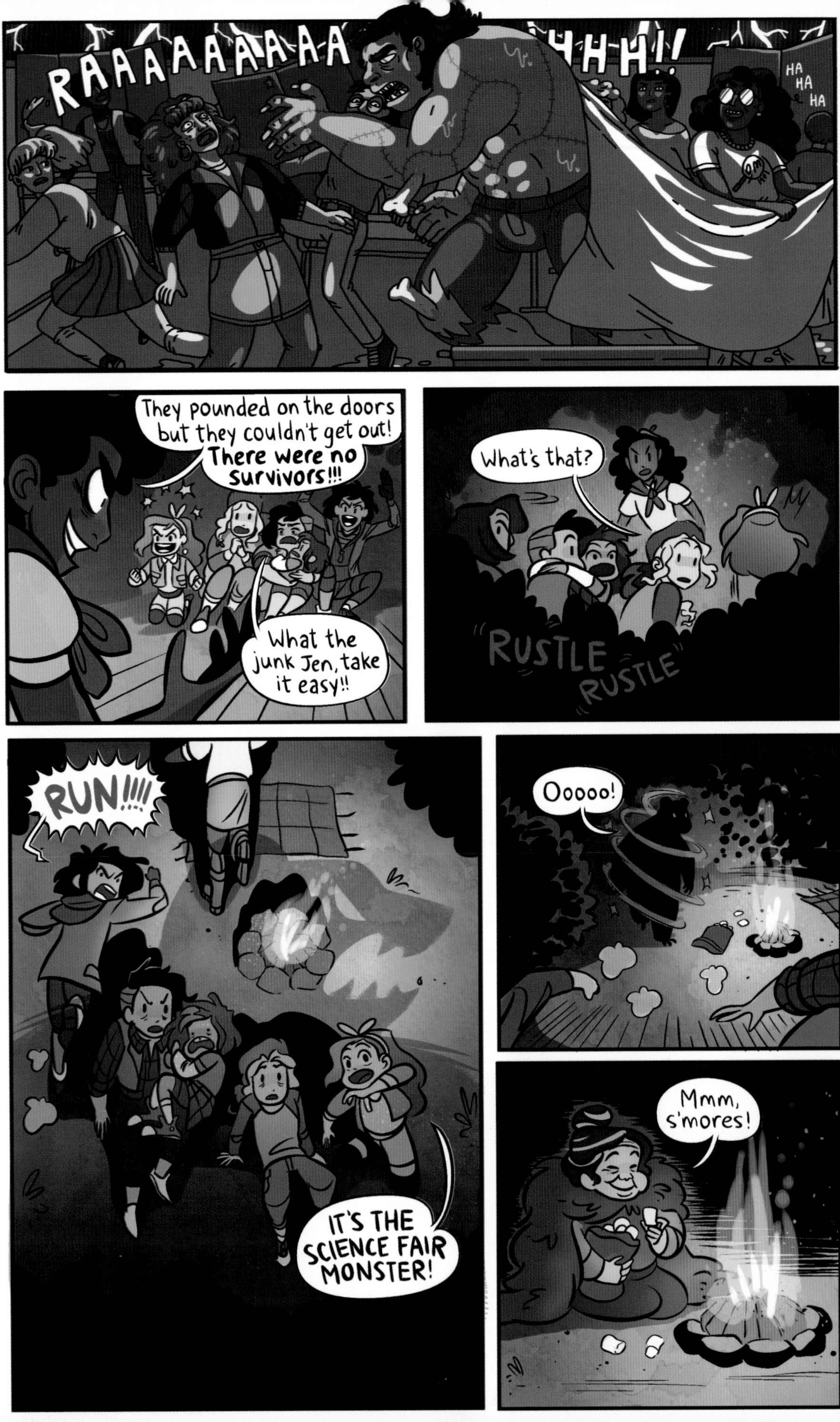
RAAAAAAAAAAAHHHH!!
HA HA HA
They pounded on the doors but they couldn't get out! There were no survivors!!!
What the junk Jen, take it easy!!
What's that?
RUSTLE RUSTLE
RUN!!!!
IT'S THE SCIENCE FAIR MONSTER!
Ooooo!
Mmm, s'mores!

will co...

The...
It he...
appearan...
dress f...
Further...
Lumber...
to have...
part in...
Thisw...
Hardc...
have...
them...

TELL US A SCARY STORY!

...E UNIFORM

...hould be worn at camp
...vents when Lumberjanes
...n may also be worn at other
...ions. It should be worn as a
...the uniform dress with
...rect shoes, and stocking or
...out grows her uniform or
...ter Lumberjane.
...a she has
...her
...her

LADIES DIG THE HAT

The...
yellow, short sle...
emb...
the w...
choose...
slacks,...
made o...
out-of-do...
green bere...
the colla...
Shoes ma...
heels, round...ings o...
socks shou...th the shoes or wi...
the uniform. Ne...es, bracelets, or othe...elry do...
belong with a Lumberjane uniform.

HOW TO WEAR T...

To look well in a unifor...
uniform be kept in good...
pressed. See that the skirt is the...
height and build, that the belt is ad...
that your shoes and stockings are in...the
uniform, that you watch your posture and c...ourself
with dignity and grace. If the beret is removed indoors,
be sure that your hair is neat and kept in place with an
insconspicuous clip or ribbon. When you wear a
Lumberjane uniform you are identified as a member of
this organization and you should be doubly careful to
conduct yourself in a way that will show everyone that
courtesy and thoughtfullness are part of being a
Lumberjane. People are likely to judge a whole nation by
the selfishness of a few individuals, to criticize a whole
family because of the misconduct of one member, and to
feel unkindly toward and organization because of the

The unifor...
helps to cre...
in a group....
active life th...
another bond...
future, and pr...
in order to b...
Lumberjane pr...
Penniquiqul Thi...ore Lady
Types, but m...s will wish to have one. They
can either bu...the uniform, or make it themselves from
materials available at the trading post.

WELCOME TO SCARE TOWN, POPULATION: YOU

LUMBERJANES FIELD MANUAL
CHAPTER TEN

Lumberjanes "Cooking" Program Field

ABSENCE MAKES THE HEART GROW FONDANT BADGE

"Fondant gives the heart diabetes, it's the circle of life."

Everyone and everything needs food to survive. It is not something that is unique only to people or to creatures and it is something everyone must acknowledge. At Lumberjane camp, every scout will learn that while food is essential, that doesn't mean we can't have some fun with it first. Now while some ladies may have been taught that it is not polite to play with their food, the Lumberjane High Council disagrees. Everything is meant to be fun and exhilarating, we should constantly be learning and improving ourselves just as we should always be laughing. Life is meant to be fun and if that means we get to bake some cakes in the process then every Lumberjane should put on her best apron and go at it.

The *Absence Makes The Heart Grow Fondant* badge represents a skill that all Lumberjanes will be taught. As a Lumberjane it will be understood that every scout should be able to rely on just herself in any situation. That means

she should not only know how to handle a bear attack without harming herself or the animals around her, but she should also know how to create an elaborate cake that will entertain all her guests not only visually but as well as in flavor. The way around the kitchen will be no match for any Lumberjane as she masters her adaptability and her problem solving skills while at this camp.

To obtain the *Absence Makes The Heart Grow Fondant* badge a Lumberjane must be participating in a bake off. She will be given an already baked cake of her choice of flavor as well as the tools to mold her frosting to the design she prefers. Once the time starts the Lumberjane scout must completely decorate her cake in a creative style that will be judged by the leader of the class, and while all art is subjective, the instructions given before the bake off will be clearly given and understood by all participants. In the end, it will be the scout who

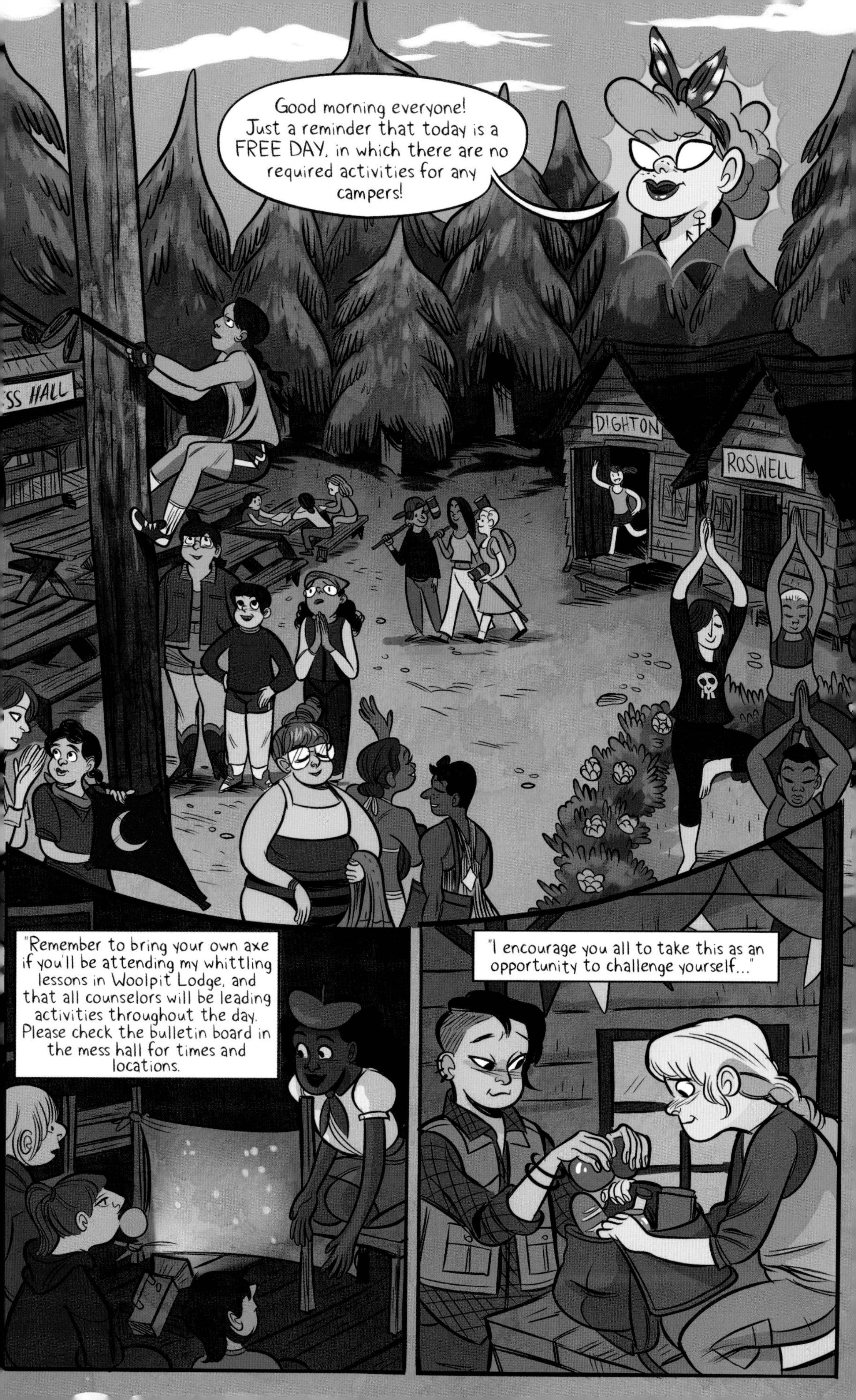
Good morning everyone! Just a reminder that today is a FREE DAY, in which there are no required activities for any campers!
SS HALL
DIGHTON
ROSWELL
"Remember to bring your own axe if you'll be attending my whittling lessons in Woolpit Lodge, and that all counselors will be leading activities throughout the day. Please check the bulletin board in the mess hall for times and locations.
"I encourage you all to take this as an opportunity to challenge yourself..."

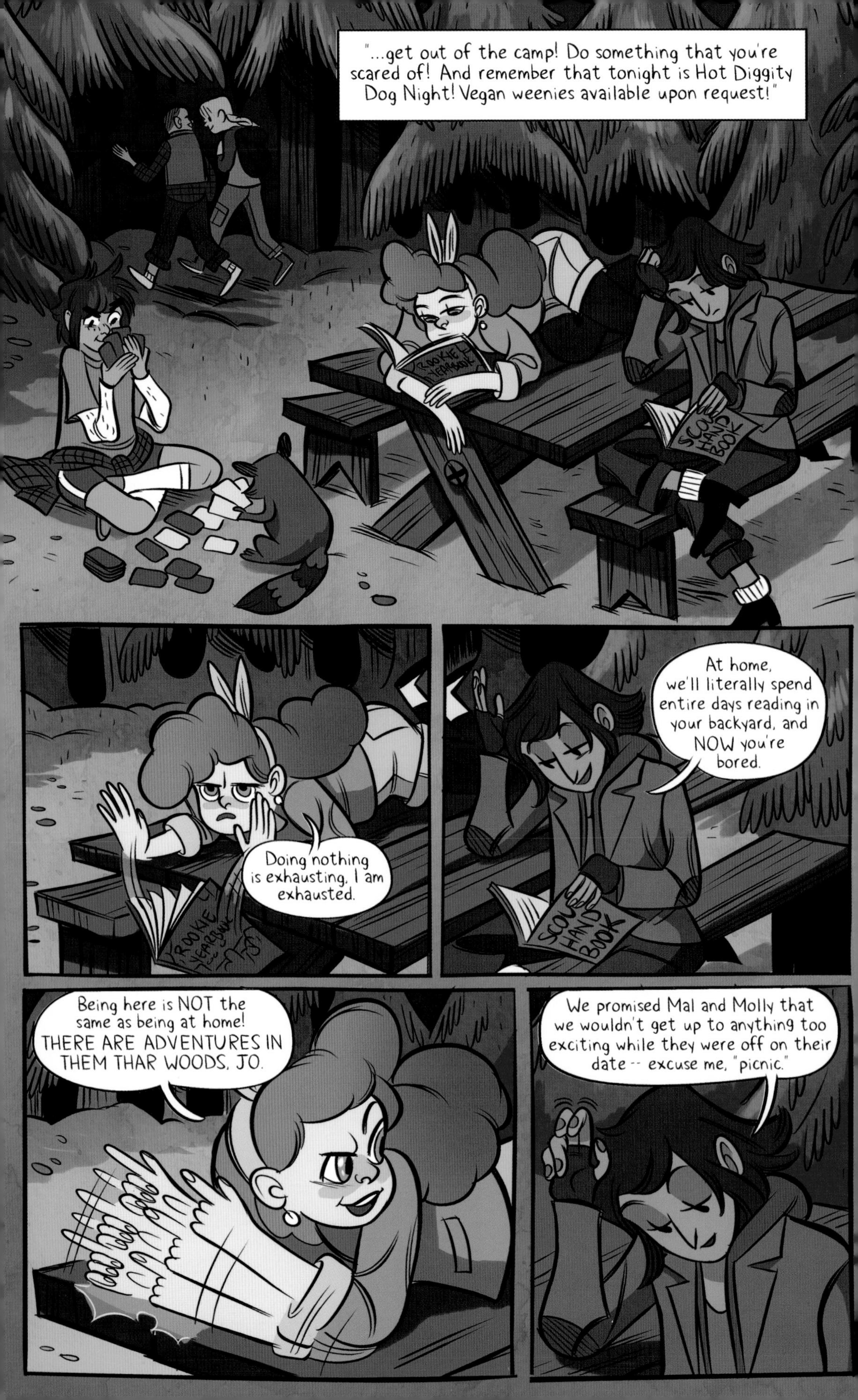
"...get out of the camp! Do something that you're scared of! And remember that tonight is Hot Diggity Dog Night! Vegan weenies available upon request!"
ROOKIE YEARBOOK
SCOUT HANDBOOK
Doing nothing is exhausting, I am exhausted.
ROOKIE YEARBOOK
At home, we'll literally spend entire days reading in your backyard, and NOW you're bored.
SCOUT HANDBOOK
Being here is NOT the same as being at home! THERE ARE ADVENTURES IN THEM THAR WOODS, JO.
We promised Mal and Molly that we wouldn't get up to anything too exciting while they were off on their date -- excuse me, "picnic."

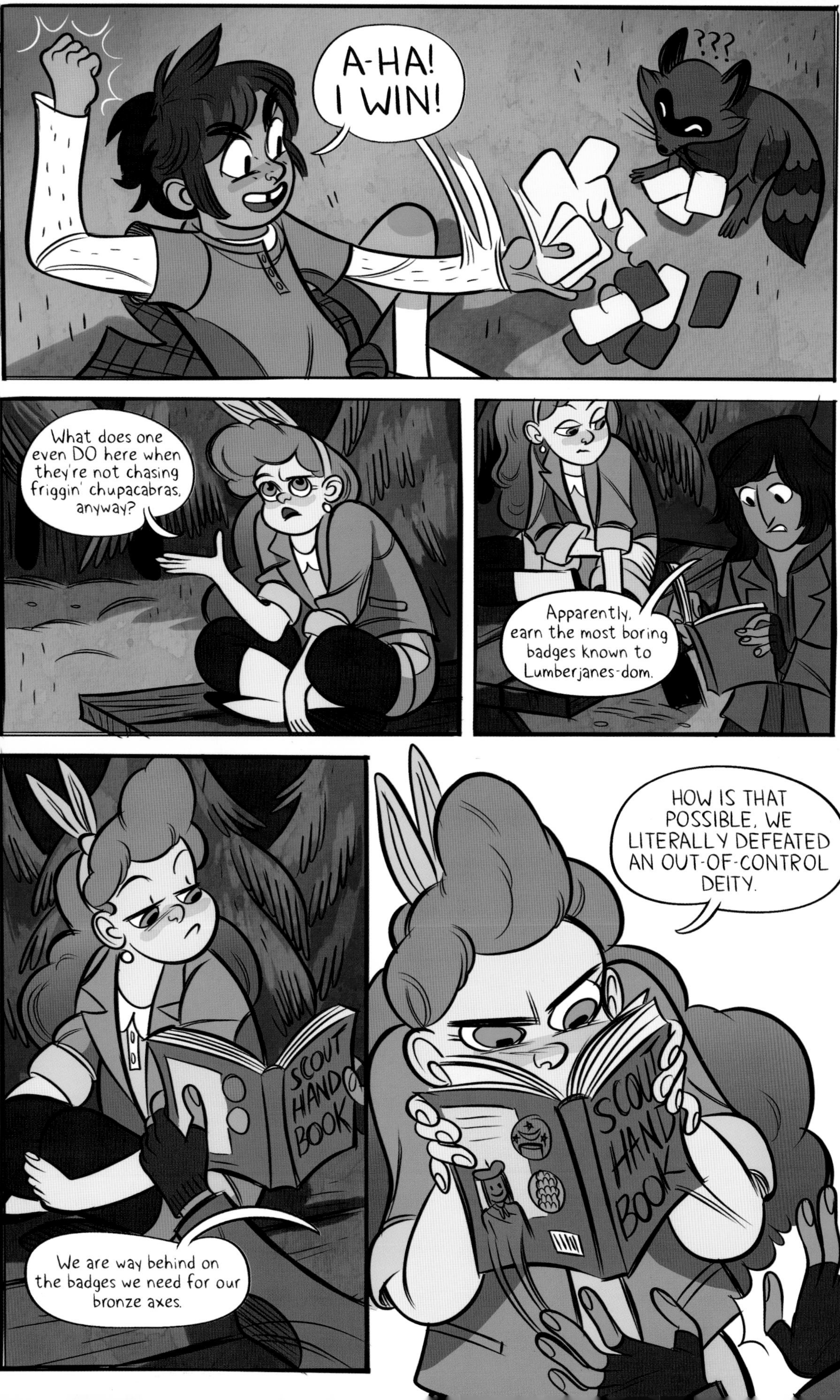
A-HA! I WIN!
???
What does one even DO here when they're not chasing friggin' chupacabras, anyway?
Apparently, earn the most boring badges known to Lumberjanes-dom.
SCOUT HAND BOOK
We are way behind on the badges we need for our bronze axes.
HOW IS THAT POSSIBLE, WE LITERALLY DEFEATED AN OUT-OF-CONTROL DEITY.
SCOUT HAND BOOK

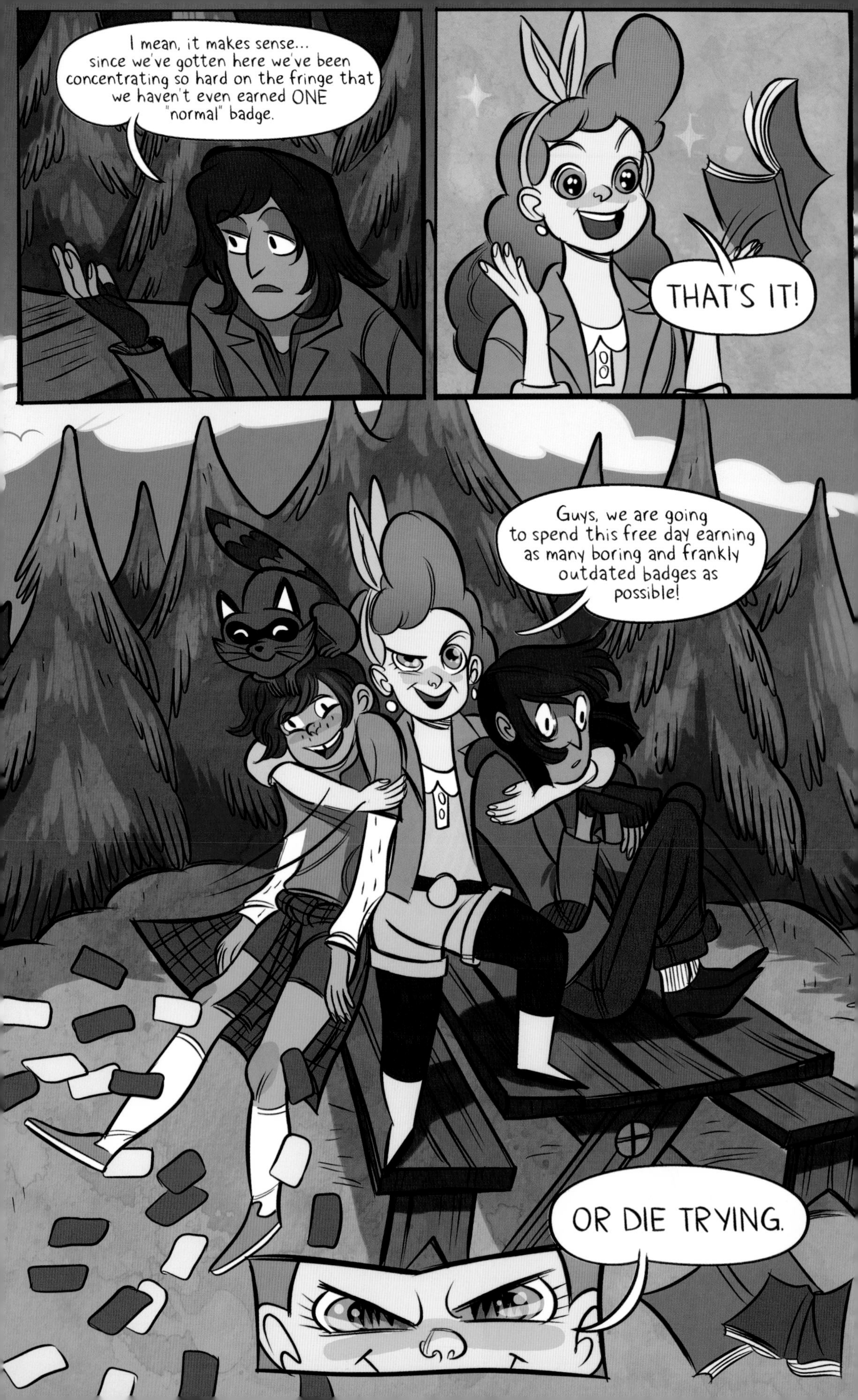
I mean, it makes sense... since we've gotten here we've been concentrating so hard on the fringe that we haven't even earned ONE "normal" badge.
THAT'S IT!
Guys, we are going to spend this free day earning as many boring and frankly outdated badges as possible!
OR DIE TRYING.

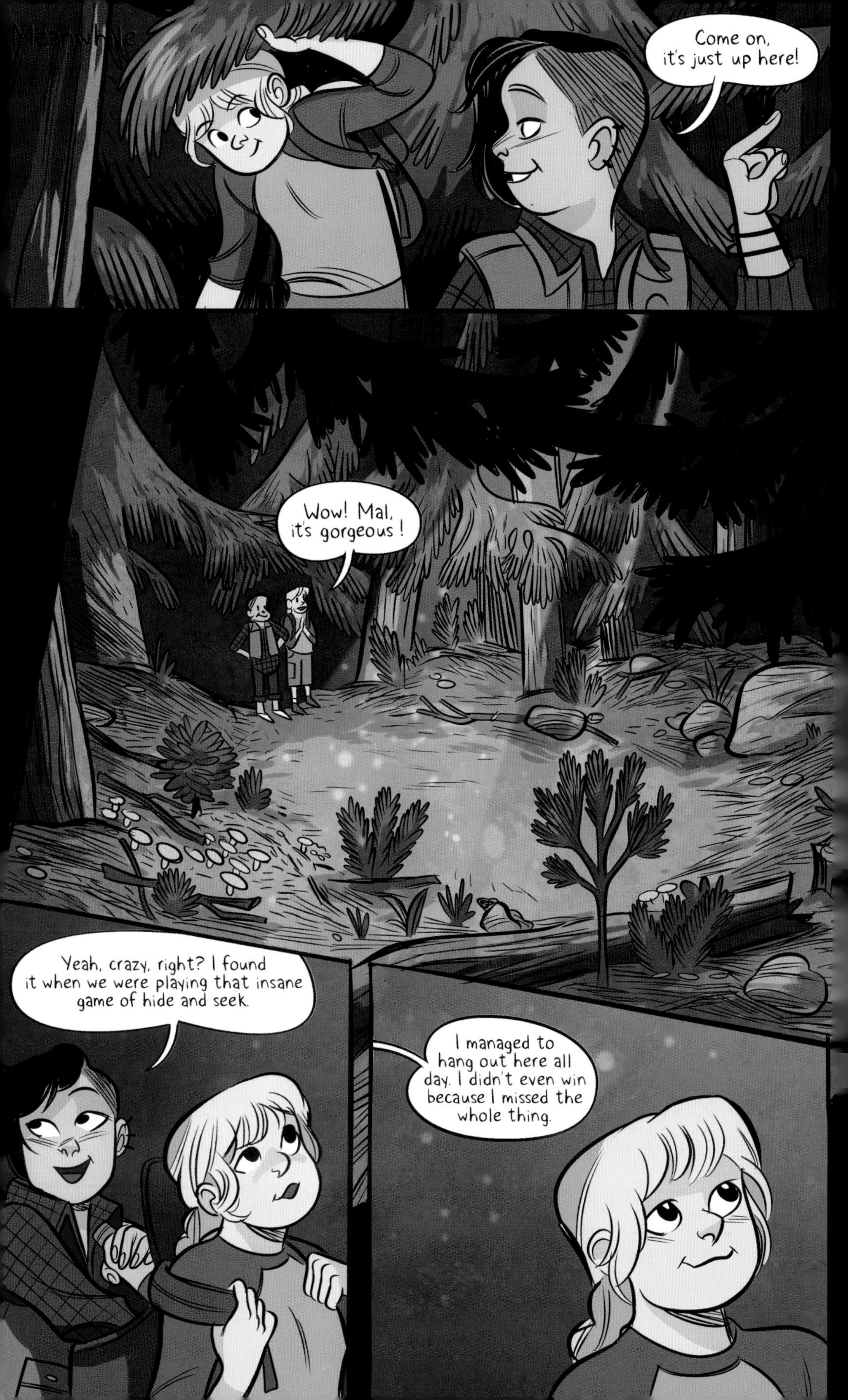
Meanwhile.
Come on, it's just up here!
Wow! Mal, it's gorgeous!
Yeah, crazy, right? I found it when we were playing that insane game of hide and seek.
I managed to hang out here all day. I didn't even win because I missed the whole thing.

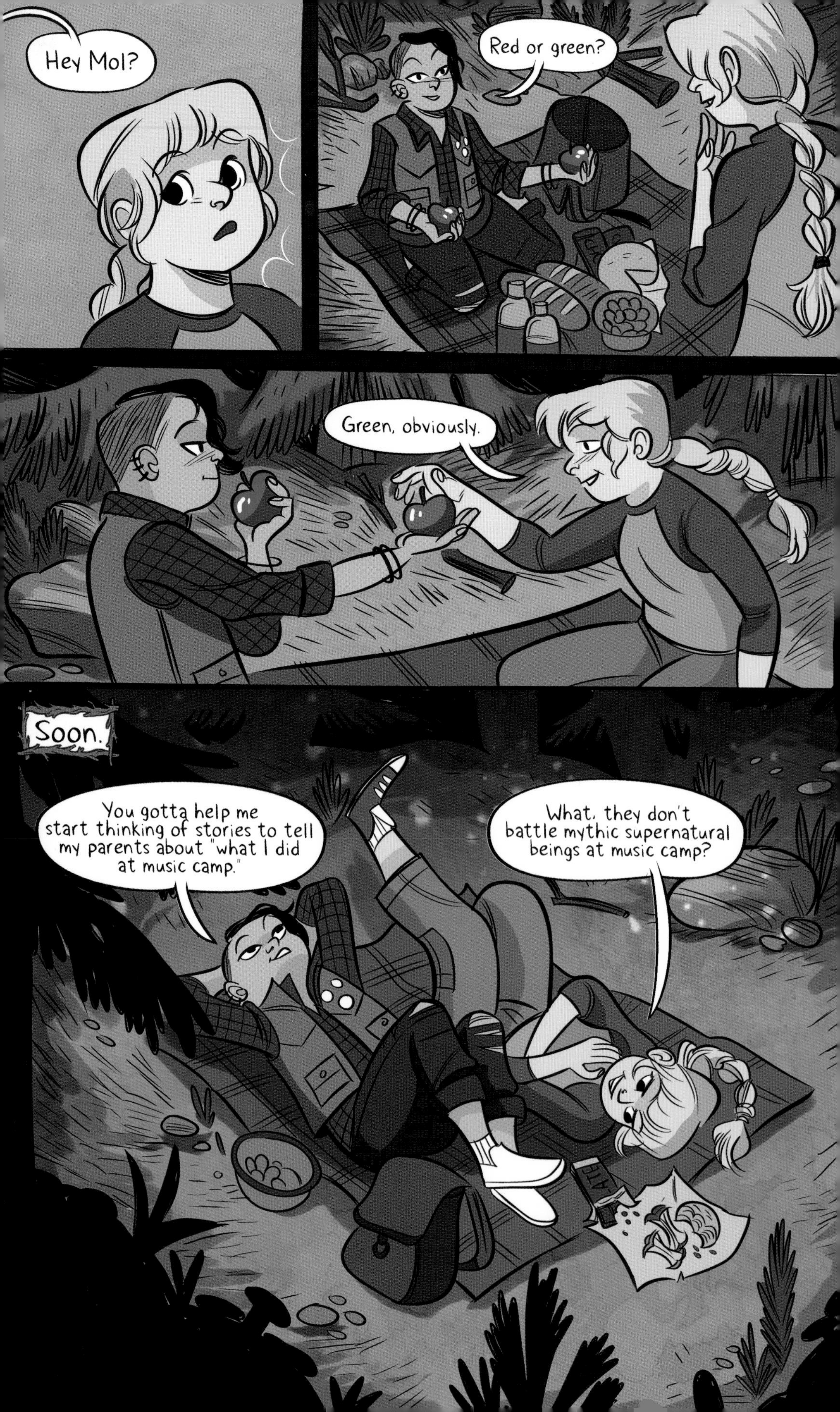
Hey Mol?
Red or green?
Green, obviously.
Soon.
You gotta help me start thinking of stories to tell my parents about "what I did at music camp."
What, they don't battle mythic supernatural beings at music camp?

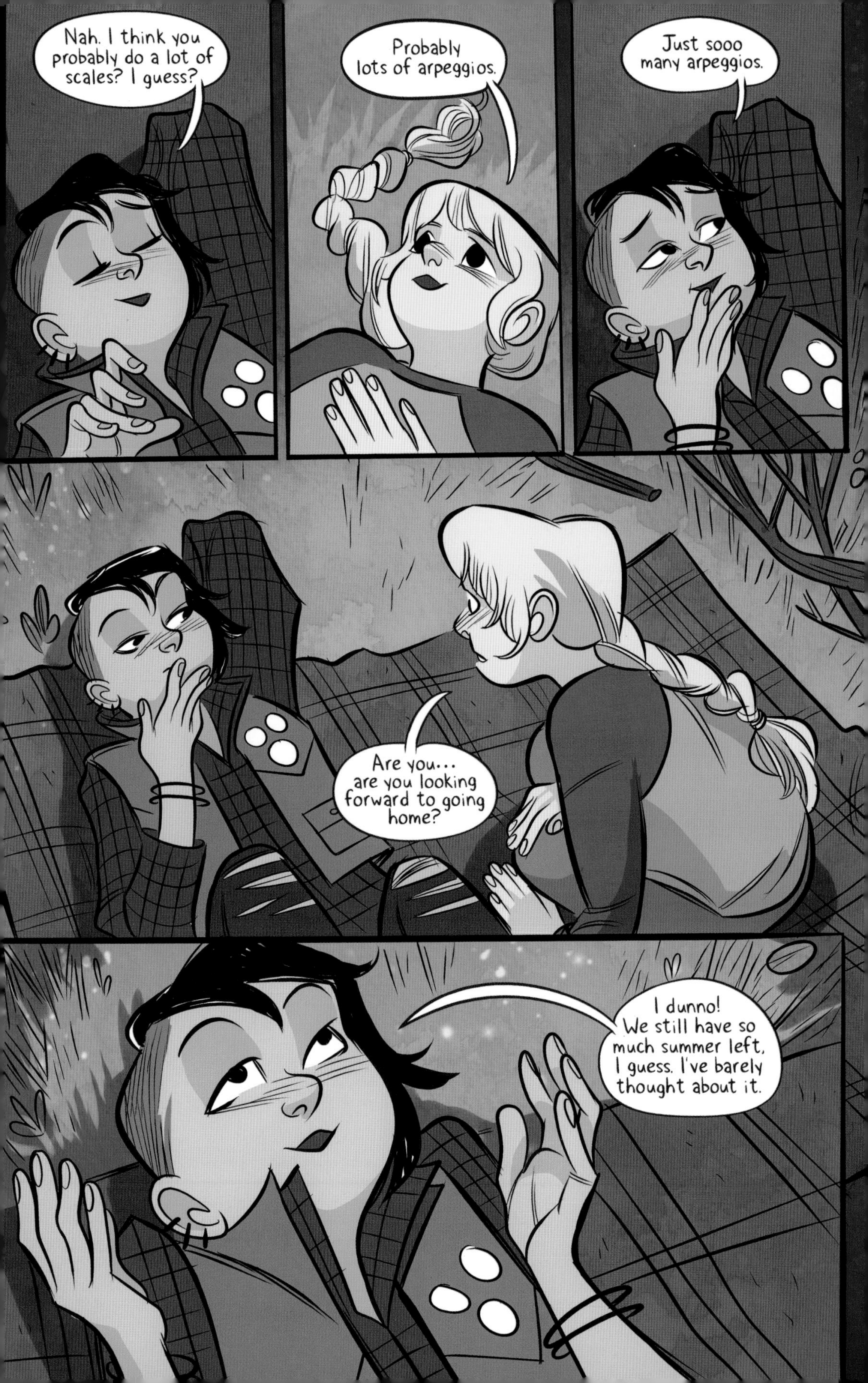
Nah. I think you probably do a lot of scales? I guess?
Probably lots of arpeggios.
Just sooo many arpeggios.
Are you... are you looking forward to going home?
I dunno! We still have so much summer left, I guess. I've barely thought about it.

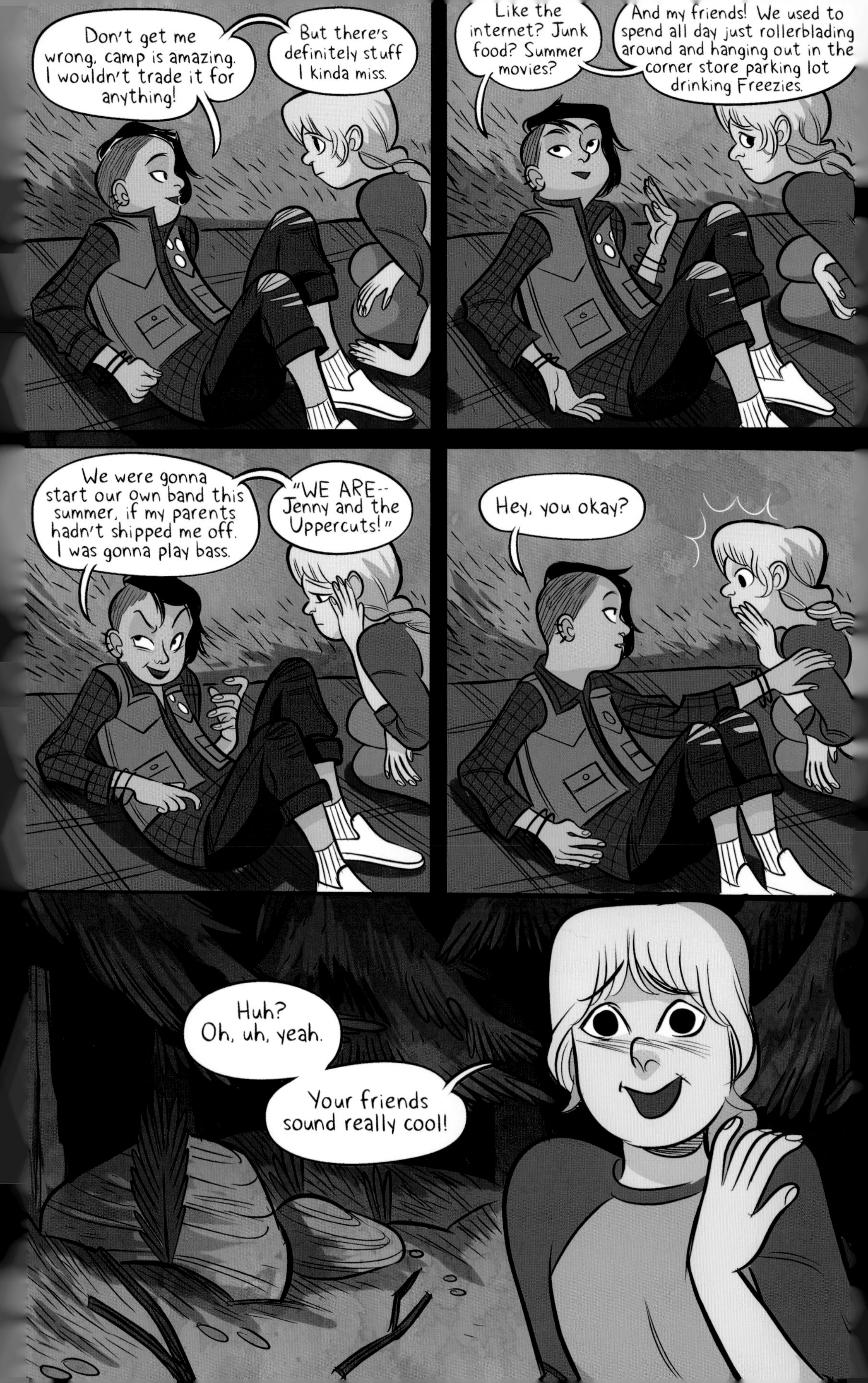
Don't get me wrong, camp is amazing. I wouldn't trade it for anything!
But there's definitely stuff I kinda miss.
Like the internet? Junk food? Summer movies?
And my friends! We used to spend all day just rollerblading around and hanging out in the corner store parking lot drinking Freezies.
We were gonna start our own band this summer, if my parents hadn't shipped me off. I was gonna play bass.
"WE ARE-- Jenny and the Uppercuts!"
Hey, you okay?
Huh? Oh, uh, yeah.
Your friends sound really cool!

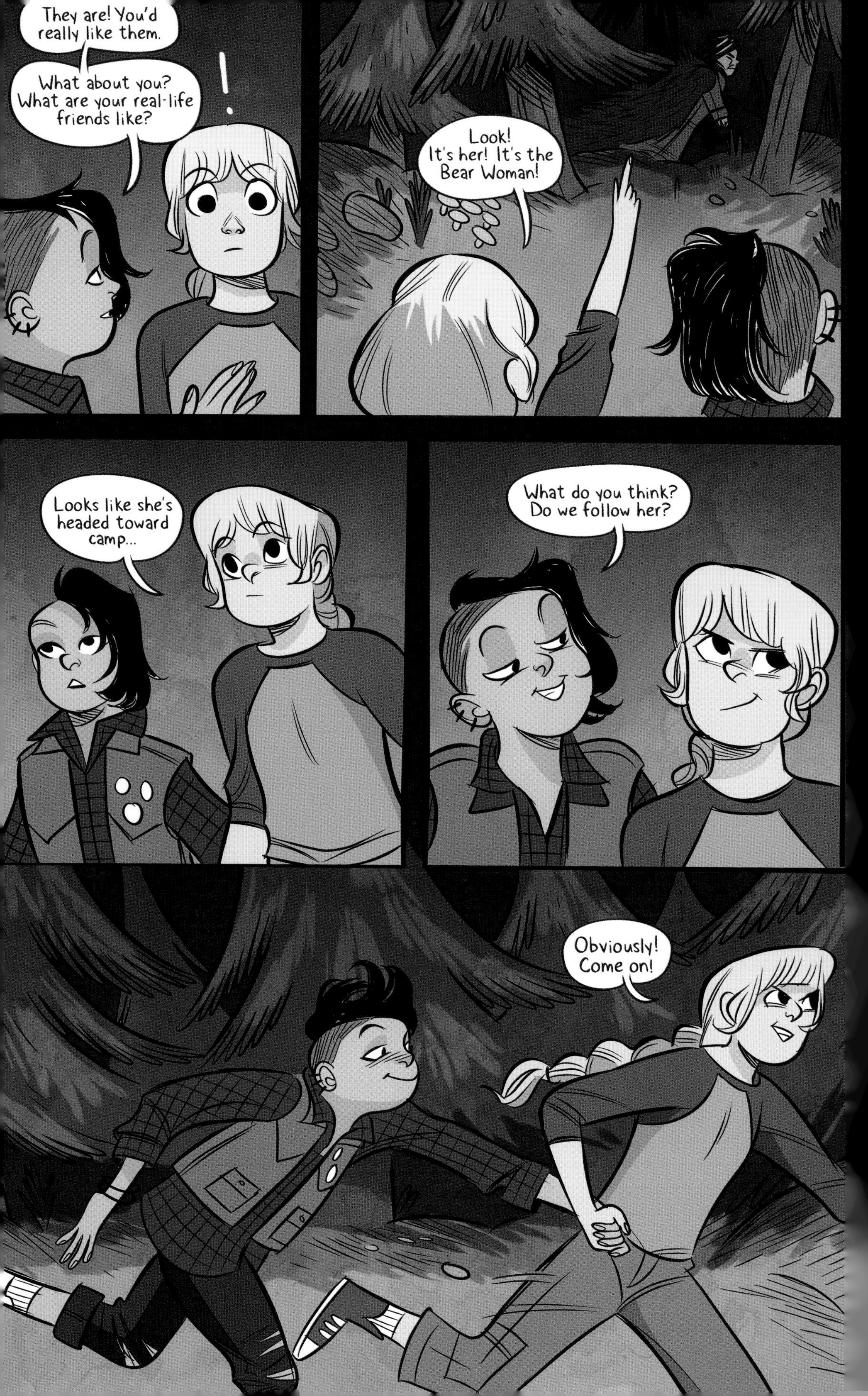
They are! You'd really like them.
What about you? What are your real-life friends like?
!
Look! It's her! It's the Bear Woman!
Looks like she's headed toward camp...
What do you think? Do we follow her?
Obviously! Come on!

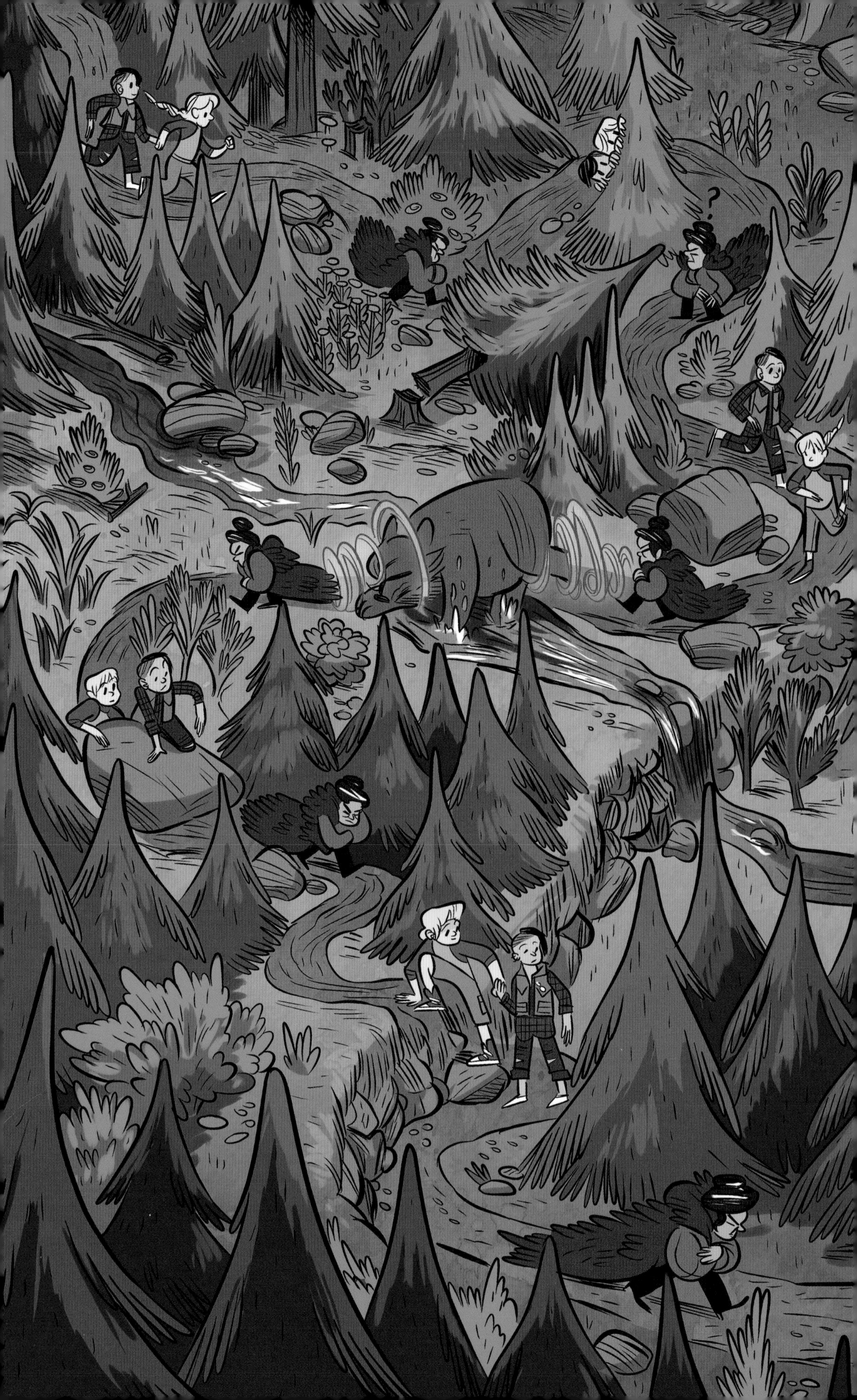

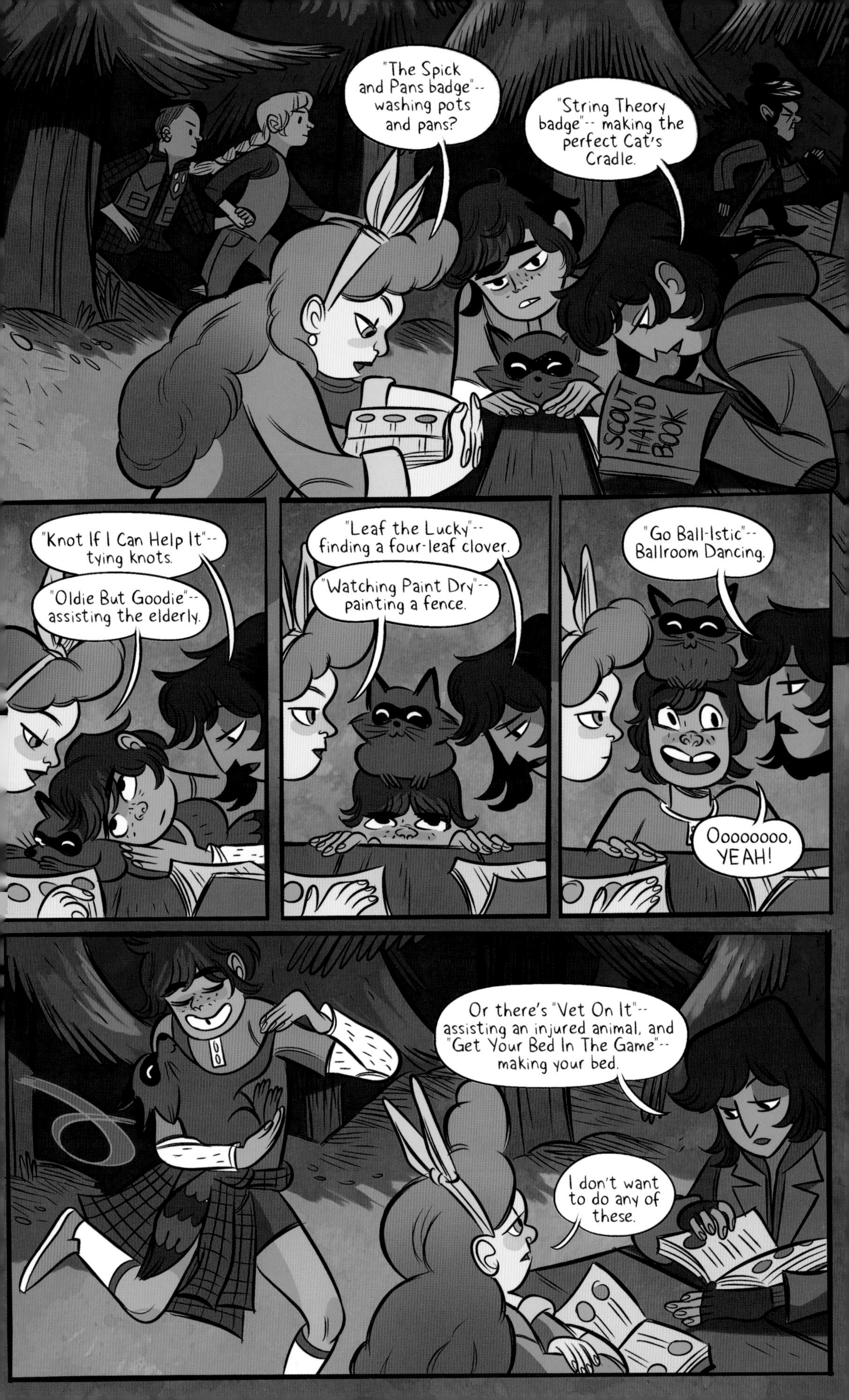
"The Spick and Pans badge"-- washing pots and pans?
"String Theory badge"-- making the perfect Cat's Cradle.
"Knot If I Can Help It"-- tying knots.
"Oldie But Goodie"-- assisting the elderly.
"Leaf the Lucky"-- finding a four-leaf clover.
"Watching Paint Dry"-- painting a fence.
"Go Ball-Istic"-- Ballroom Dancing.
Oooooooo, YEAH!
SCOUT HAND BOOK
Or there's "Vet On It"-- assisting an injured animal, and "Get Your Bed In The Game"-- making your bed.
I don't want to do any of these.

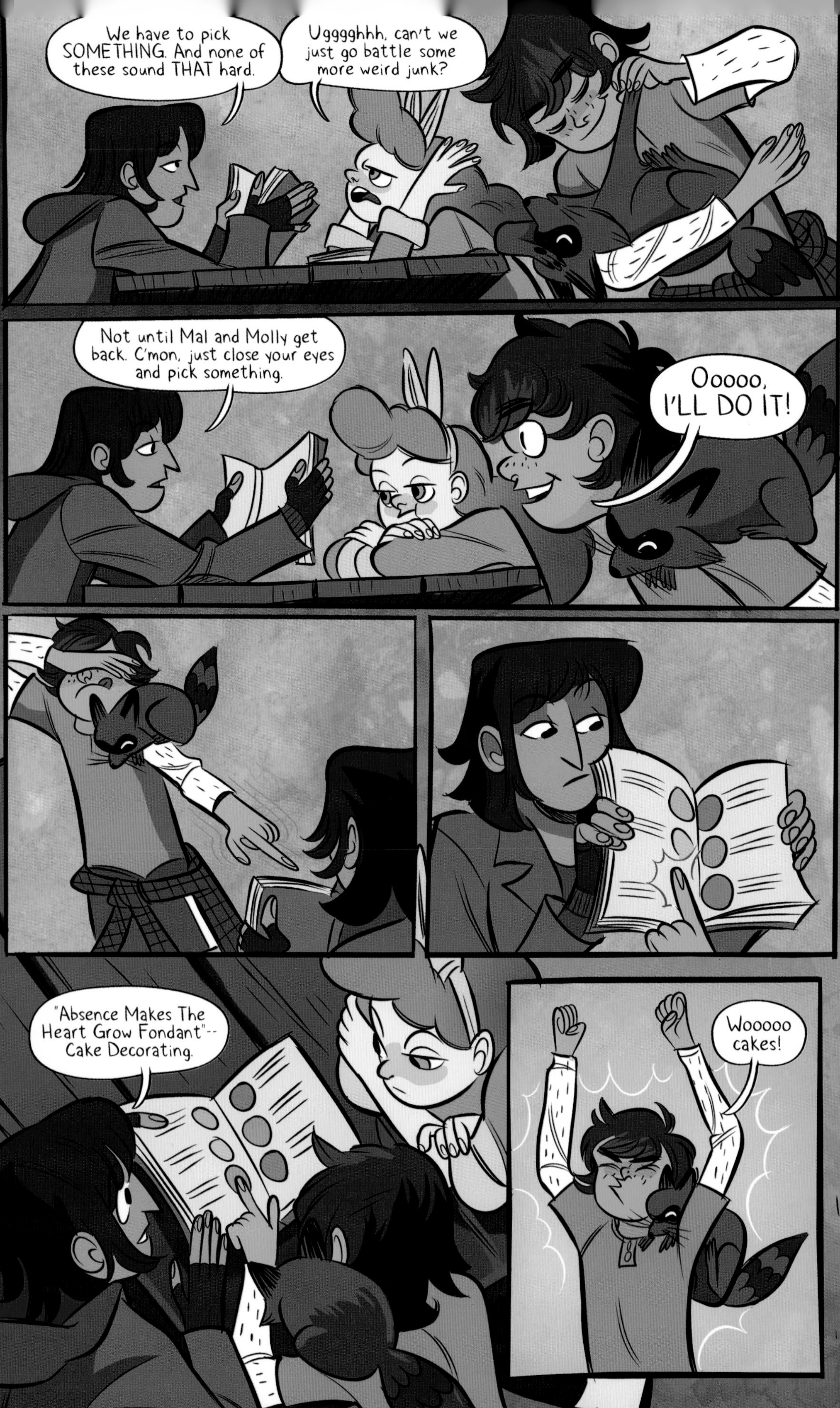
We have to pick SOMETHING. And none of these sound THAT hard.
Ugggghhh, can't we just go battle some more weird junk?
Not until Mal and Molly get back. C'mon, just close your eyes and pick something.
Ooooo, I'LL DO IT!
"Absence Makes The Heart Grow Fondant"-- Cake Decorating.
Wooooo cakes!

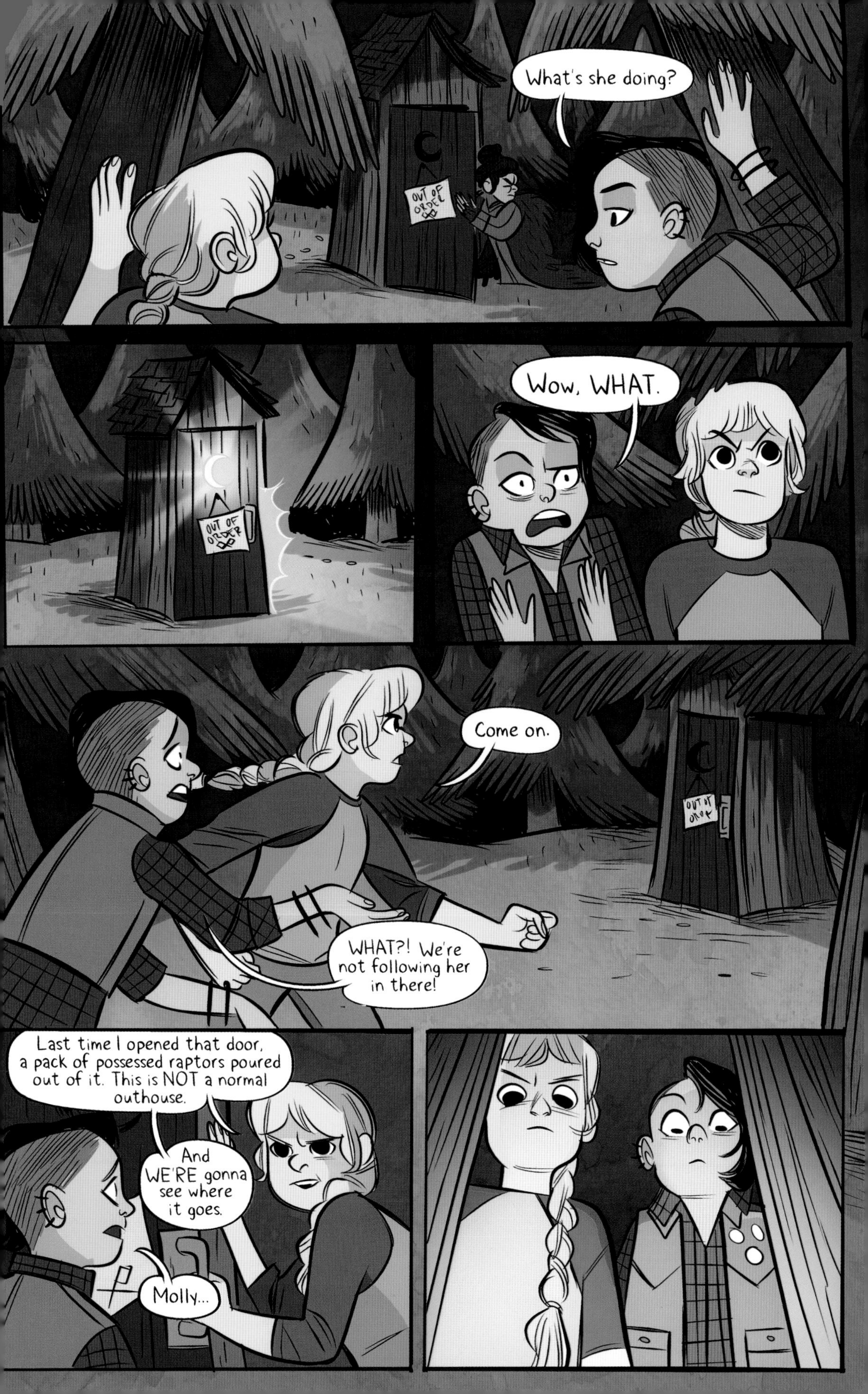
What's she doing?
OUT OF ORDER
OUT OF ORDER
Wow, WHAT.
Come on.
WHAT?! We're not following her in there!
Last time I opened that door, a pack of possessed raptors poured out of it. This is NOT a normal outhouse.
And WE'RE gonna see where it goes.
Molly...

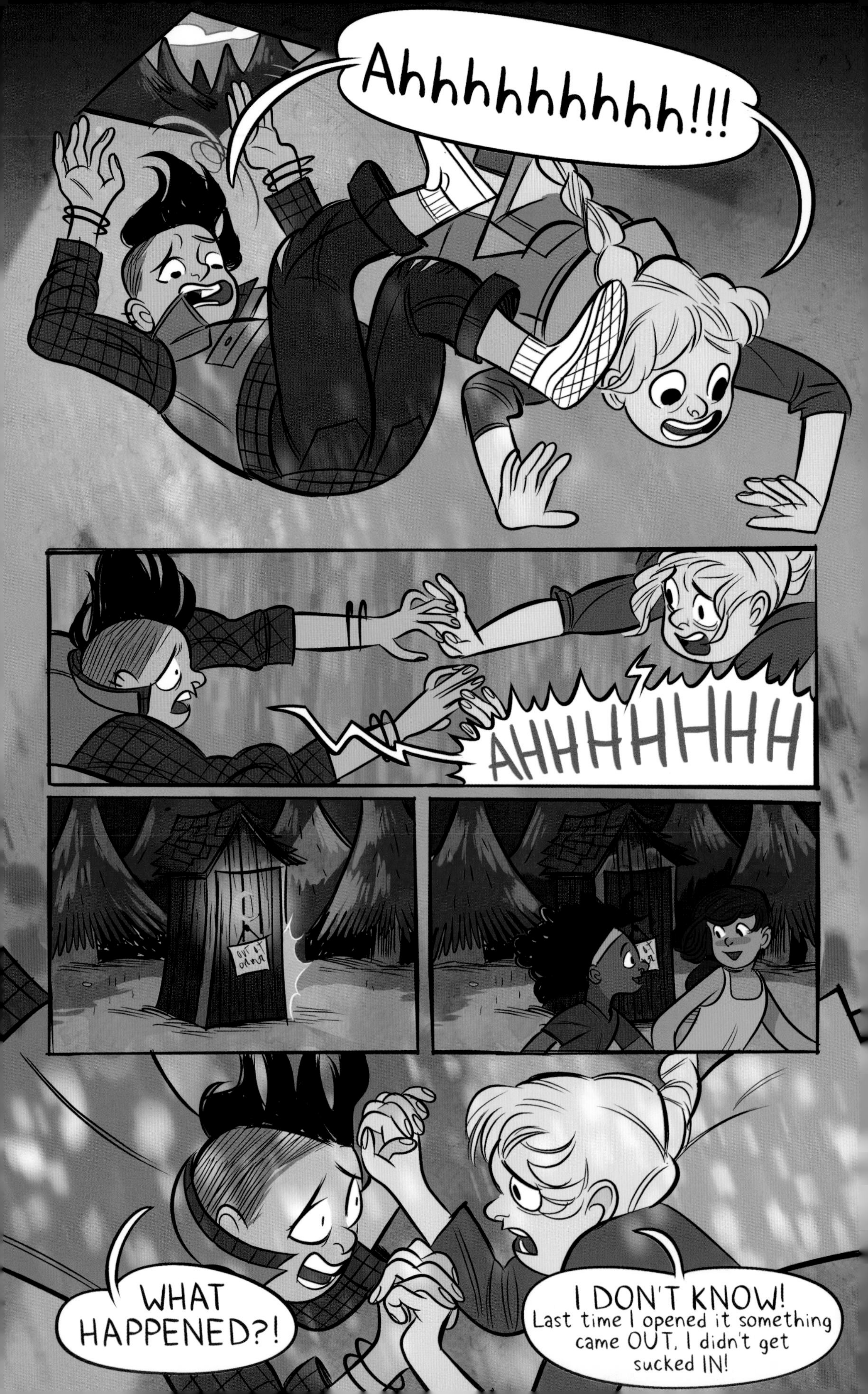
Ahhhhhhhhhh!!!
AHHHHHHH
OUT OF ORDER
WHAT HAPPENED?!
I DON'T KNOW! Last time I opened it something came OUT, I didn't get sucked IN!

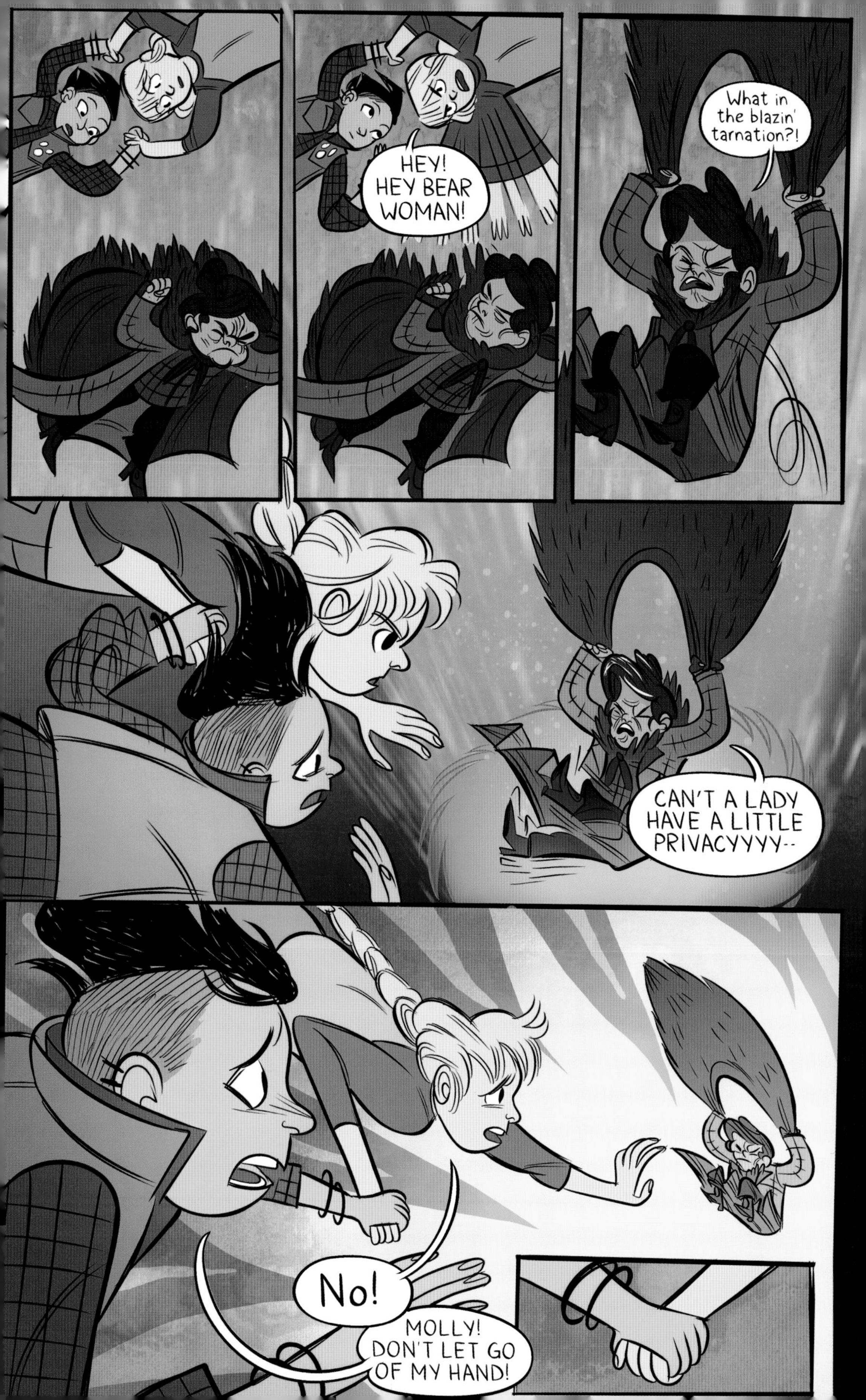
HEY!
HEY BEAR WOMAN!
What in the blazin' tarnation?!
CAN'T A LADY HAVE A LITTLE PRIVACYYYY--
No!
MOLLY! DON'T LET GO OF MY HAND!

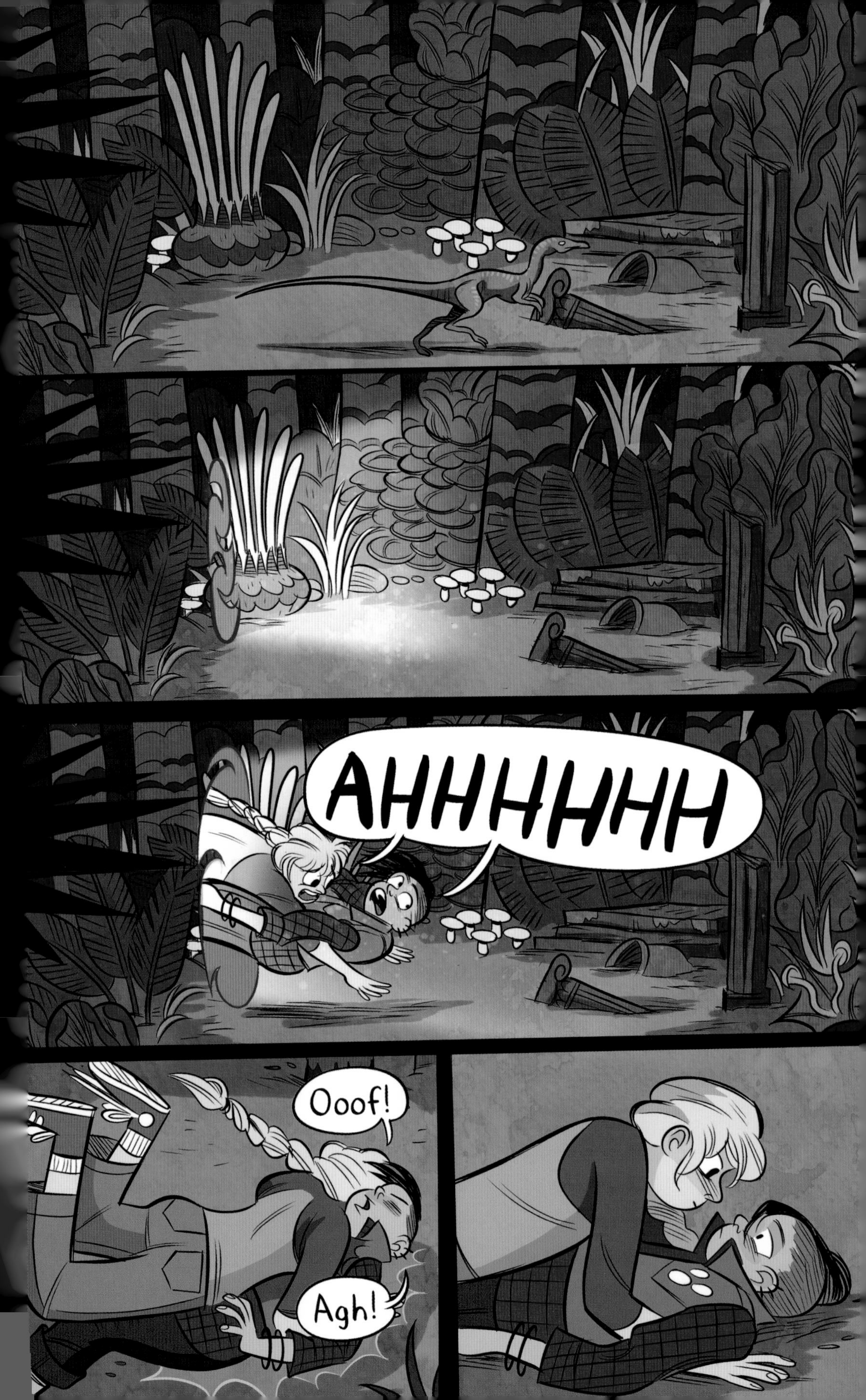
AHHHHHH
Ooof!
Agh!

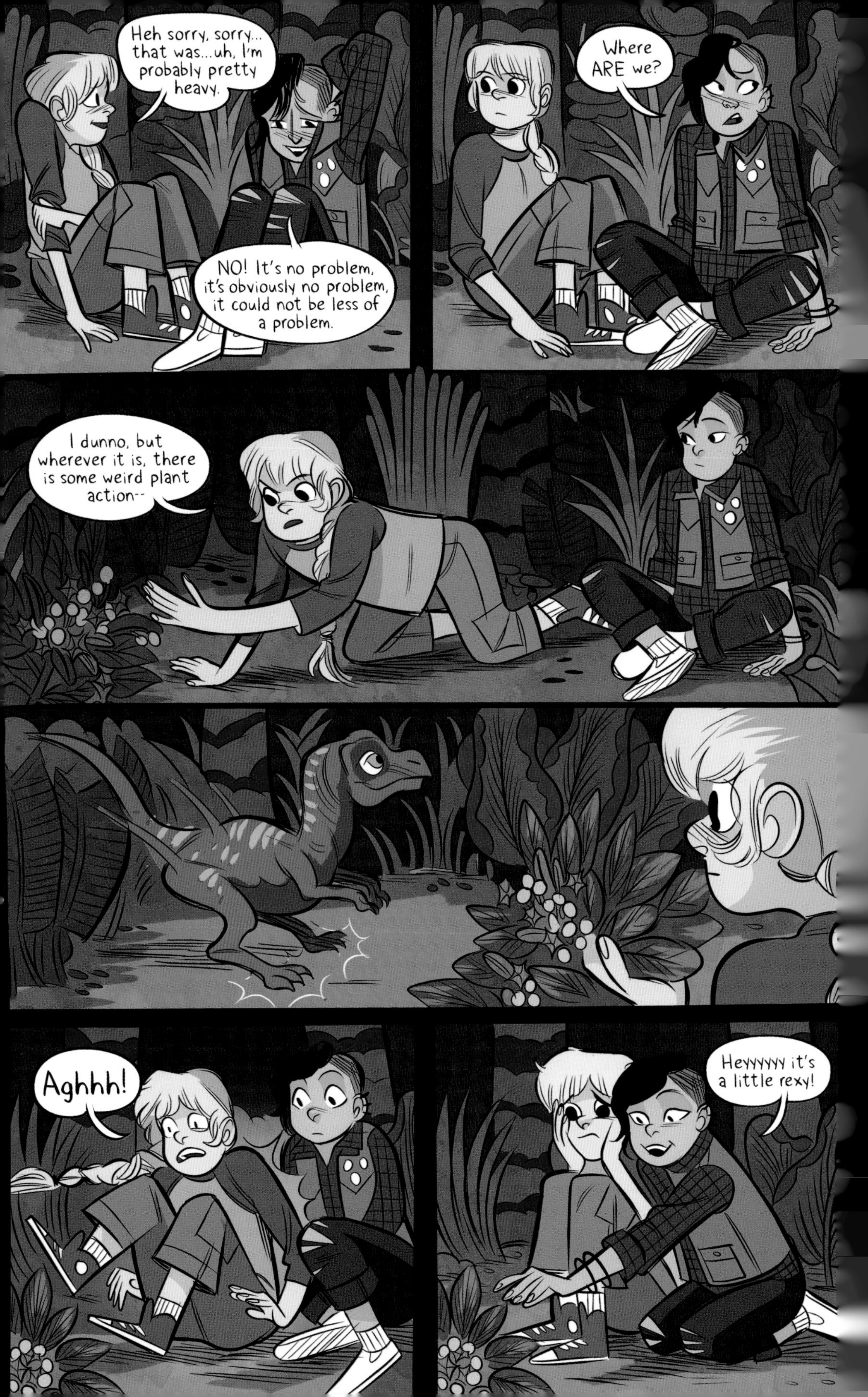
Heh sorry, sorry... that was...uh, I'm probably pretty heavy.
NO! It's no problem, it's obviously no problem, it could not be less of a problem.
Where ARE we?
I dunno, but wherever it is, there is some weird plant action--
Aghhh!
Heyyyyyy it's a little rexy!

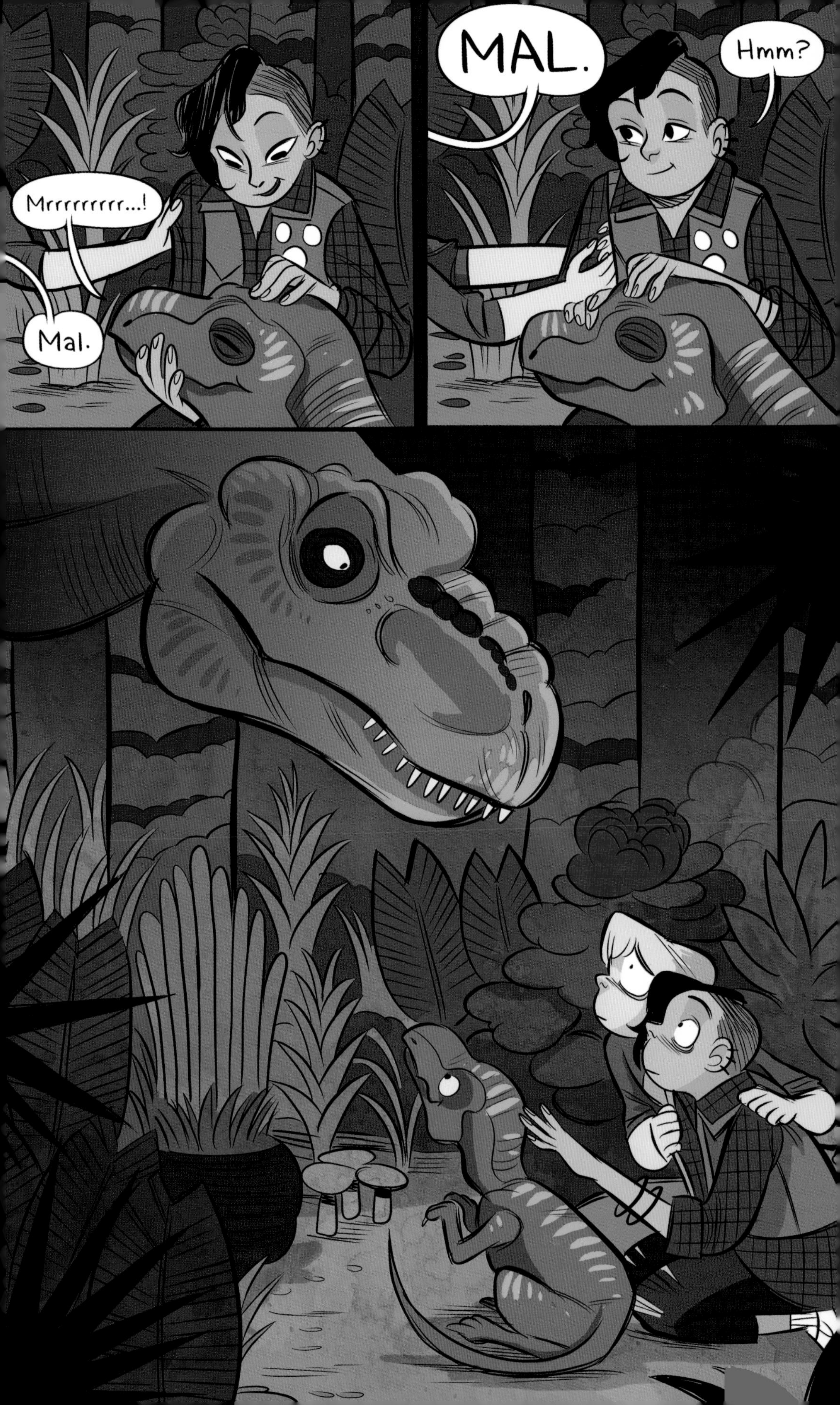
Mrrrrrrrrr...!
Mal.
MAL.
Hmm?

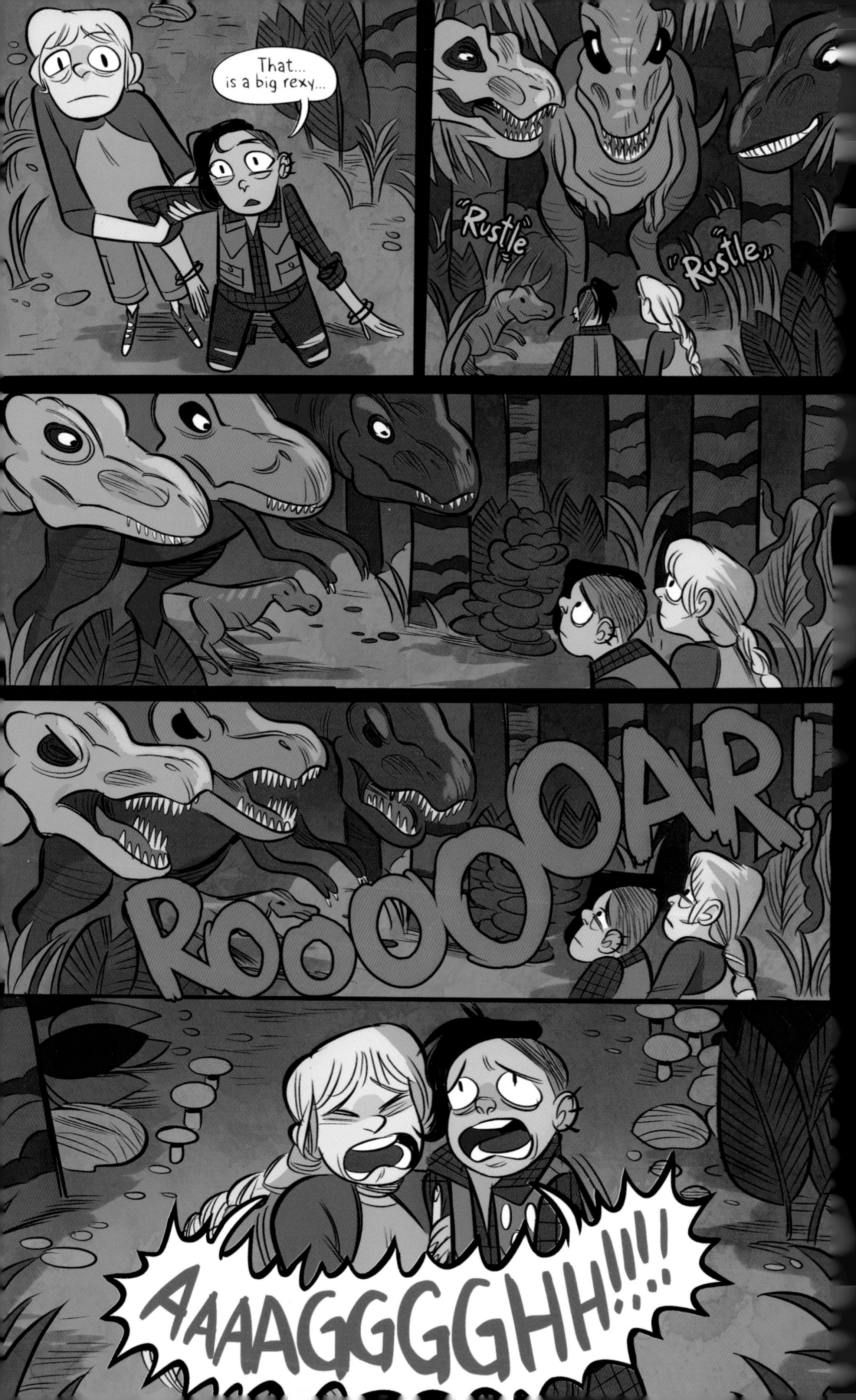
That... is a big rexy...
"Rustle"
"Rustle"
ROOOOOOAR!
AAAAGGGGHH!!!!

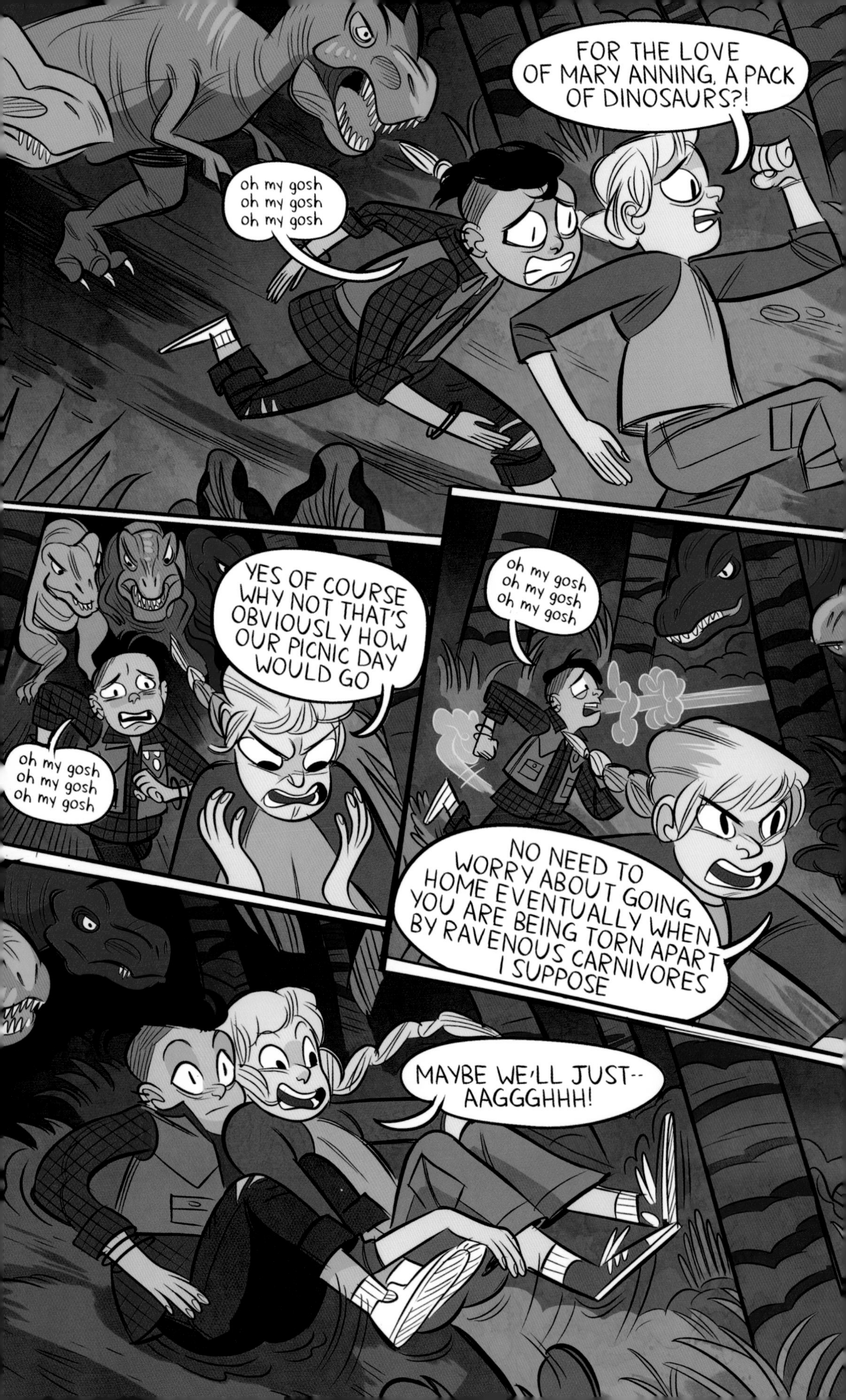
FOR THE LOVE OF MARY ANNING, A PACK OF DINOSAURS?!
oh my gosh oh my gosh oh my gosh
YES OF COURSE WHY NOT THAT'S OBVIOUSLY HOW OUR PICNIC DAY WOULD GO
oh my gosh oh my gosh oh my gosh
oh my gosh oh my gosh oh my gosh
NO NEED TO WORRY ABOUT GOING HOME EVENTUALLY WHEN YOU ARE BEING TORN APART BY RAVENOUS CARNIVORES I SUPPOSE
MAYBE WE'LL JUST-- AAGGGHHH!

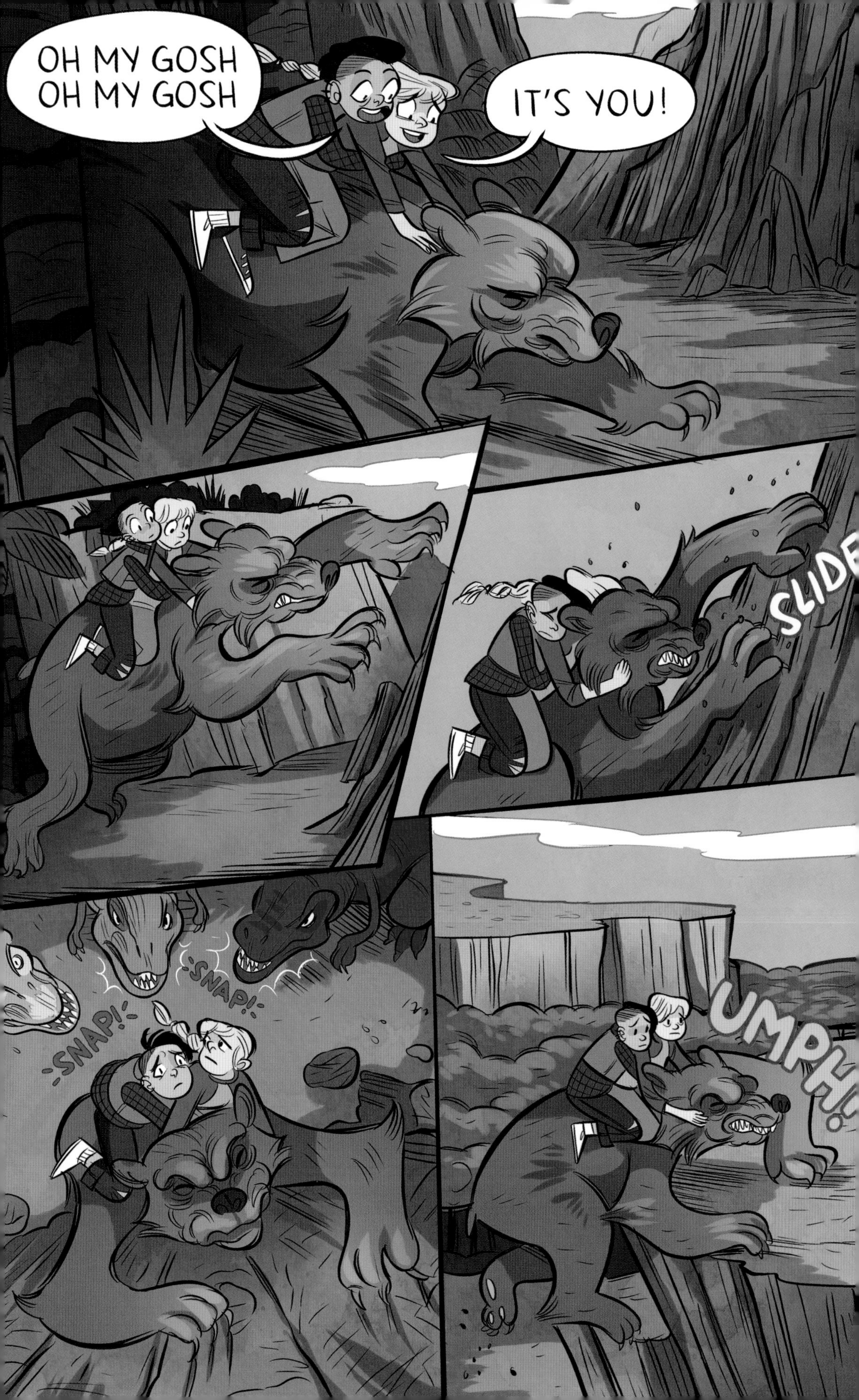
OH MY GOSH
OH MY GOSH
IT'S YOU!
SLIDE
SNAP!
SNAP!
UMPH!

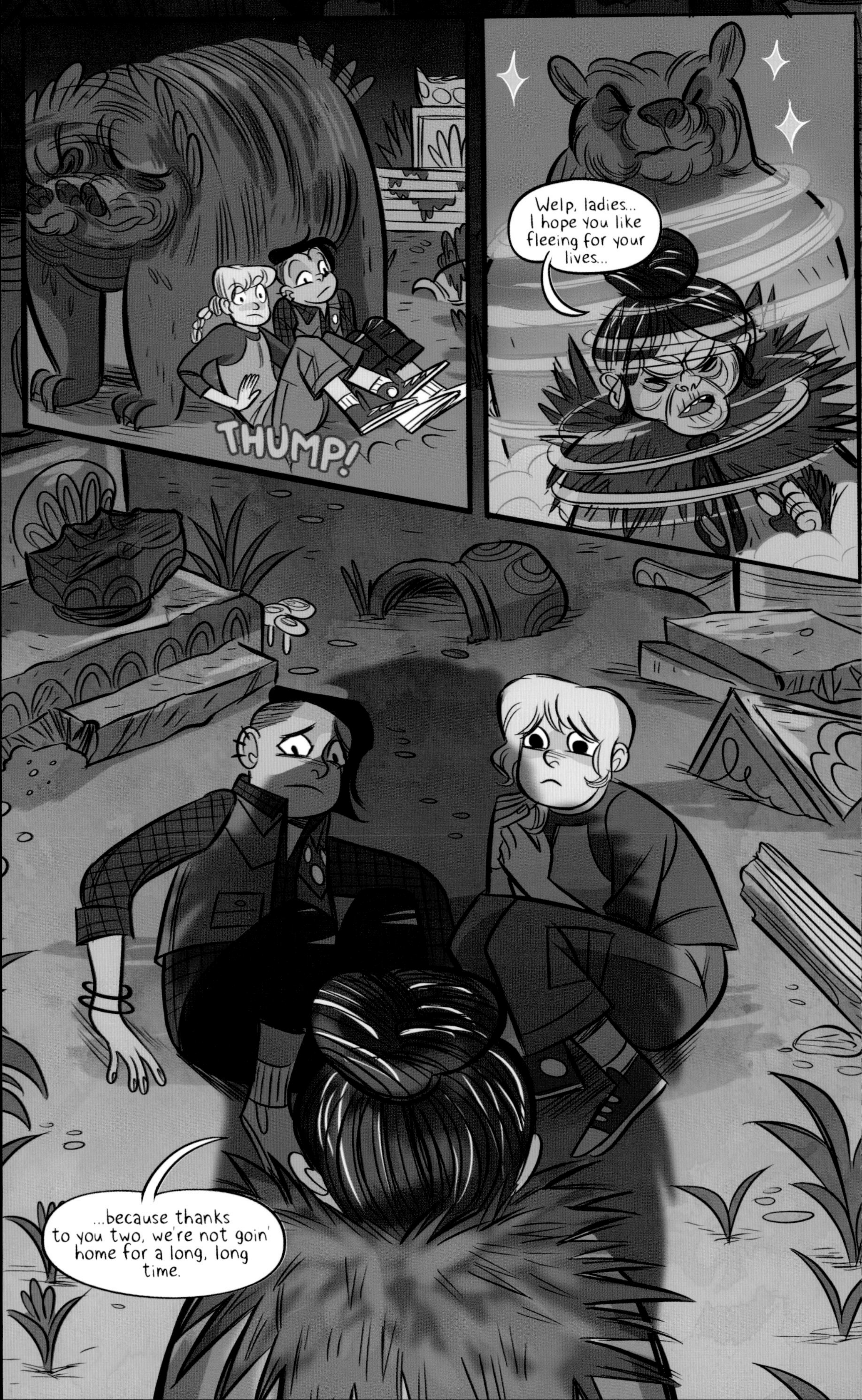
THUMP!
Welp, ladies... I hope you like fleeing for your lives...
...because thanks to you two, we're not goin' home for a long, long time.

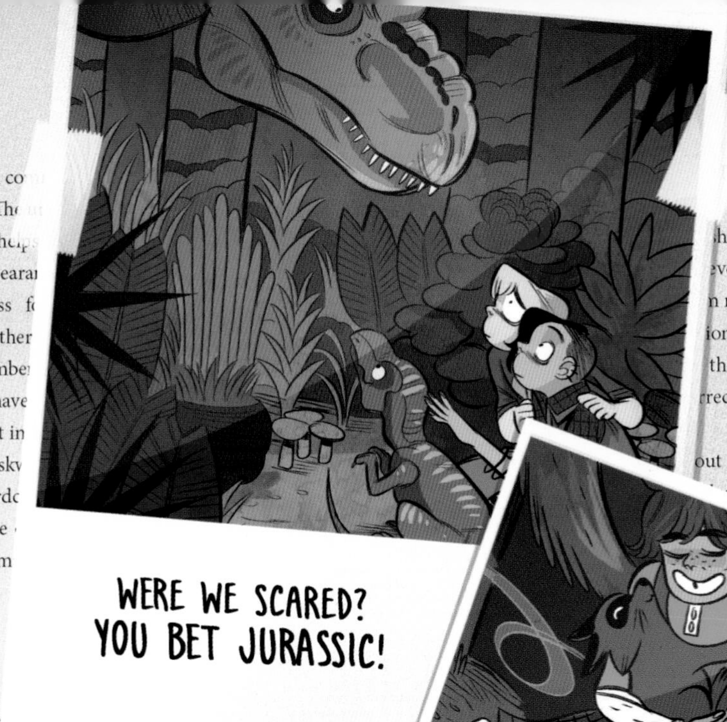
WERE WE SCARED?
YOU BET JURASSIC!

will co
Th
It h
appeara
dress f
Further
Lumbe
to have
part in
Thiskv
Hardc
have
them

HE UNIFORM

hould be worn at camp
events when Lumberjanes
n may also be worn at other
ions. It should be worn as a
the uniform dress with
rrect shoes, and stocking or

out grows her uniform or
ter Lumberjane.
a she has
her
her

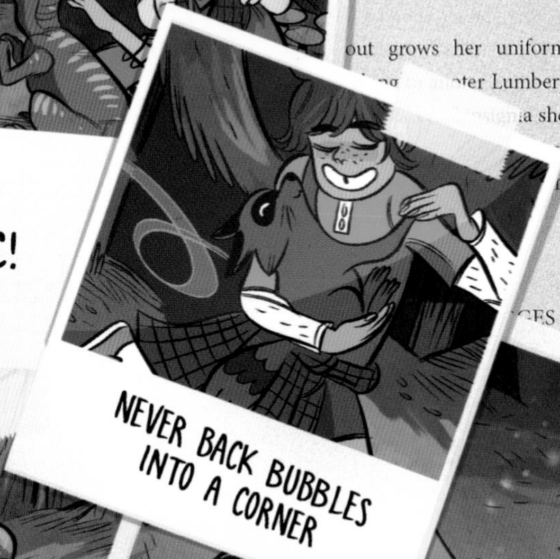
NEVER BACK BUBBLES
INTO A CORNER

The
yellow, short sl
emb
the w
choos
slacks,
made o
out-of-do
green bere
the colla
Shoes ma
heels, rou … kings or
socks shou … with the shoes or wi
the uniform. Ne… es, bracelets, or other jewelry do
belong with a Lumberjane uniform.

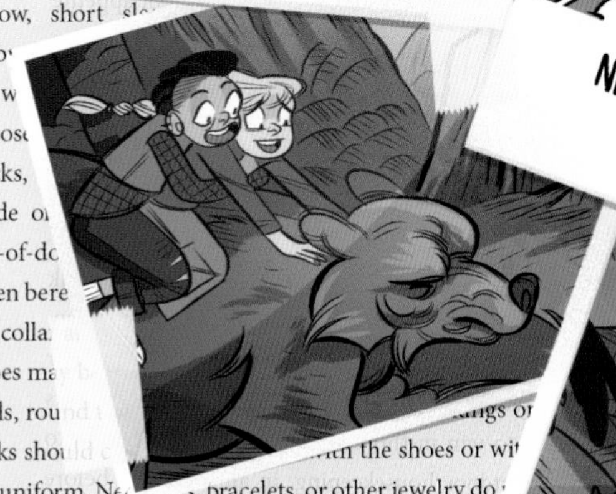

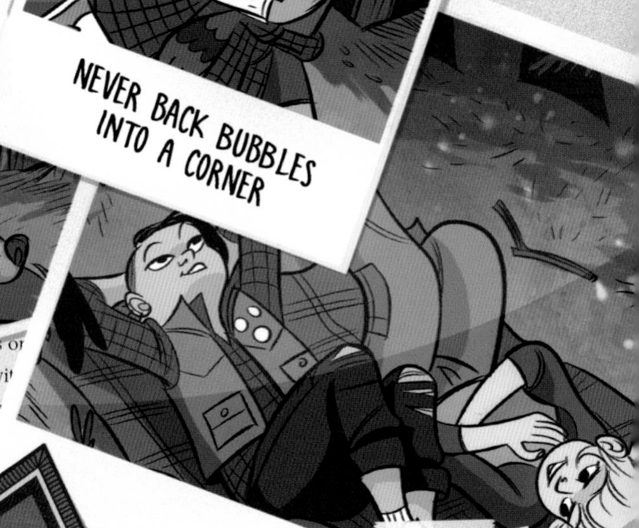

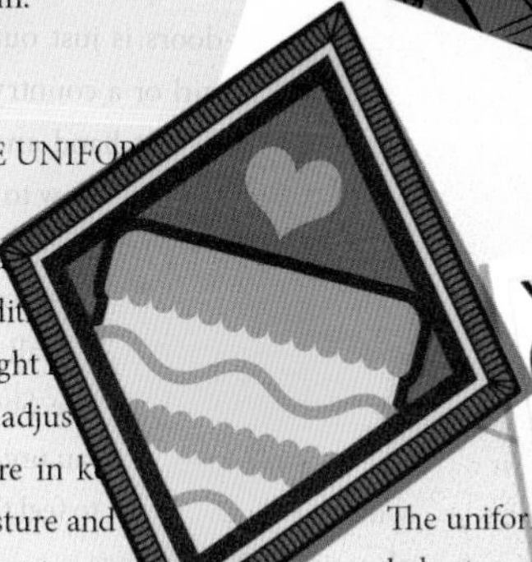

HOW TO WEAR THE UNIFO

To look well in a uniform dema… uniform be kept in good condit… pressed. See that the skirt is the right … height and build, that the belt is adjus… that your shoes and stockings are in k… uniform, that you watch your posture and … with dignity and grace. If the beret is remo…rs, be sure that your hair is neat and kept in pla… with an insonspicuous clip or ribbon. When you wear a Lumberjane uniform you are identified as a member of this organization and you should be doubly careful to conduct yourself in a way that will show everyone that courtesy and thoughtfullness are part of being a Lumberjane. People are likely to judge a whole nation by the selfishness of a few individuals, to criticize a whole family because of the misconduct of one member, and to feel unkindly toward and organization because of the

The unifor
helps to cre
in a group.
active life th
another bond
future, and pr
in order to b
Lumberjane pr
Penniquiqul Thi … ore Lady
Types, but m… will wish to have one. They
can either bu… uniform, or make it themselves from
materials available at the trading post.

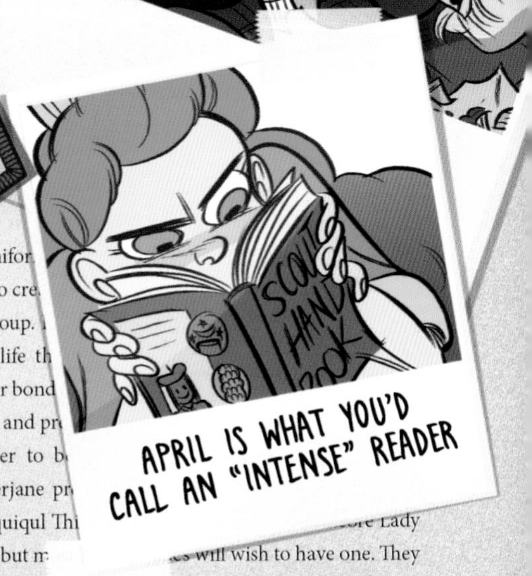
APRIL IS WHAT YOU'D
CALL AN "INTENSE" READER

LUMBERJANES FIELD MANUAL
CHAPTER ELEVEN

Lumberjanes "Arts and Crafts" Program Field

GO BALL-ISTIC BADGE
"Dance like your life depends on it."

There are many things that a Lumberjane will learn while at camp, but one of the camp favorites over these many years has been ballroom dancing. Ballroom dancing is a stress reliever and will teach any Lumberjane scout to put the pressure of the world behind her. The feel and styles of ballroom dances brings the feeling of comfort and great social interaction. Not only that, but it has been shown to help Lumberjanes discover true passion and joy of their life. As a Lumberjanes, she will learn important ballroom dance elements, which include flexibility, superior mental ability, endurance, and strength.

The *Go Ball-istic* badge is not just another step for a Lumberjane on her personal journey in this camp but something much more. Just as many of the other Lumberjane classes will be able to teach and mold the scouts of this camp, it will be ballroom dancing that will show them that not is grace not a weakness, it is a powerful tool that can be used in almost any situation. The style of ballroom dances will make any Lumberjane more confident with a fresh sense of creativity, motivation and energy. The different forms of ballroom dancing not only give a great learning experience but will also show the importance of working in pairs and the ability to rely on a partner who is separate but at the same time an extension of the dancer.

To obtain the *Go Ball-istic* badge, a Lumberjanes must be able to perform one of the many dances available from start to finish with her partner. As partners, they will hold each other up and help each other if needed as they complete the dance to the best of their abilities. The lesson from this badge is something a Lumberjane will take with her for the rest of her life as she learns to understand the influence she will have on those around her. Confidence and strength is something that

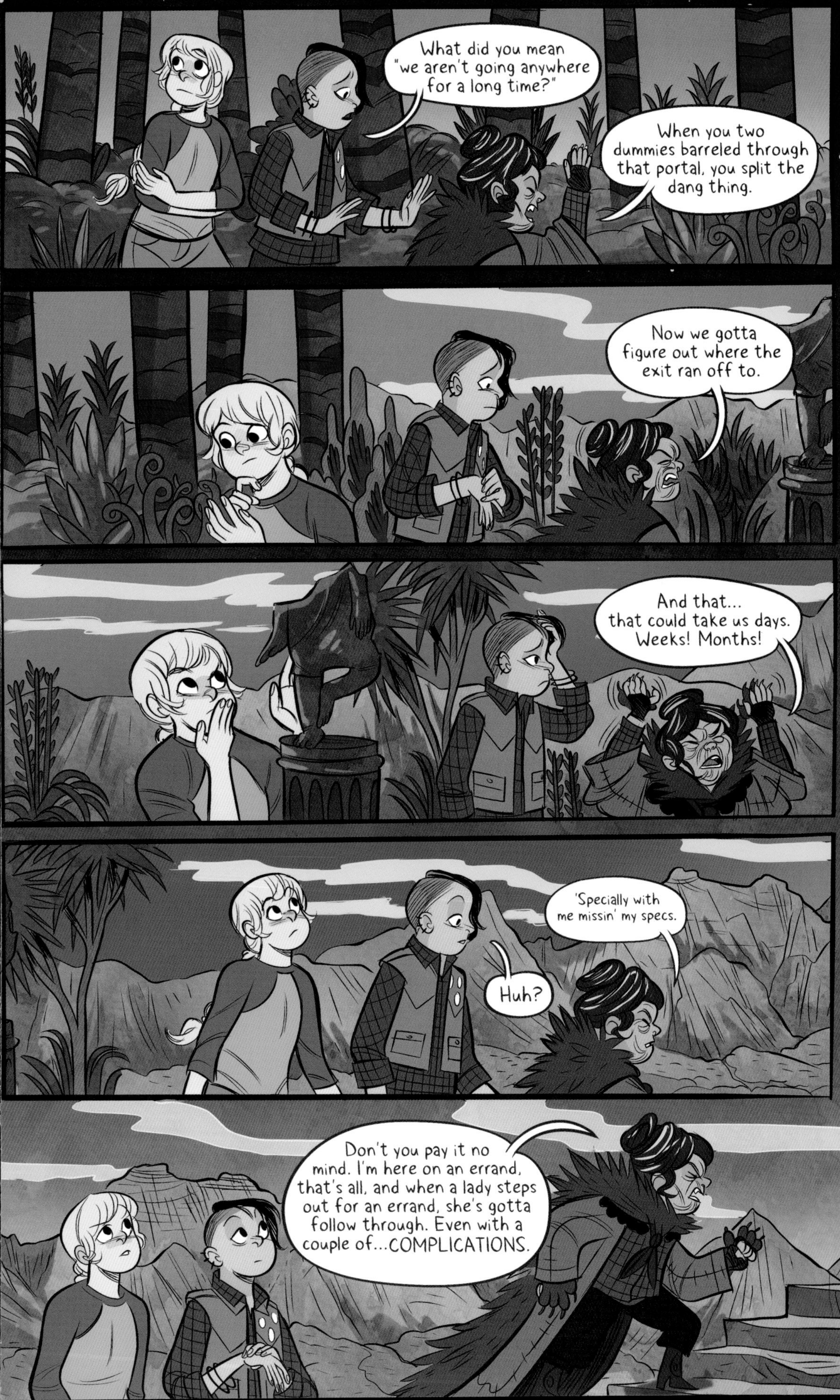
What did you mean "we aren't going anywhere for a long time?"
When you two dummies barreled through that portal, you split the dang thing.
Now we gotta figure out where the exit ran off to.
And that... that could take us days. Weeks! Months!
'Specially with me missin' my specs.
Huh?
Don't you pay it no mind. I'm here on an errand, that's all, and when a lady steps out for an errand, she's gotta follow through. Even with a couple of...COMPLICATIONS.

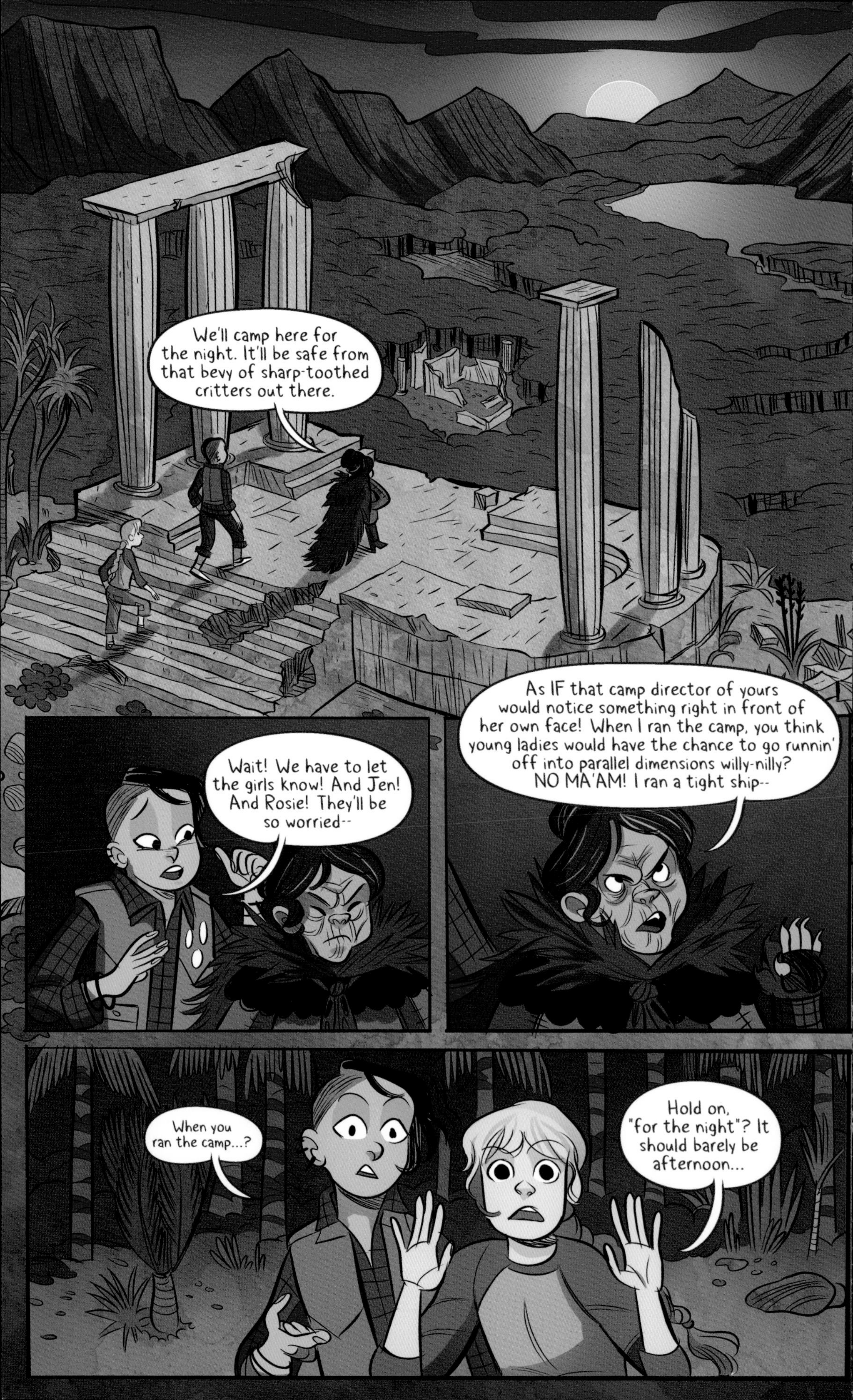
We'll camp here for the night. It'll be safe from that bevy of sharp-toothed critters out there.
Wait! We have to let the girls know! And Jen! And Rosie! They'll be so worried--
As IF that camp director of yours would notice something right in front of her own face! When I ran the camp, you think young ladies would have the chance to go runnin' off into parallel dimensions willy-nilly? NO MA'AM! I ran a tight ship--
When you ran the camp...?
Hold on, "for the night"? It should barely be afternoon...

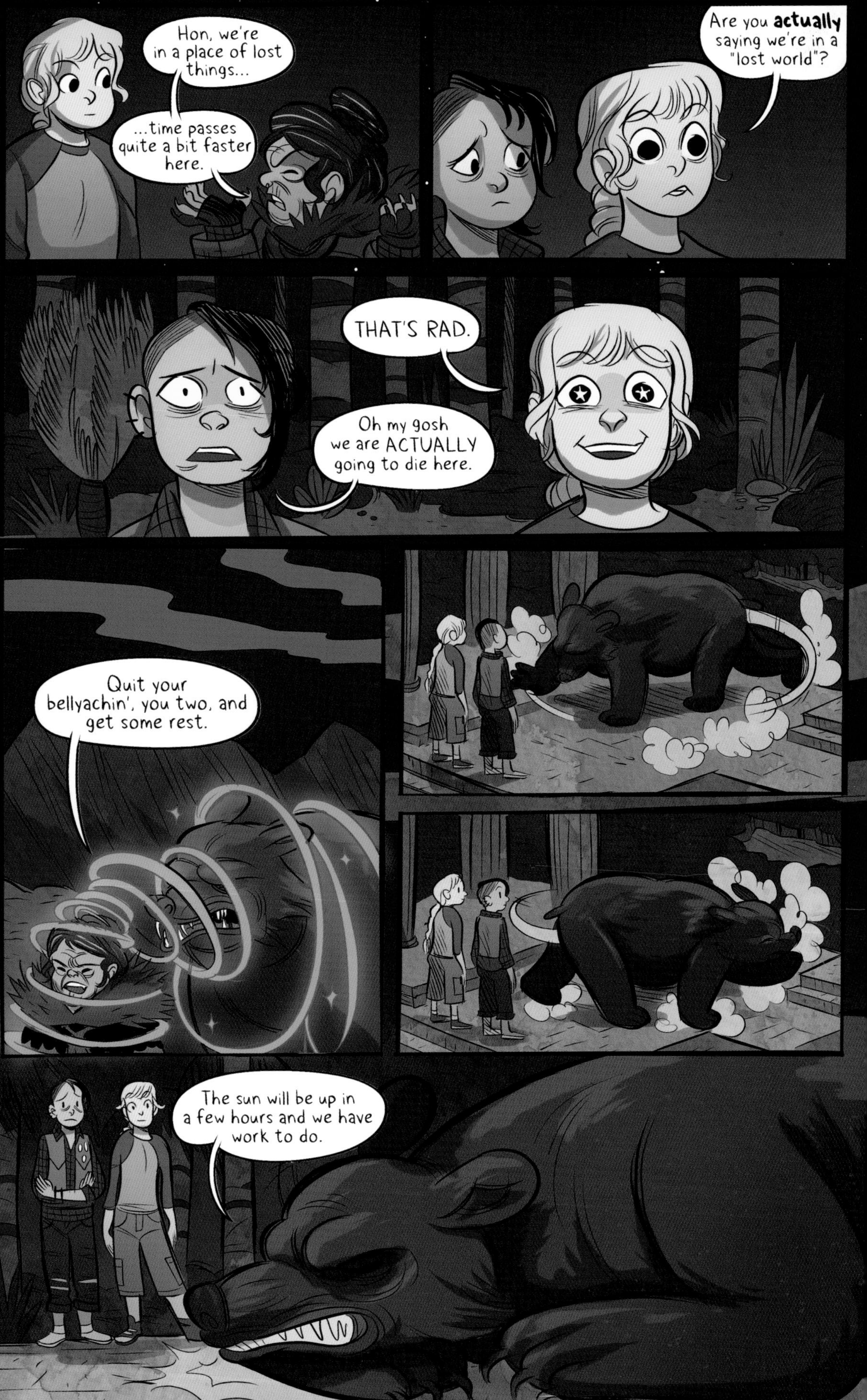
Hon, we're in a place of lost things...
...time passes quite a bit faster here.
Are you **actually** saying we're in a "lost world"?
THAT'S RAD.
Oh my gosh we are ACTUALLY going to die here.
Quit your bellyachin', you two, and get some rest.
The sun will be up in a few hours and we have work to do.

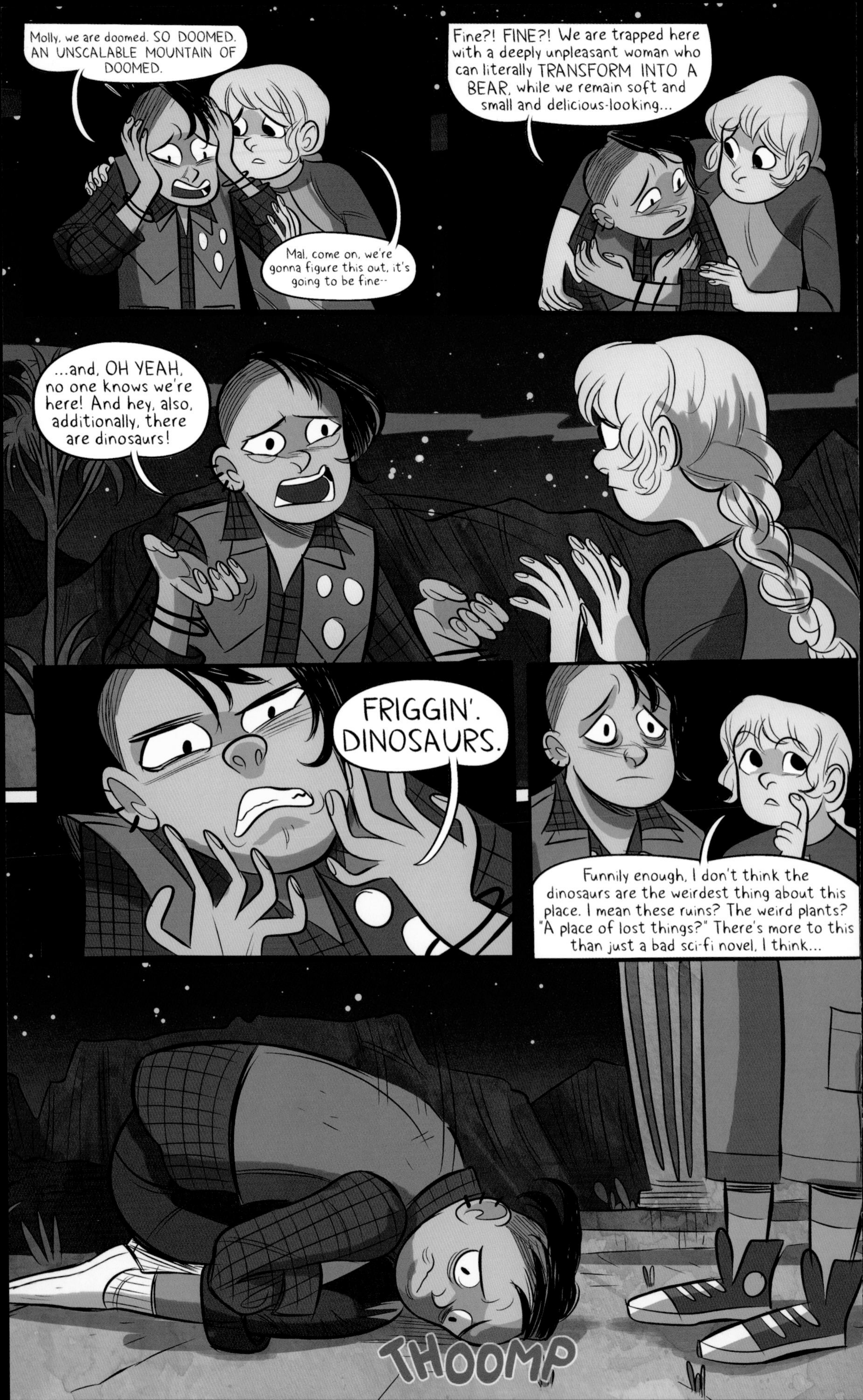
Molly, we are doomed. SO DOOMED. AN UNSCALABLE MOUNTAIN OF DOOMED.
Mal, come on, we're gonna figure this out, it's going to be fine--
Fine?! FINE?! We are trapped here with a deeply unpleasant woman who can literally TRANSFORM INTO A BEAR, while we remain soft and small and delicious-looking...
...and, OH YEAH, no one knows we're here! And hey, also, additionally, there are dinosaurs!
FRIGGIN'. DINOSAURS.
Funnily enough, I don't think the dinosaurs are the weirdest thing about this place. I mean these ruins? The weird plants? "A place of lost things?" There's more to this than just a bad sci-fi novel, I think...
THOOMP

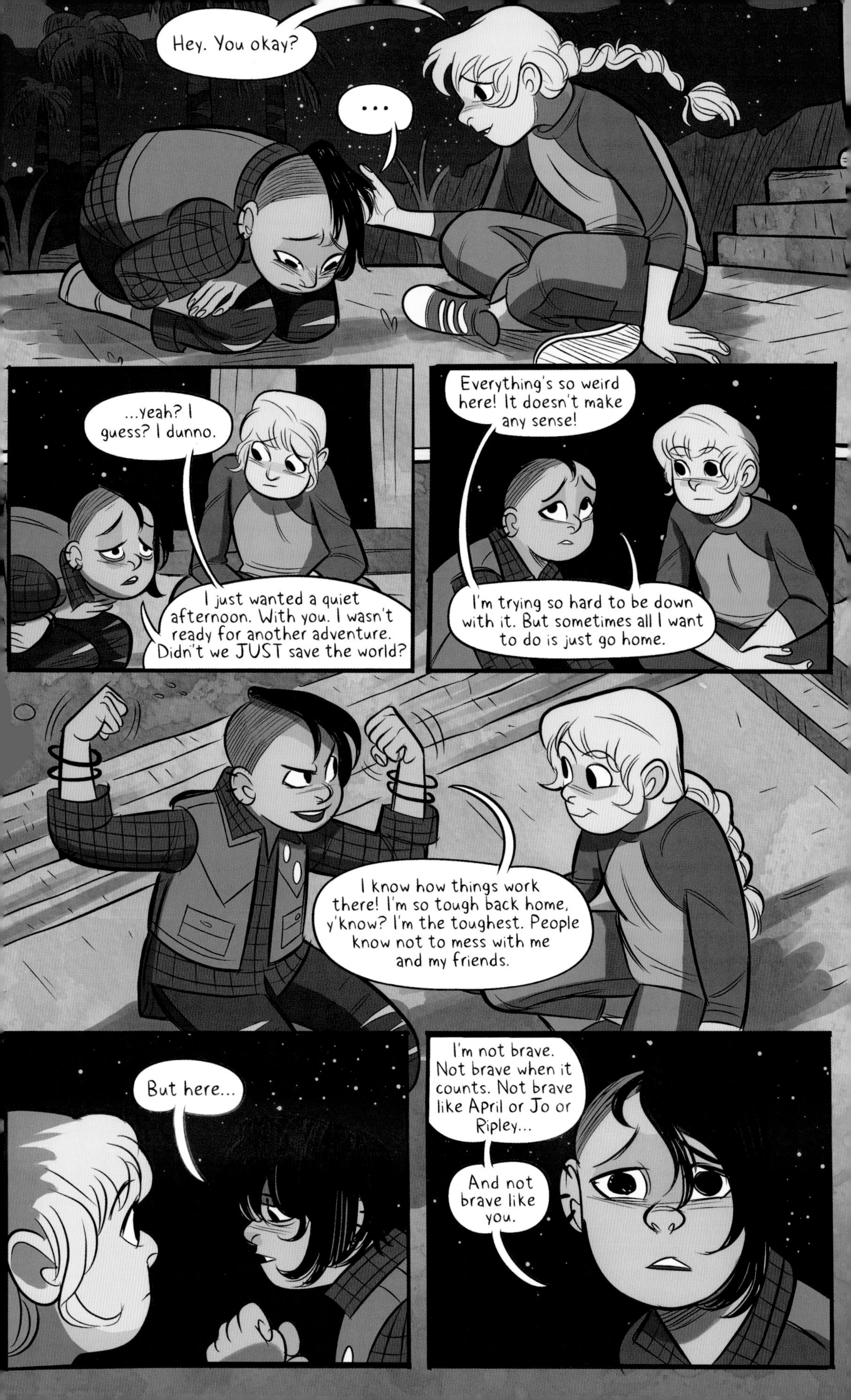
Hey. You okay?
...
...yeah? I guess? I dunno.
I just wanted a quiet afternoon. With you. I wasn't ready for another adventure. Didn't we JUST save the world?
Everything's so weird here! It doesn't make any sense!
I'm trying so hard to be down with it. But sometimes all I want to do is just go home.
I know how things work there! I'm so tough back home, y'know? I'm the toughest. People know not to mess with me and my friends.
But here...
I'm not brave. Not brave when it counts. Not brave like April or Jo or Ripley...
And not brave like you.

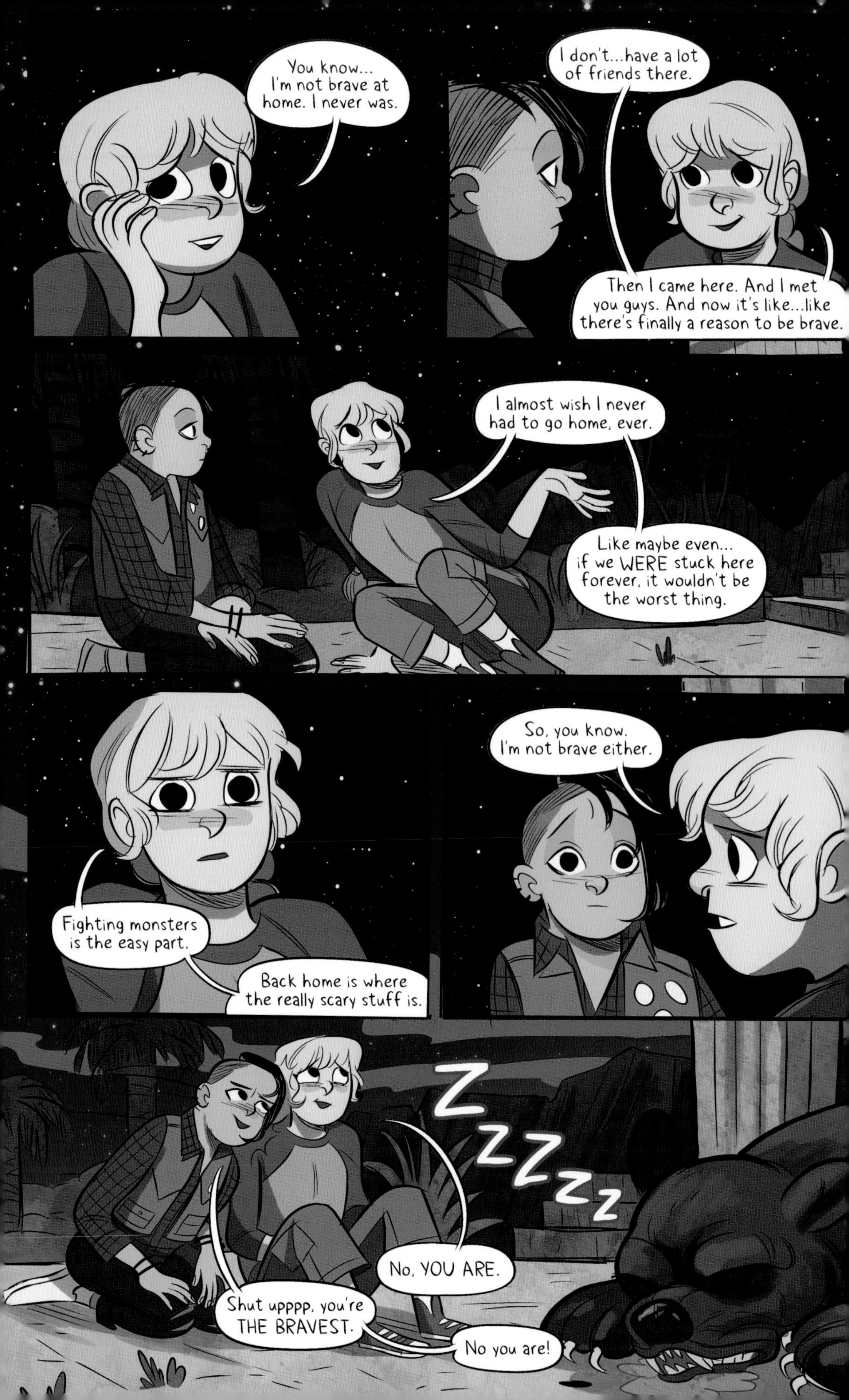
You know... I'm not brave at home. I never was.
I don't...have a lot of friends there.
Then I came here. And I met you guys. And now it's like...like there's finally a reason to be brave.
I almost wish I never had to go home, ever.
Like maybe even... if we WERE stuck here forever, it wouldn't be the worst thing.
Fighting monsters is the easy part.
Back home is where the really scary stuff is.
So, you know. I'm not brave either.
ZZZZZ
Shut upppp, you're THE BRAVEST.
No, YOU ARE.
No you are!

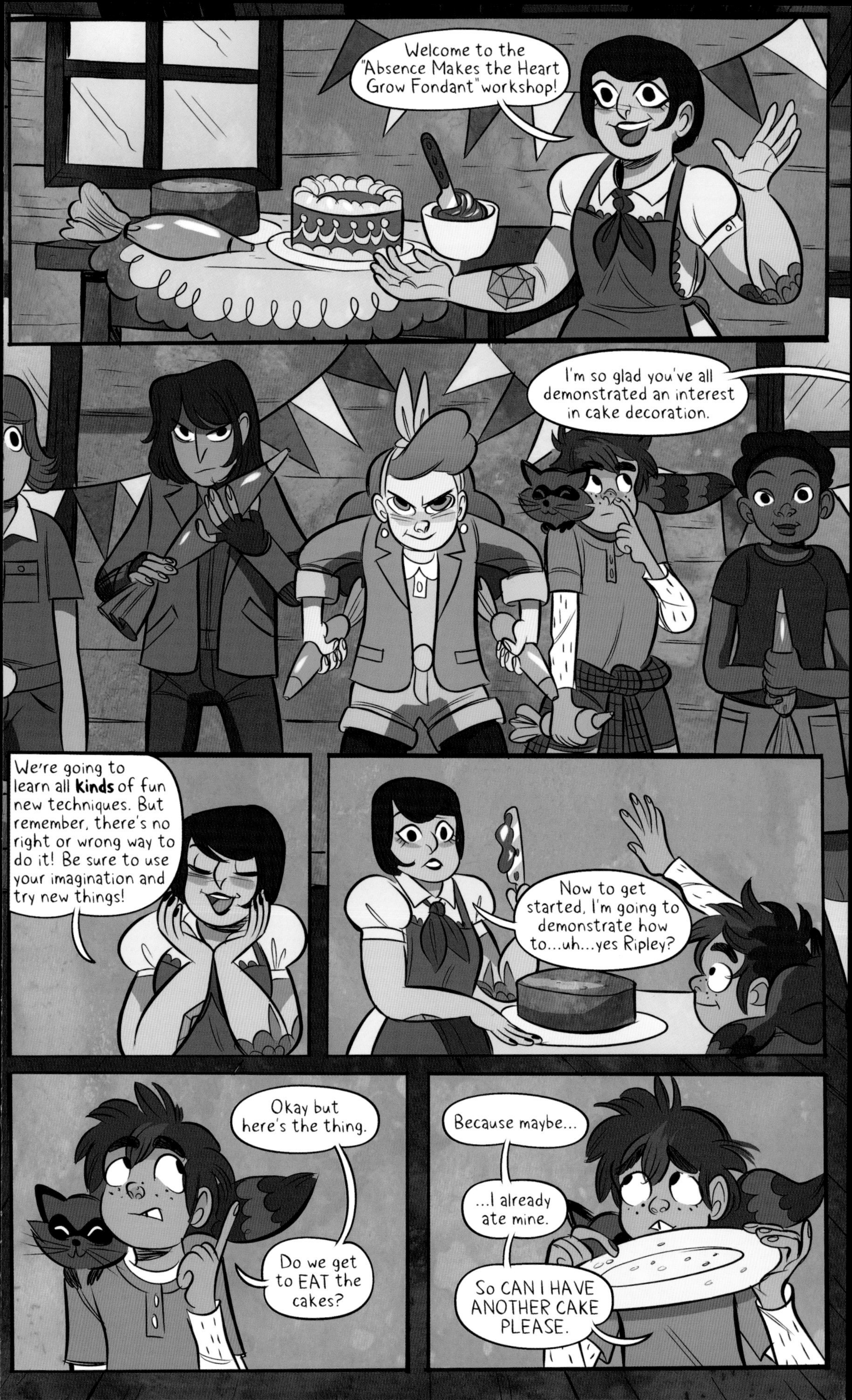
Welcome to the "Absence Makes the Heart Grow Fondant" workshop!
I'm so glad you've all demonstrated an interest in cake decoration.
We're going to learn all **Kinds** of fun new techniques. But remember, there's no right or wrong way to do it! Be sure to use your imagination and try new things!
Now to get started, I'm going to demonstrate how to...uh...yes Ripley?
Okay but here's the thing.
Do we get to EAT the cakes?
Because maybe...
...I already ate mine.
So CAN I HAVE ANOTHER CAKE PLEASE.

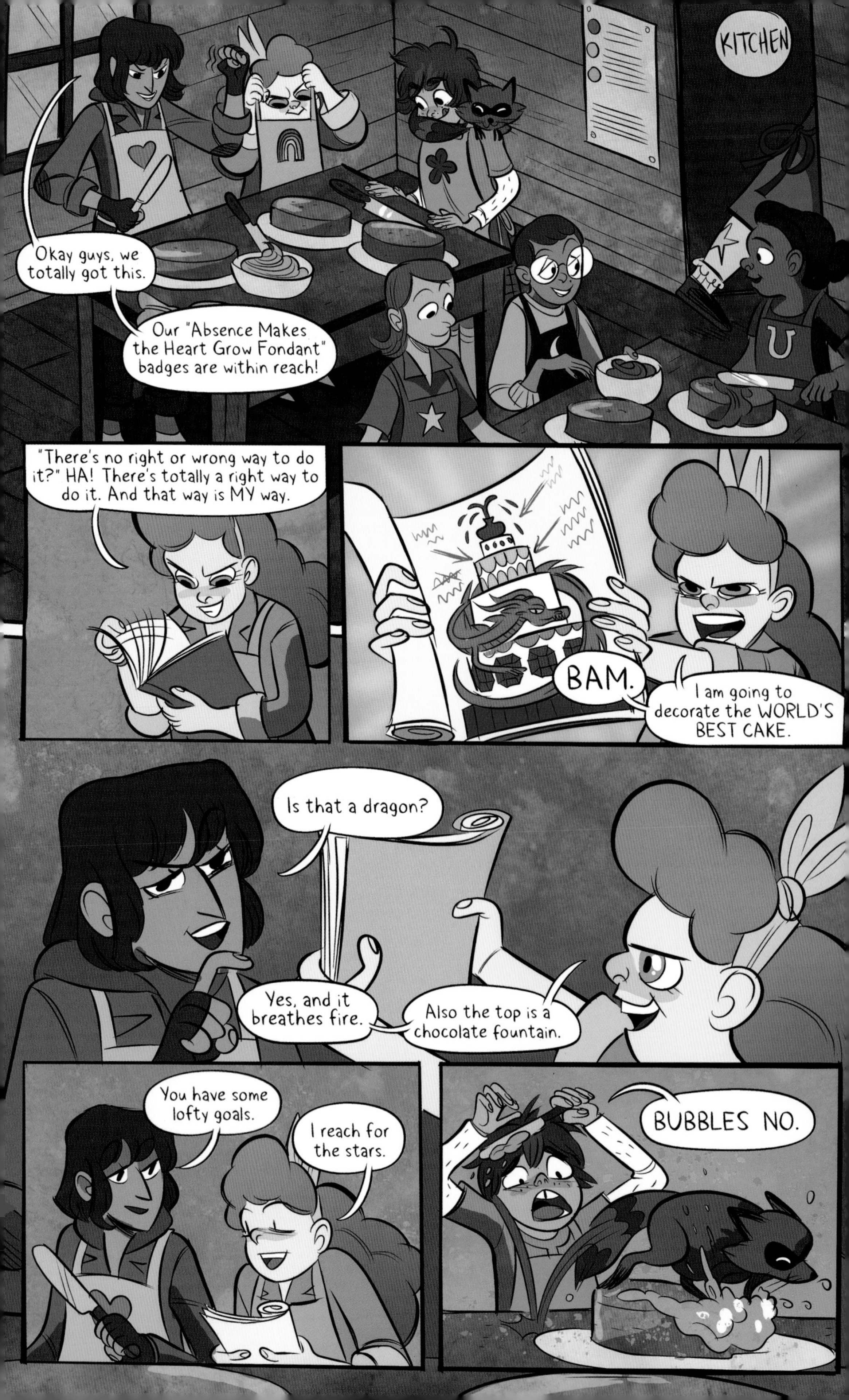
KITCHEN
Okay guys, we totally got this.
Our "Absence Makes the Heart Grow Fondant" badges are within reach!
"There's no right or wrong way to do it?" HA! There's totally a right way to do it. And that way is MY way.
BAM.
I am going to decorate the WORLD'S BEST CAKE.
Is that a dragon?
Yes, and it breathes fire.
Also the top is a chocolate fountain.
You have some lofty goals.
I reach for the stars.
BUBBLES NO.

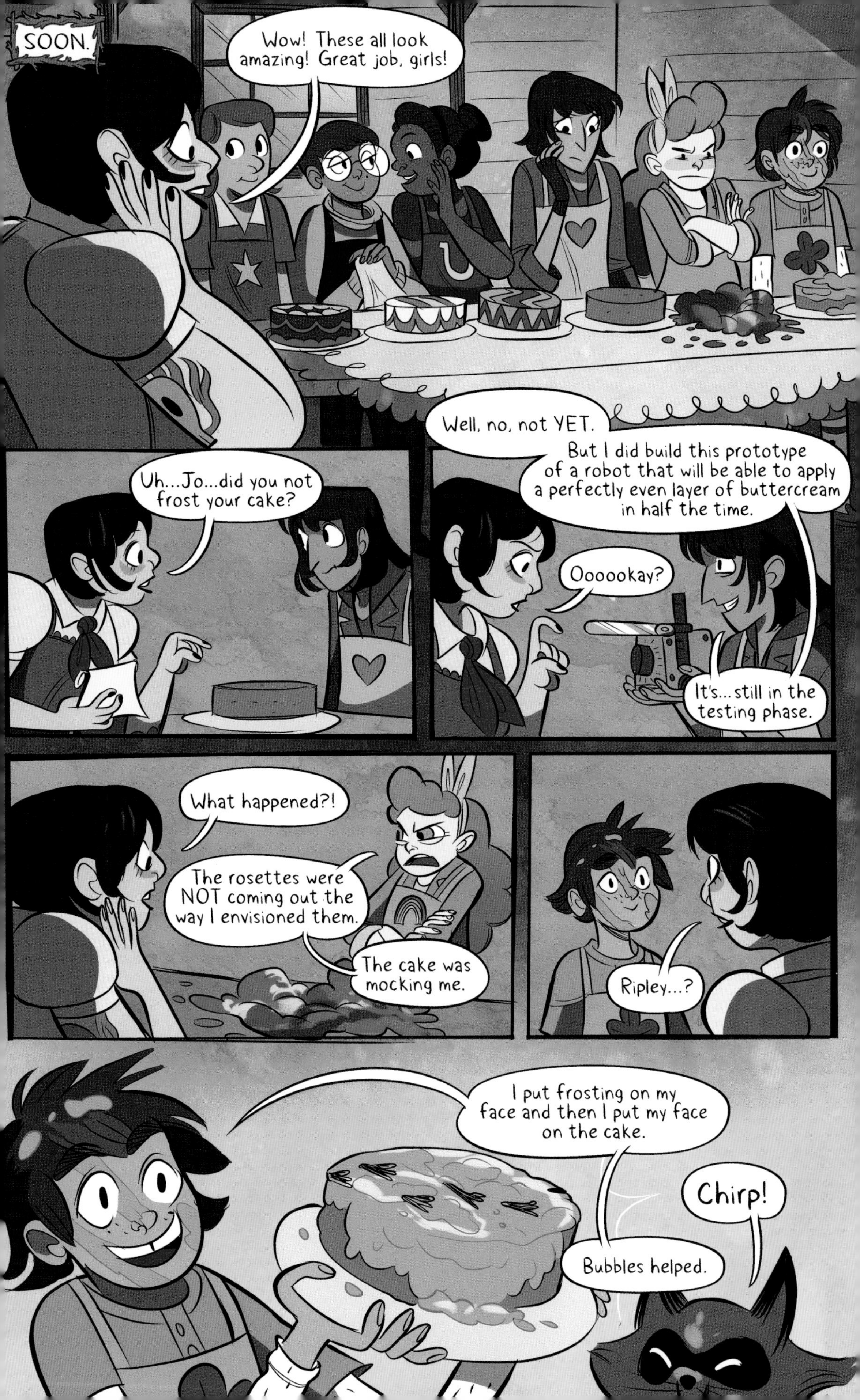
SOON.
Wow! These all look amazing! Great job, girls!
Uh...Jo...did you not frost your cake?
Well, no, not YET.
But I did build this prototype of a robot that will be able to apply a perfectly even layer of buttercream in half the time.
Oooookay?
It's... still in the testing phase.
What happened?!
The rosettes were NOT coming out the way I envisioned them.
The cake was mocking me.
Ripley...?
I put frosting on my face and then I put my face on the cake.
Bubbles helped.
Chirp!

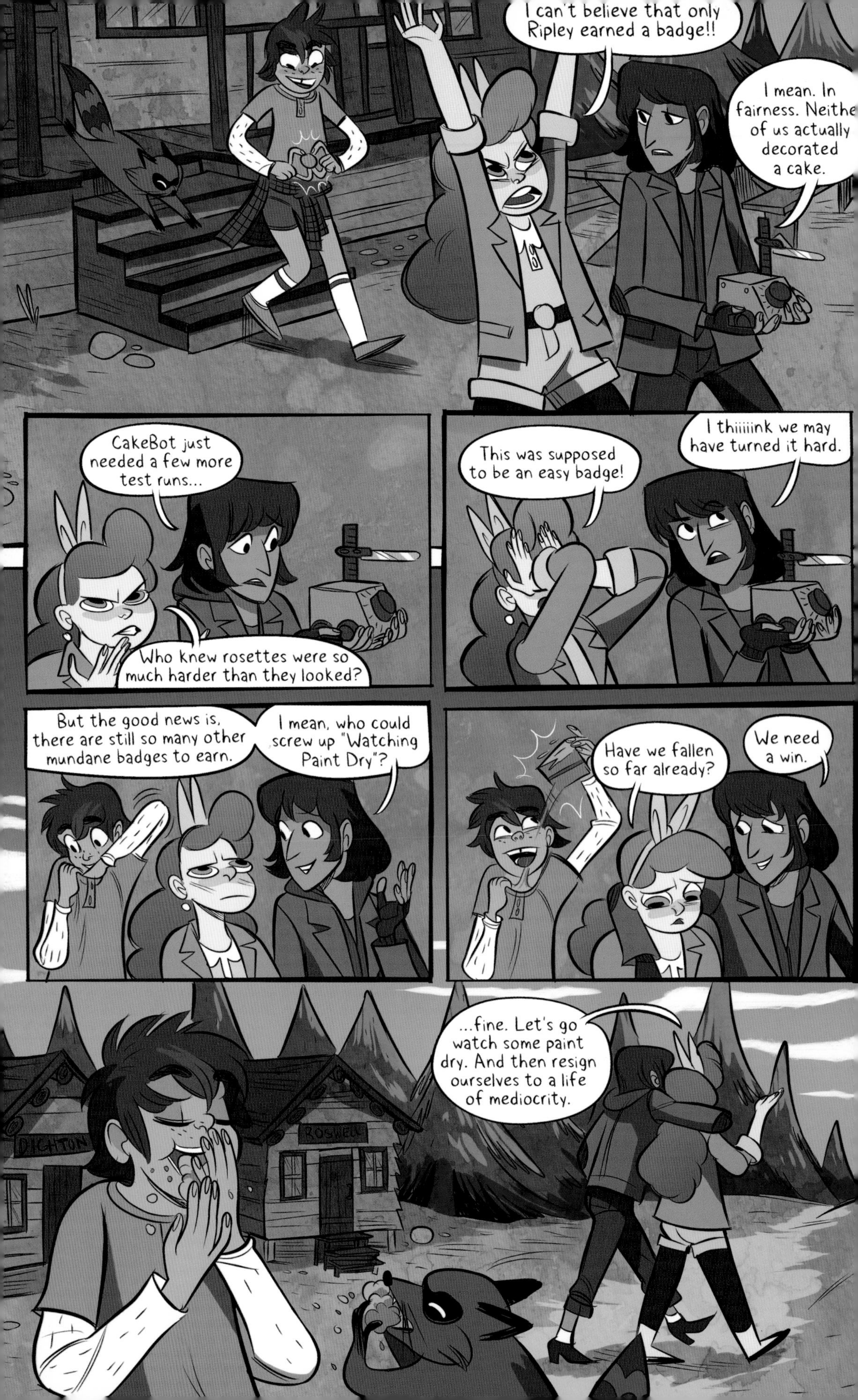
I can't believe that only Ripley earned a badge!!
I mean. In fairness. Neithe of us actually decorated a cake.
CakeBot just needed a few more test runs...
Who knew rosettes were so much harder than they looked?
This was supposed to be an easy badge!
I thiiiiink we may have turned it hard.
But the good news is, there are still so many other mundane badges to earn.
I mean, who could screw up "Watching Paint Dry"?
Have we fallen so far already?
We need a win.
...fine. Let's go watch some paint dry. And then resign ourselves to a life of mediocrity.
DIGHTON
ROSWELL

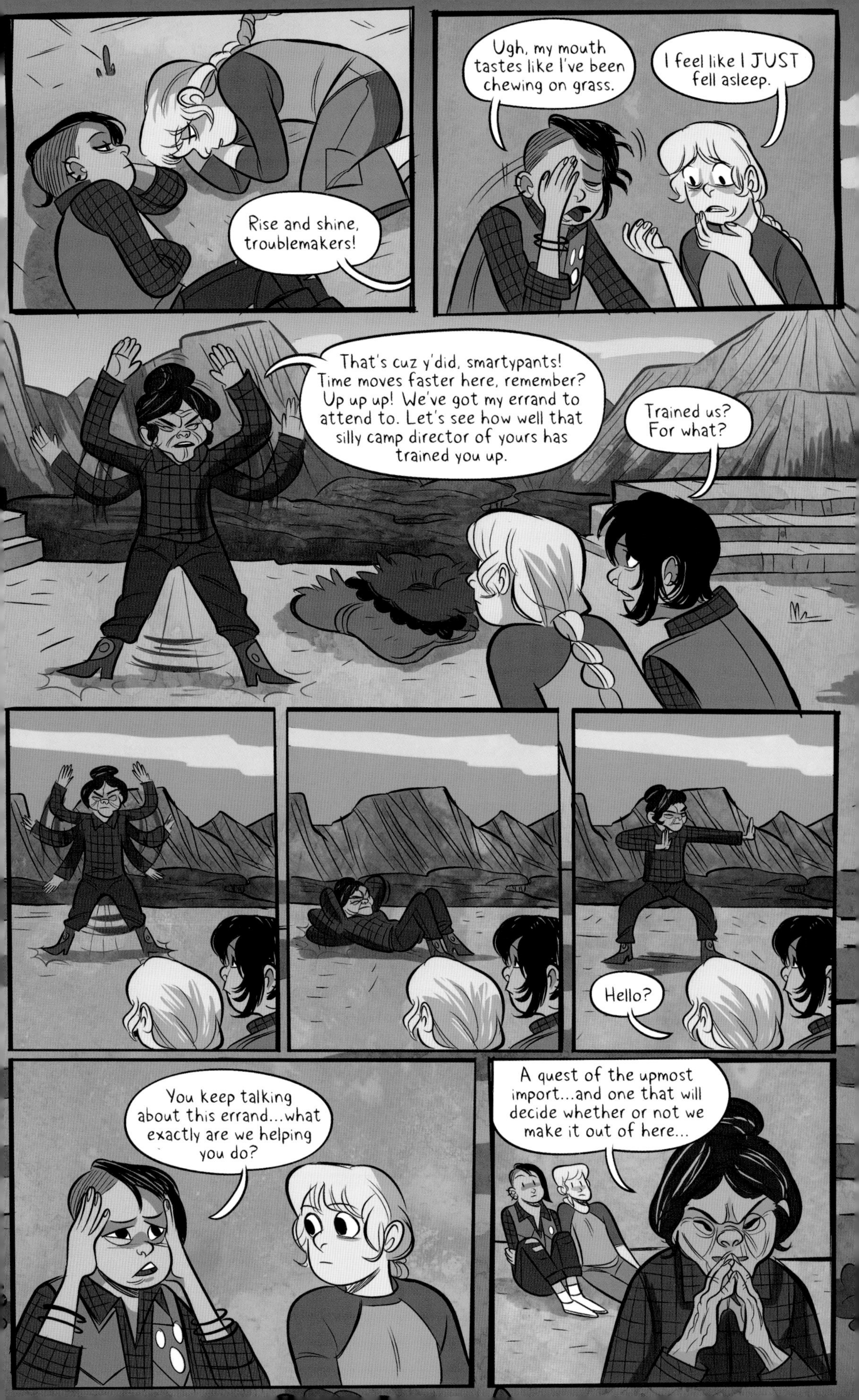
Rise and shine, troublemakers!
Ugh, my mouth tastes like I've been chewing on grass.
I feel like I JUST fell asleep.
That's cuz y'did, smartypants! Time moves faster here, remember? Up up up! We've got my errand to attend to. Let's see how well that silly camp director of yours has trained you up.
Trained us? For what?
Hello?
You keep talking about this errand...what exactly are we helping you do?
A quest of the upmost import...and one that will decide whether or not we make it out of here...

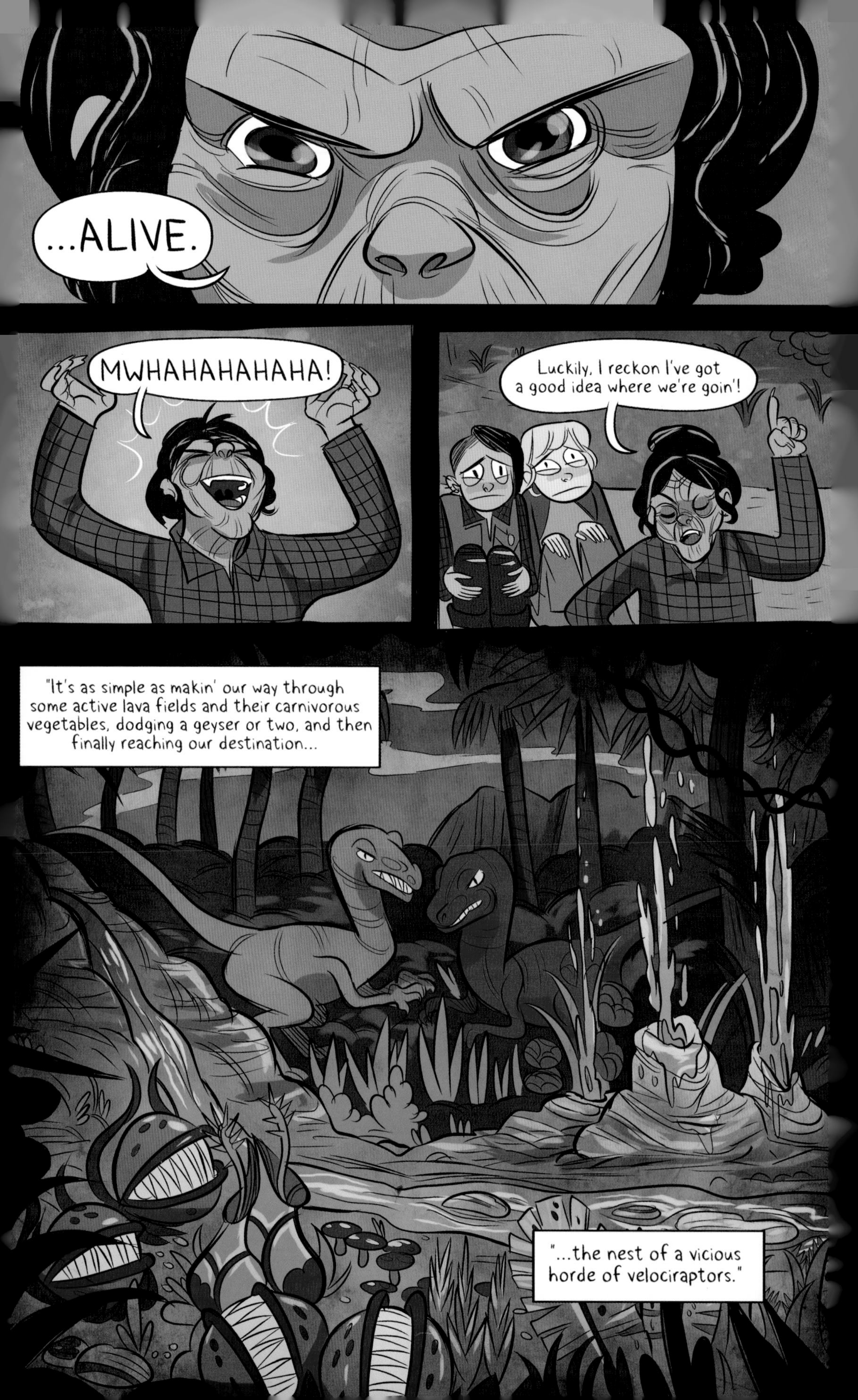
...ALIVE.
MWHAHAHAHAHA!
Luckily, I reckon I've got a good idea where we're goin'!
"It's as simple as makin' our way through some active lava fields and their carnivorous vegetables, dodging a geyser or two, and then finally reaching our destination...
"...the nest of a vicious horde of velociraptors."

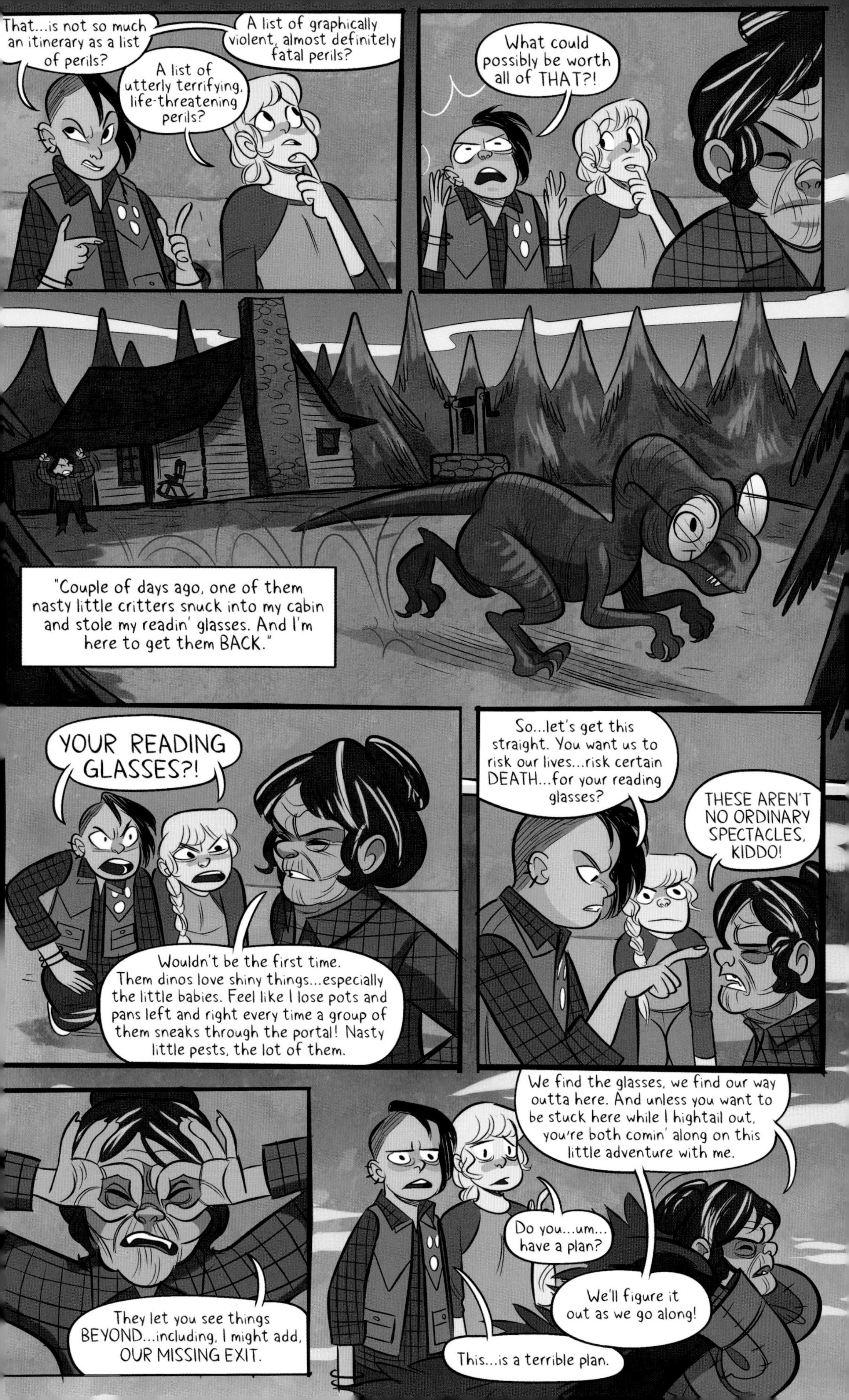
That...is not so much an itinerary as a list of perils?
A list of graphically violent, almost definitely fatal perils?
A list of utterly terrifying, life-threatening perils?
What could possibly be worth all of THAT?!
"Couple of days ago, one of them nasty little critters snuck into my cabin and stole my readin' glasses. And I'm here to get them BACK."
YOUR READING GLASSES?!
Wouldn't be the first time. Them dinos love shiny things...especially the little babies. Feel like I lose pots and pans left and right every time a group of them sneaks through the portal! Nasty little pests, the lot of them.
So...let's get this straight. You want us to risk our lives...risk certain DEATH...for your reading glasses?
THESE AREN'T NO ORDINARY SPECTACLES, KIDDO!
They let you see things BEYOND...including, I might add, OUR MISSING EXIT.
We find the glasses, we find our way outta here. And unless you want to be stuck here while I hightail out, you're both comin' along on this little adventure with me.
Do you...um... have a plan?
We'll figure it out as we go along!
This...is a terrible plan.

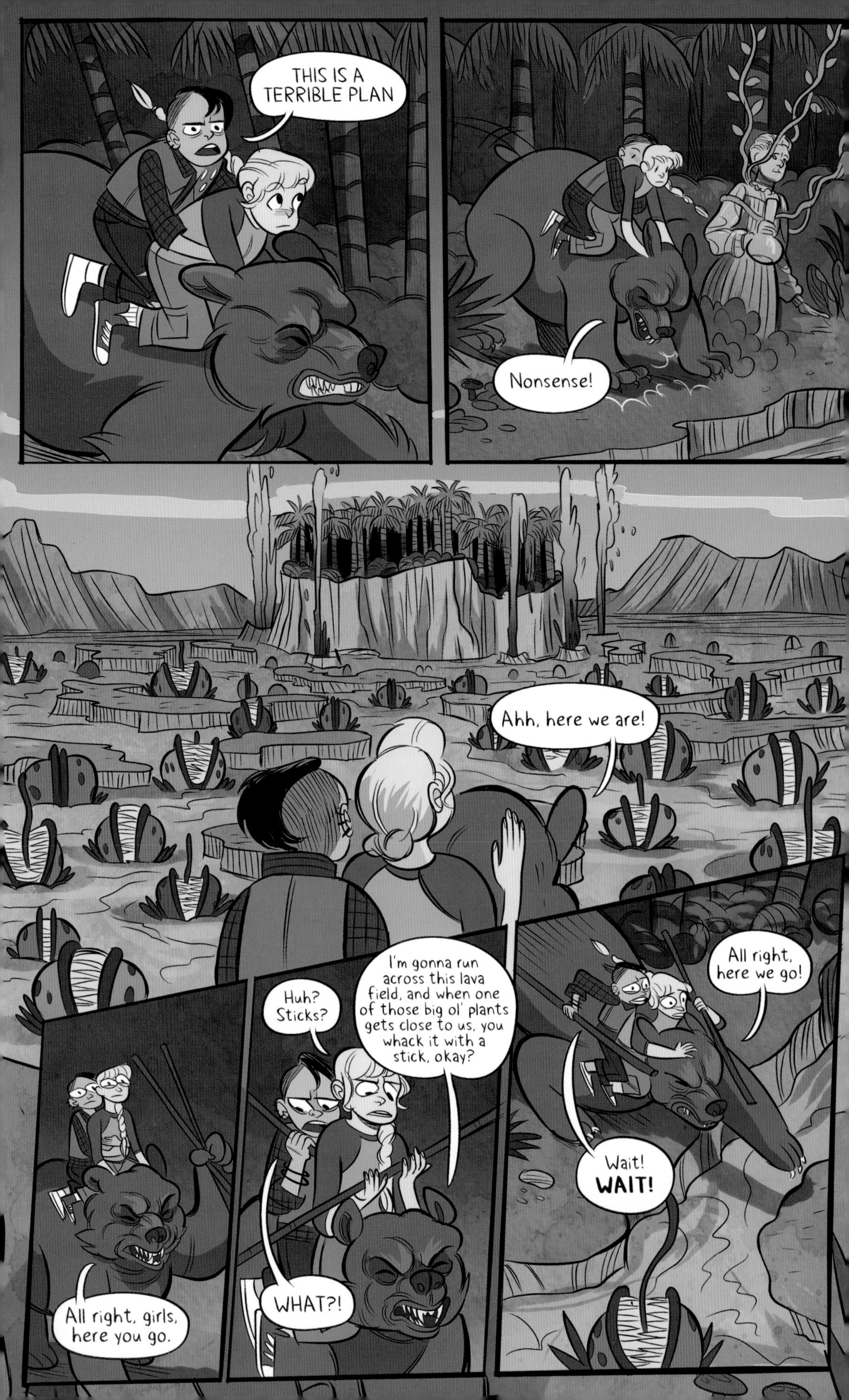
THIS IS A TERRIBLE PLAN
Nonsense!
Ahh, here we are!
All right, girls, here you go.
Huh? Sticks?
I'm gonna run across this lava field, and when one of those big ol' plants gets close to us, you whack it with a stick, okay?
WHAT?!
All right, here we go!
Wait! WAIT!

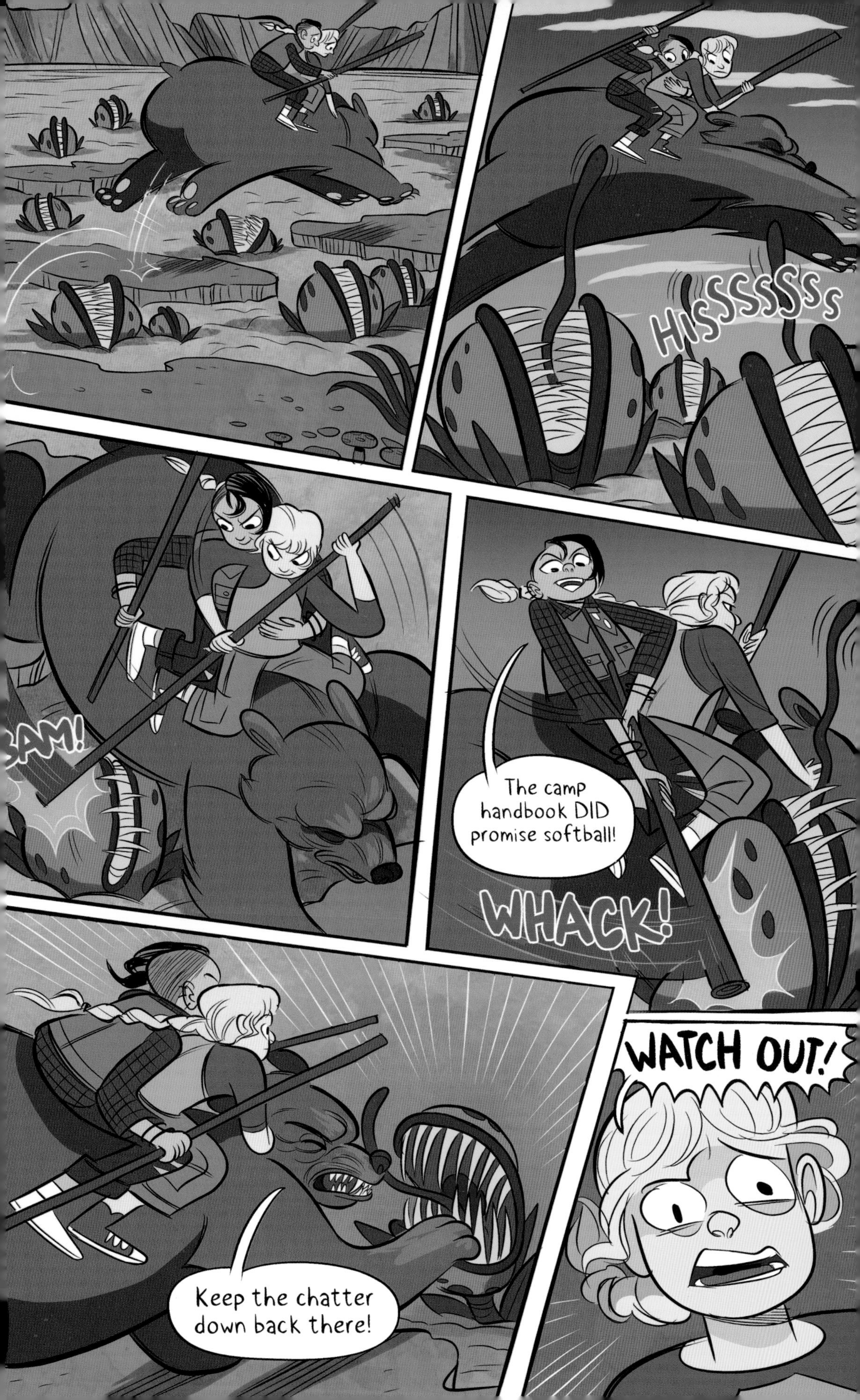
HISSSSSSS
BAM!
The camp handbook DID promise softball!
WHACK!
Keep the chatter down back there!
WATCH OUT!

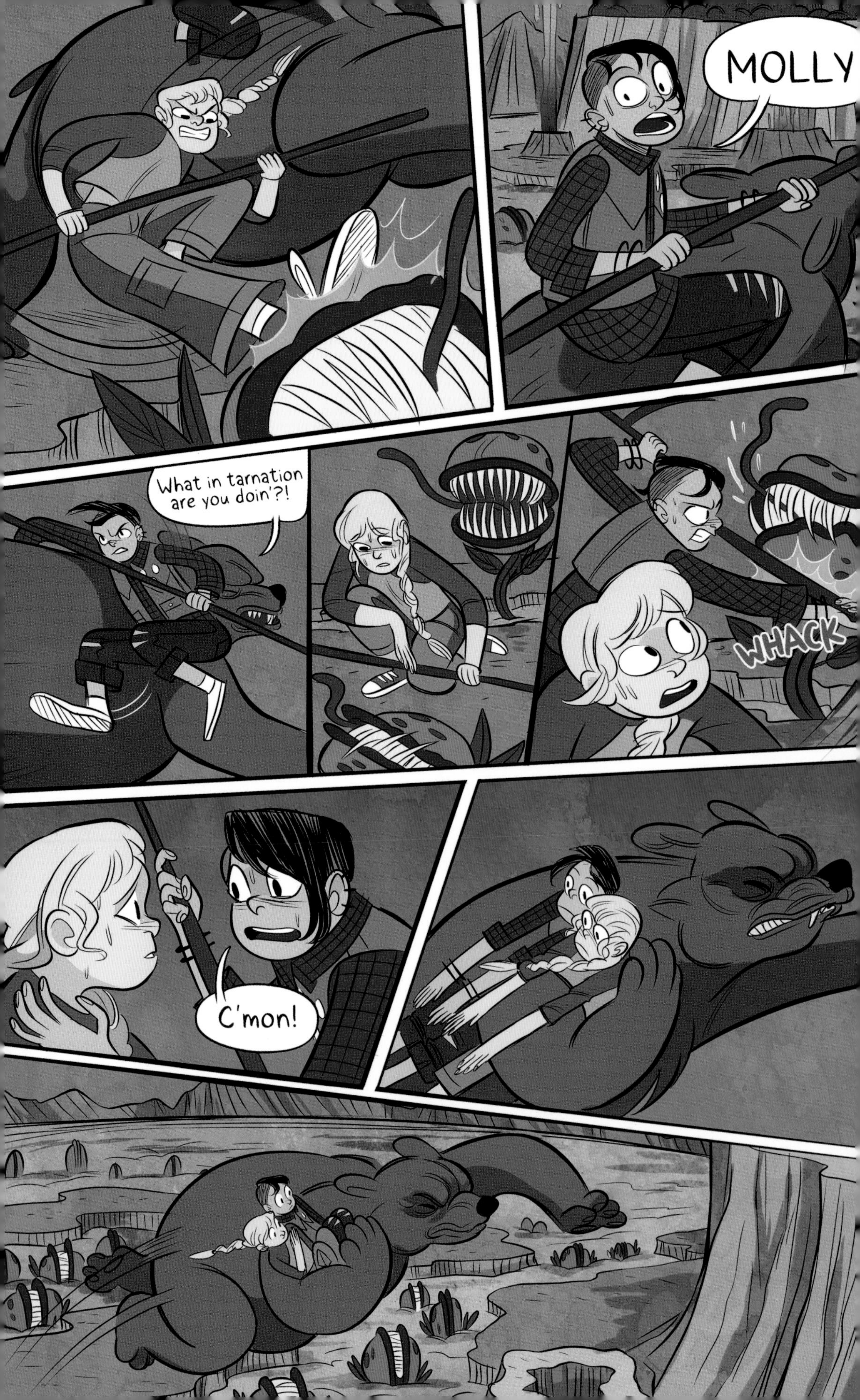
MOLLY
What in tarnation are you doin'?!
WHACK
C'mon!

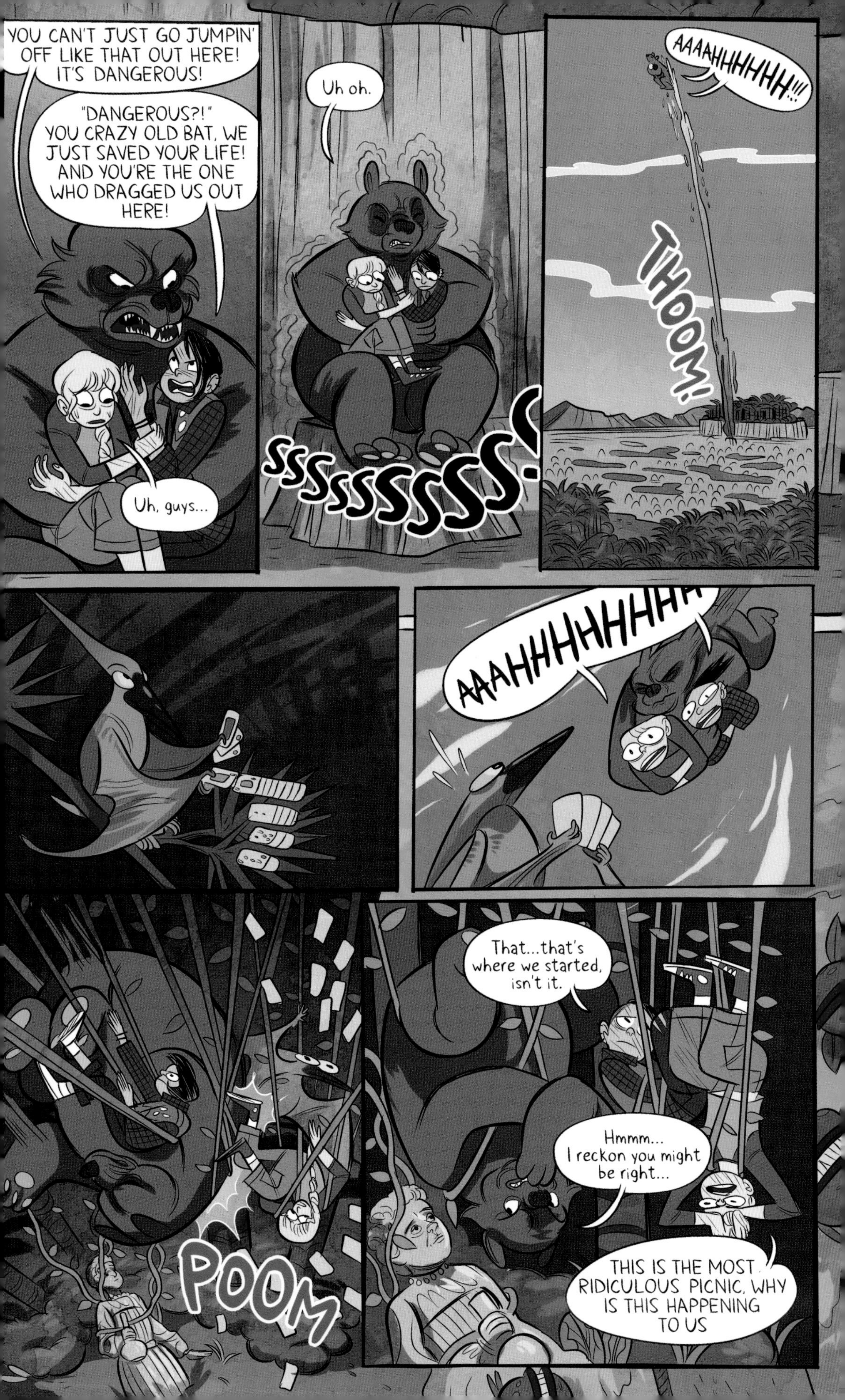
YOU CAN'T JUST GO JUMPIN' OFF LIKE THAT OUT HERE! IT'S DANGEROUS!
"DANGEROUS?!" YOU CRAZY OLD BAT, WE JUST SAVED YOUR LIFE! AND YOU'RE THE ONE WHO DRAGGED US OUT HERE!
Uh, guys...
Uh oh.
SSSSSSSSS!
AAAAHHHHHH!!!
THOOOM!
AAAHHHHHHHH
POOM
That...that's where we started, isn't it.
Hmmm... I reckon you might be right...
THIS IS THE MOST RIDICULOUS PICNIC, WHY IS THIS HAPPENING TO US

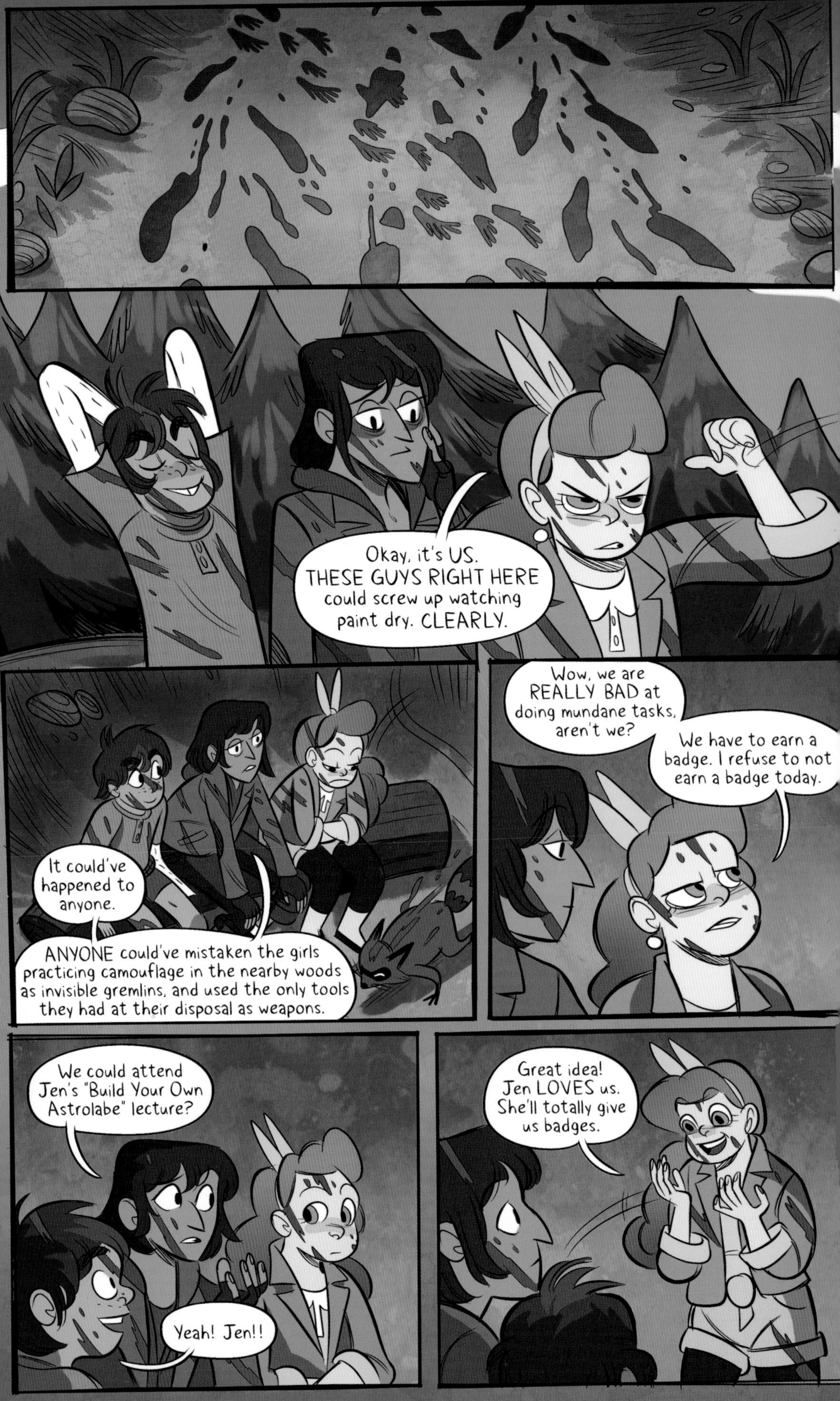

Okay, it's US. THESE GUYS RIGHT HERE could screw up watching paint dry. CLEARLY.
It could've happened to anyone.
ANYONE could've mistaken the girls practicing camouflage in the nearby woods as invisible gremlins, and used the only tools they had at their disposal as weapons.
Wow, we are REALLY BAD at doing mundane tasks, aren't we?
We have to earn a badge. I refuse to not earn a badge today.
We could attend Jen's "Build Your Own Astrolabe" lecture?
Yeah! Jen!!
Great idea! Jen LOVES us. She'll totally give us badges.

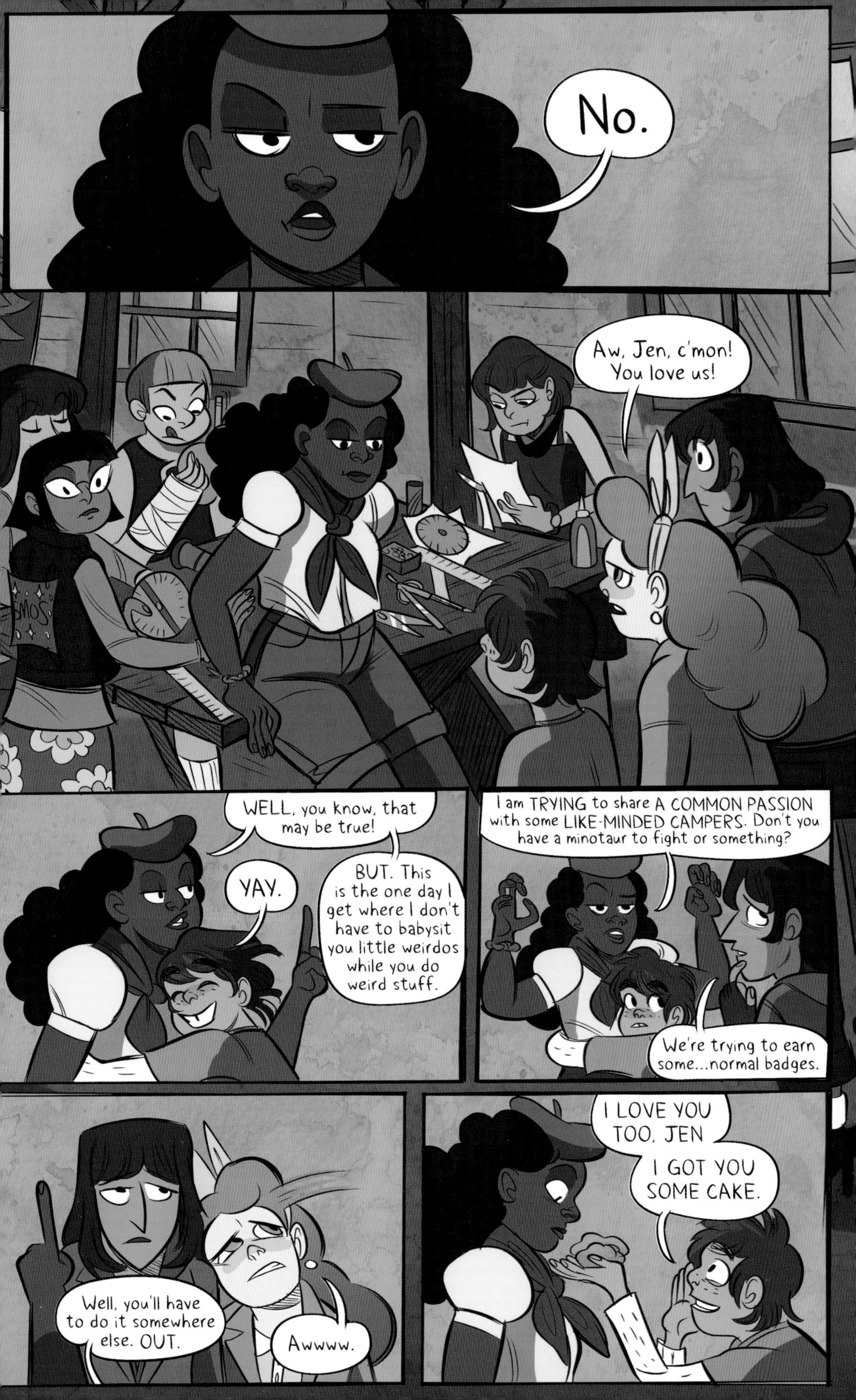
No.
Aw, Jen, c'mon! You love us!
WELL, you know, that may be true!
YAY.
BUT. This is the one day I get where I don't have to babysit you little weirdos while you do weird stuff.
I am TRYING to share A COMMON PASSION with some LIKE-MINDED CAMPERS. Don't you have a minotaur to fight or something?
We're trying to earn some...normal badges.
Well, you'll have to do it somewhere else. OUT.
Awwww.
I LOVE YOU TOO, JEN
I GOT YOU SOME CAKE.

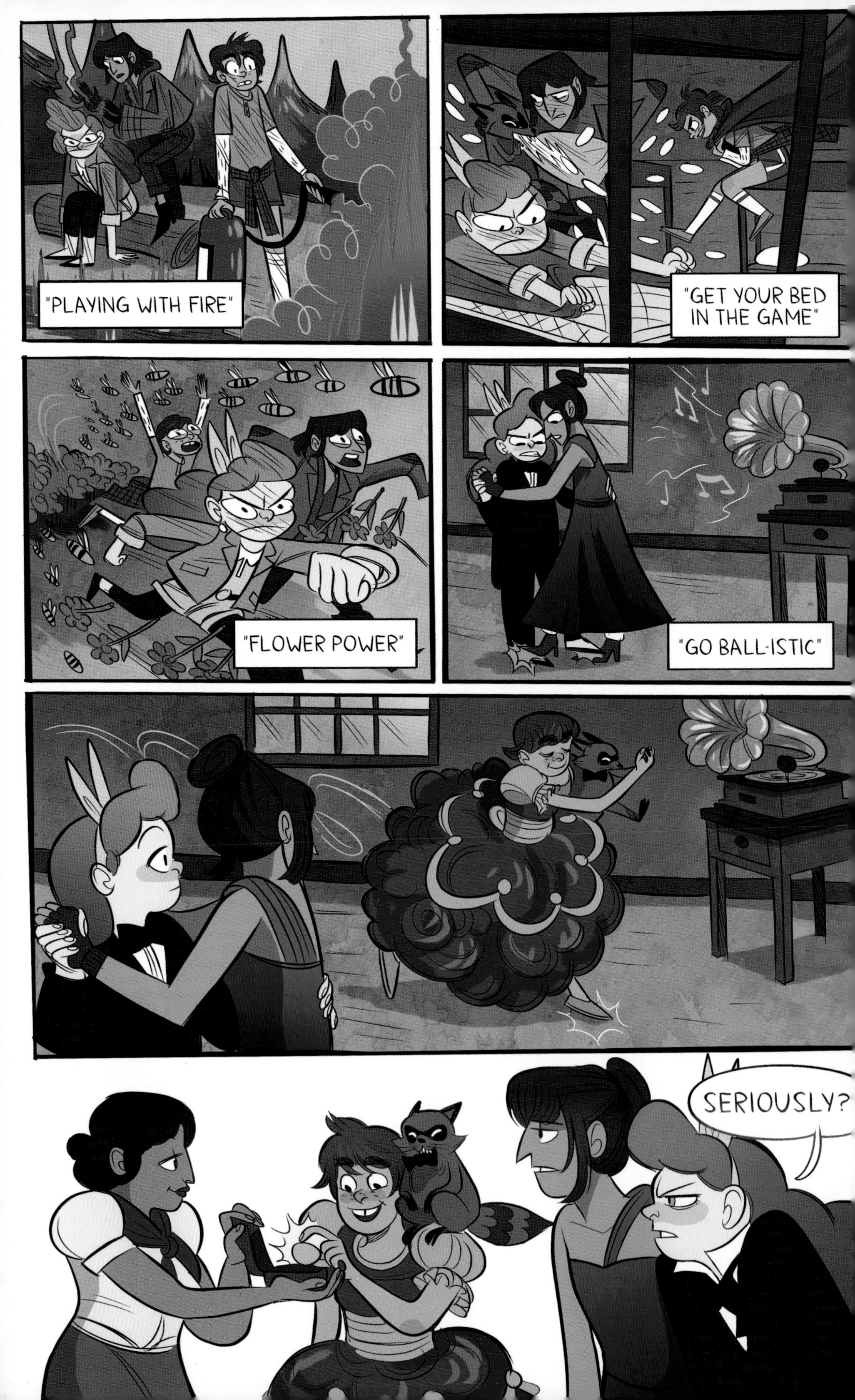
"PLAYING WITH FIRE"
"GET YOUR BED IN THE GAME"
"FLOWER POWER"
"GO BALL-ISTIC"
SERIOUSLY?

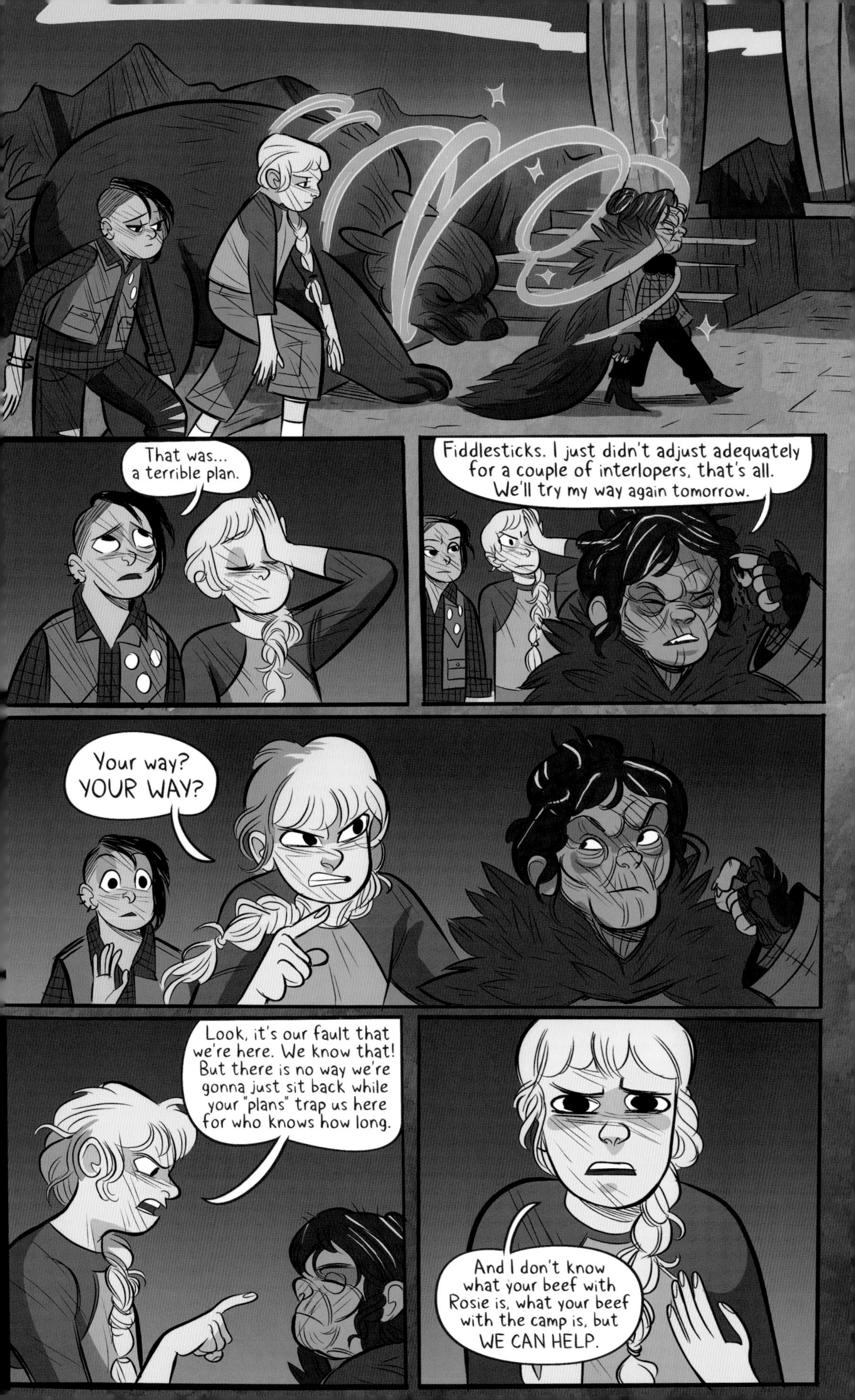
That was... a terrible plan.
Fiddlesticks. I just didn't adjust adequately for a couple of interlopers, that's all. We'll try my way again tomorrow.
Your way? YOUR WAY?
Look, it's our fault that we're here. We know that! But there is no way we're gonna just sit back while your "plans" trap us here for who knows how long.
And I don't know what your beef with Rosie is, what your beef with the camp is, but WE CAN HELP.

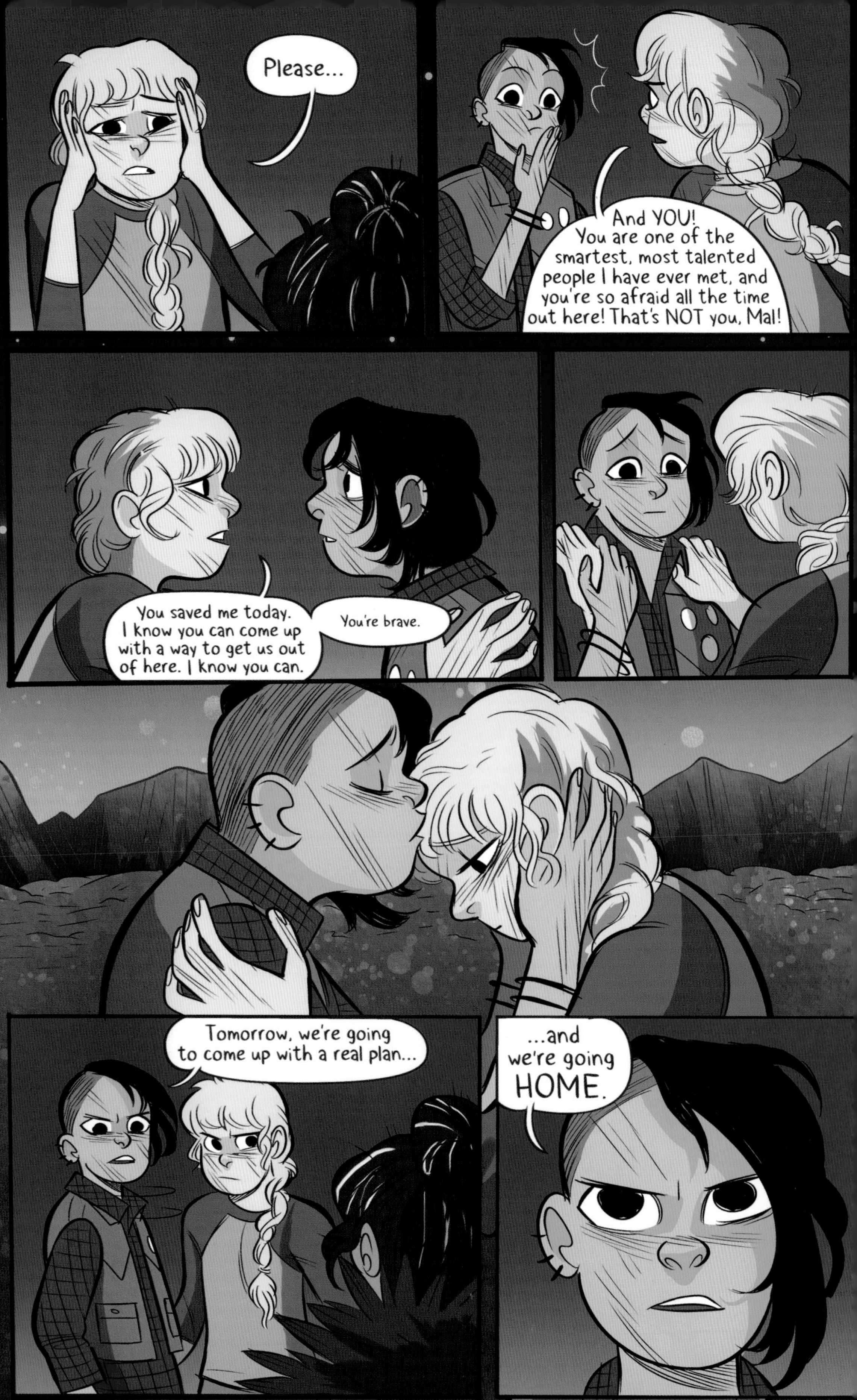
Please...
And YOU! You are one of the smartest, most talented people I have ever met, and you're so afraid all the time out here! That's NOT you, Mal!
You saved me today. I know you can come up with a way to get us out of here. I know you can.
You're brave.
Tomorrow, we're going to come up with a real plan...
...and we're going HOME.

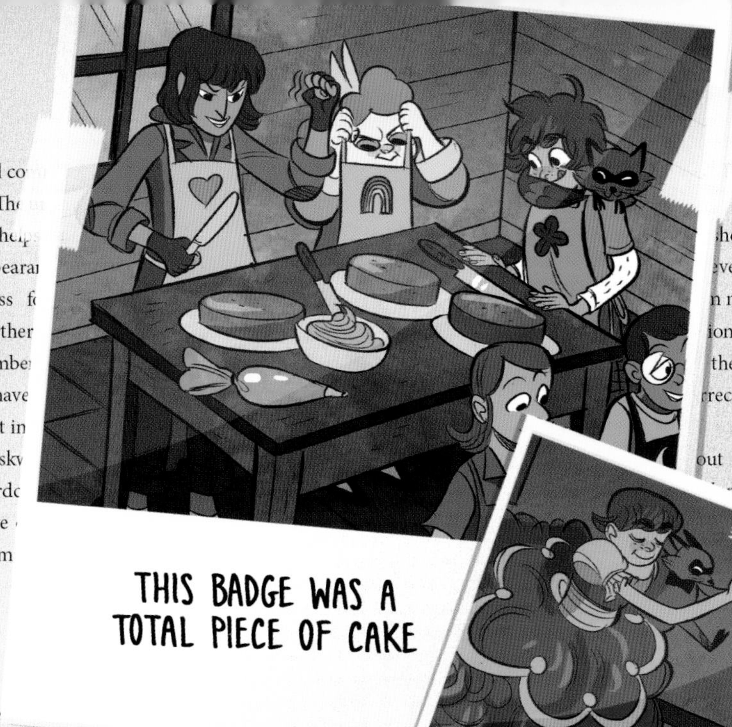
THIS BADGE WAS A
TOTAL PIECE OF CAKE

will co

The

It helps

appearan

dress fo

Further

Lumbe

to have

part in

Thiskv

Hardc

have

them

HE UNIFORM

should be worn at camp events when Lumberjanes n may also be worn at other ions. It should be worn as a the uniform dress with rrect shoes, and stocking or

out grows her uniform or ter Lumberjane. a she has her her

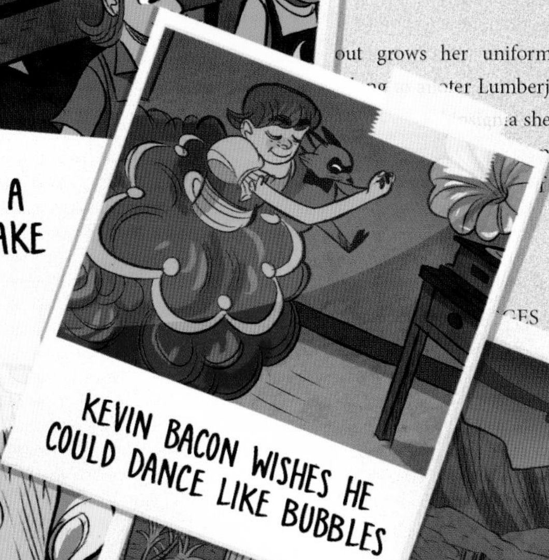
KEVIN BACON WISHES HE
COULD DANCE LIKE BUBBLES

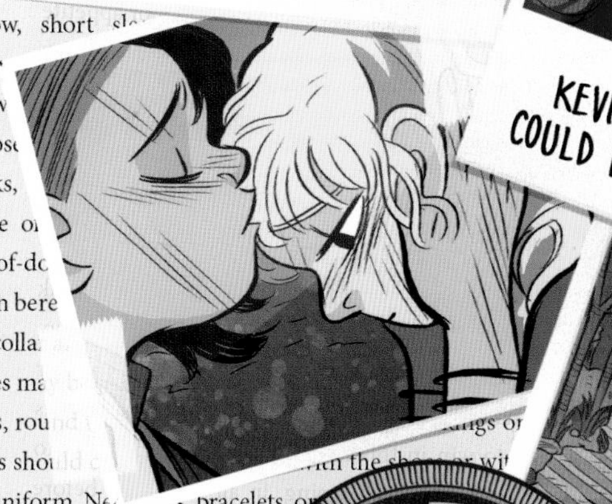

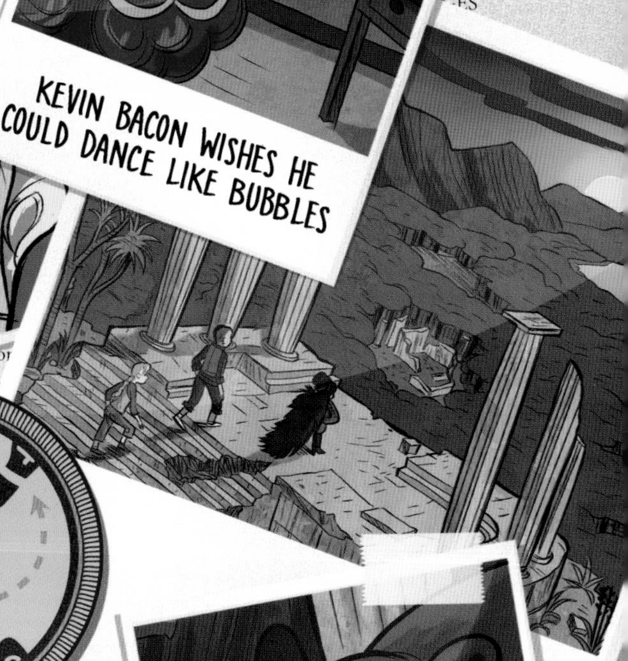

The yellow, short sl emb the w choose slacks, made o out-of-do green bere the colla Shoes ma heels, rou ings or socks shou with the shoes or wi the uniform. Ne bracelets, o belong with a Lumberjane unifo

GES

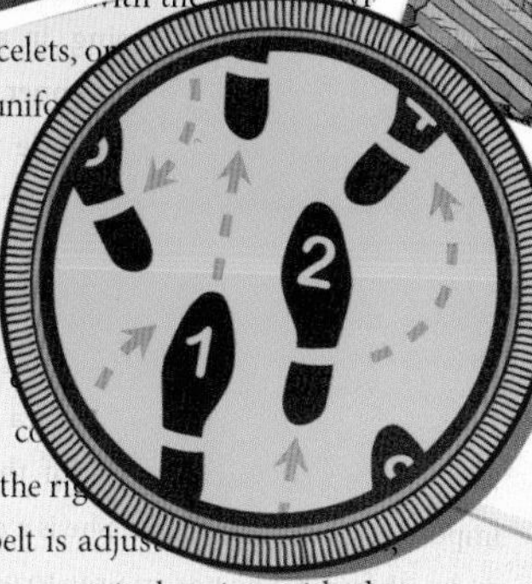

HOW TO WEA

To look well in a uniform uniform be kept in good co pressed. See that the skirt is the ri height and build, that the belt is adjus that your shoes and stockings are in keeping with the uniform, that you watch your posture and carry yourself with dignity and grace. If the beret is removed indoors, be sure that your hair is neat and kept in place with an insonspicuous clip or ribbon. When you wear a Lumberjane uniform you are identified as a member of this organization and you should be doubly careful to conduct yourself in a way that will show everyone that courtesy and thoughtfullness are part of being a Lumberjane. People are likely to judge a whole nation by the selfishness of a few individuals, to criticize a whole family because of the misconduct of one member, and to feel unkindly toward and organization because of the

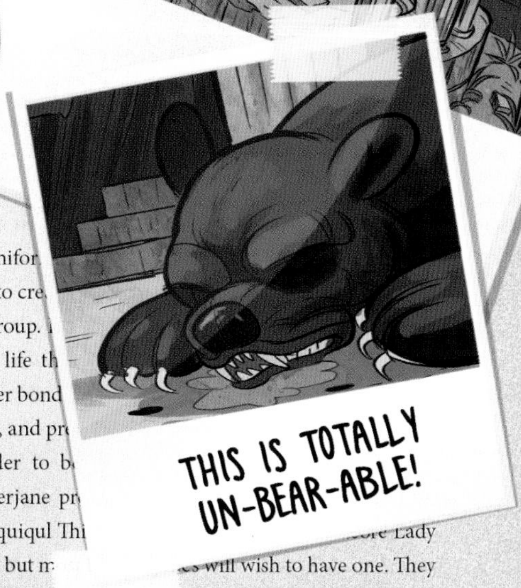
THIS IS TOTALLY
UN-BEAR-ABLE!

The unifor helps to cre in a group. active life th another bond future, and pr in order to b Lumberjane pr Penniquiqul Thi Lady Types, but m will wish to have one. They can either b , or make it themselves from materials available at the trading post.

LUMBERJANES FIELD MANUAL
CHAPTER TWELVE

Lumberjanes "Arts and Crafts" Program Field

OLDIE BUT GOODIE BADGE

"Helping history stay alive."

Every year we grow older and mature as women. Like any well rounded Lumberjane, we will understand that the experiences of those older than ourselves are meant to help guide us on our path. They are the ropes on the walkway of our journey, hinting at directions that should be taken while not forcing us to stay on just one path. Being a Lumberjane is more than learning skills for the great outdoors, it is also a chance to learn from this community of unique individuals. 'Respect your elders' is not a term that is taken lightly at Lumberjane camp and it never will be. All women learn from the follies of their youth, just as each young woman could learn a different lesson from the same problem it is up to all the Lumberjanes to seek guidance in their counselors, their peers, and their elders.

The importance of the *Oldie But Goodie* badge is that it teaches respect, and how to value all the lives around

you, even if they don't visibly affect your own. We are all connected under the same sky and one decision from a young scout fifty years in the past can still affect the decisions of young Lumberjanes attending camp this day. History is important, it is a chance for us to learn from the actions of others, to see the courses that were already taken and to take a step in an all-new direction. Even our own personal histories are used as guides in every decision we make as we continue on our personal journeys.

To obtain the *Oldie But Goodie* badge a Lumberjane must help an elder in the camp. In this performance they will be able to see what is needed to assist and will do all that they can to make sure that they are able to help. They are not required to perform on their own as to be a Lumberjane means to be constantly surrounded by friends, and in this badge, all who help out will each earn their own *Oldie But Goodie* badge. It is

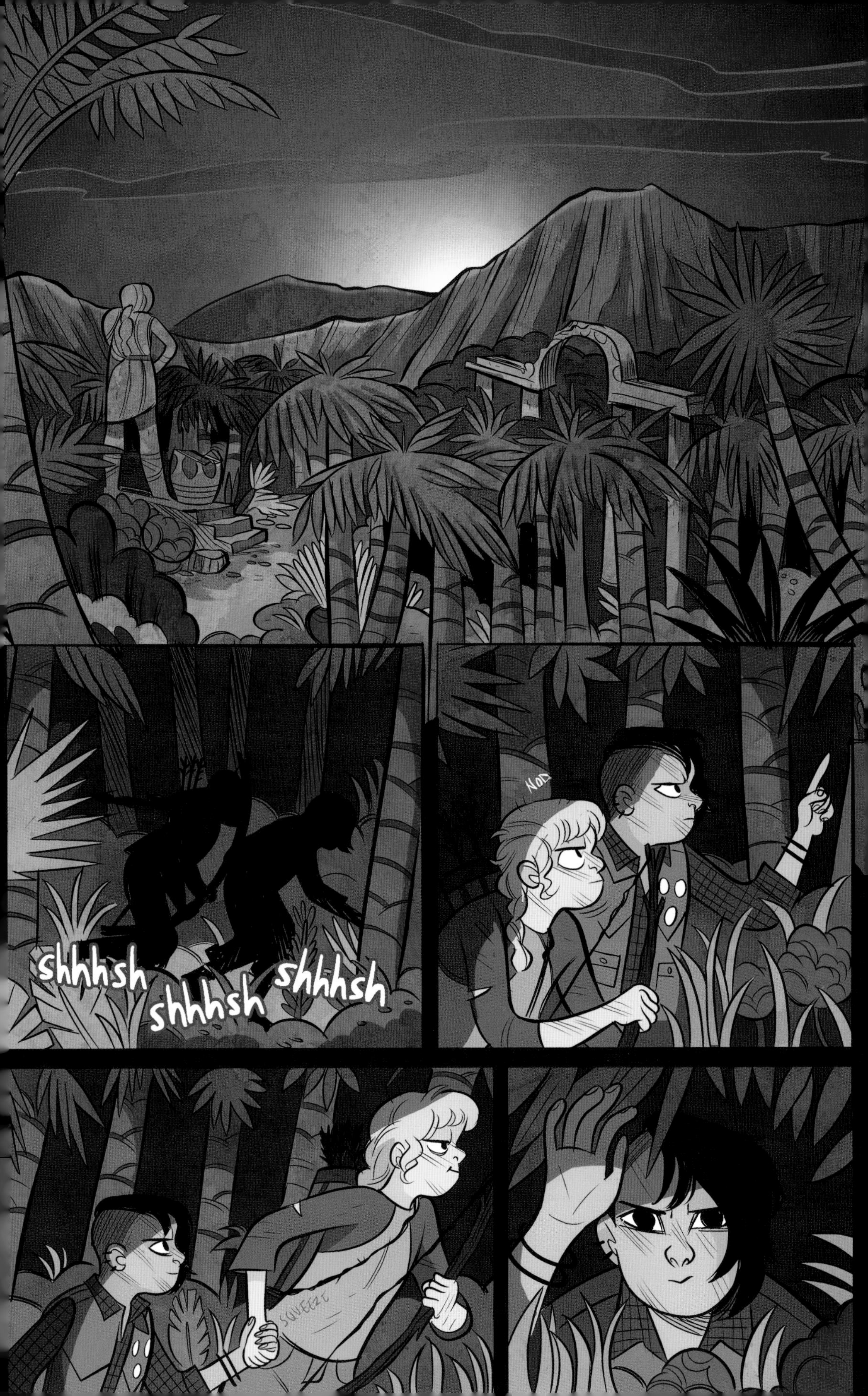
shhhsh
shhhsh
shhhsh
NOD
SQUEEZE

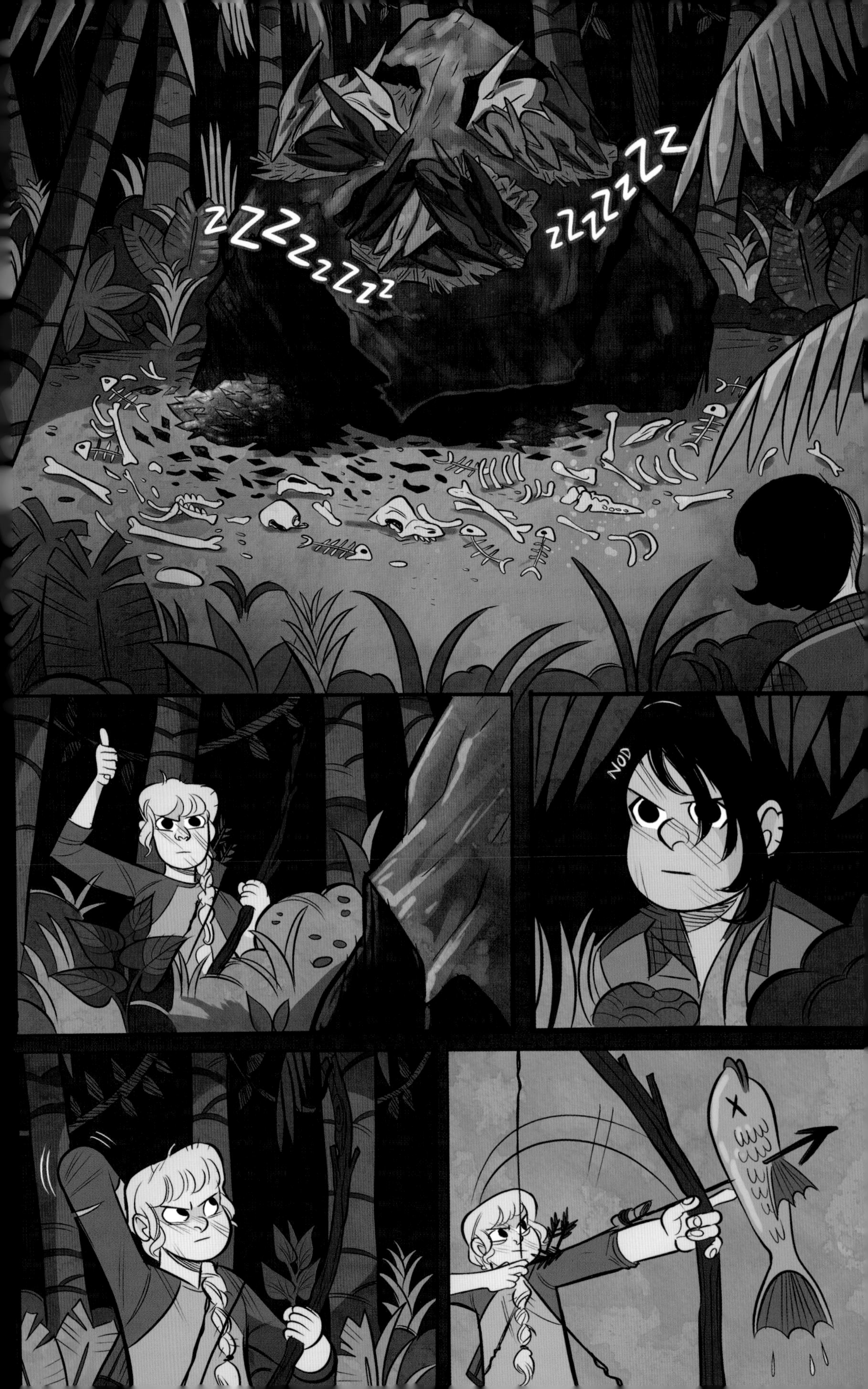
zZZZzzZzz
zzzzzZZ
NOD

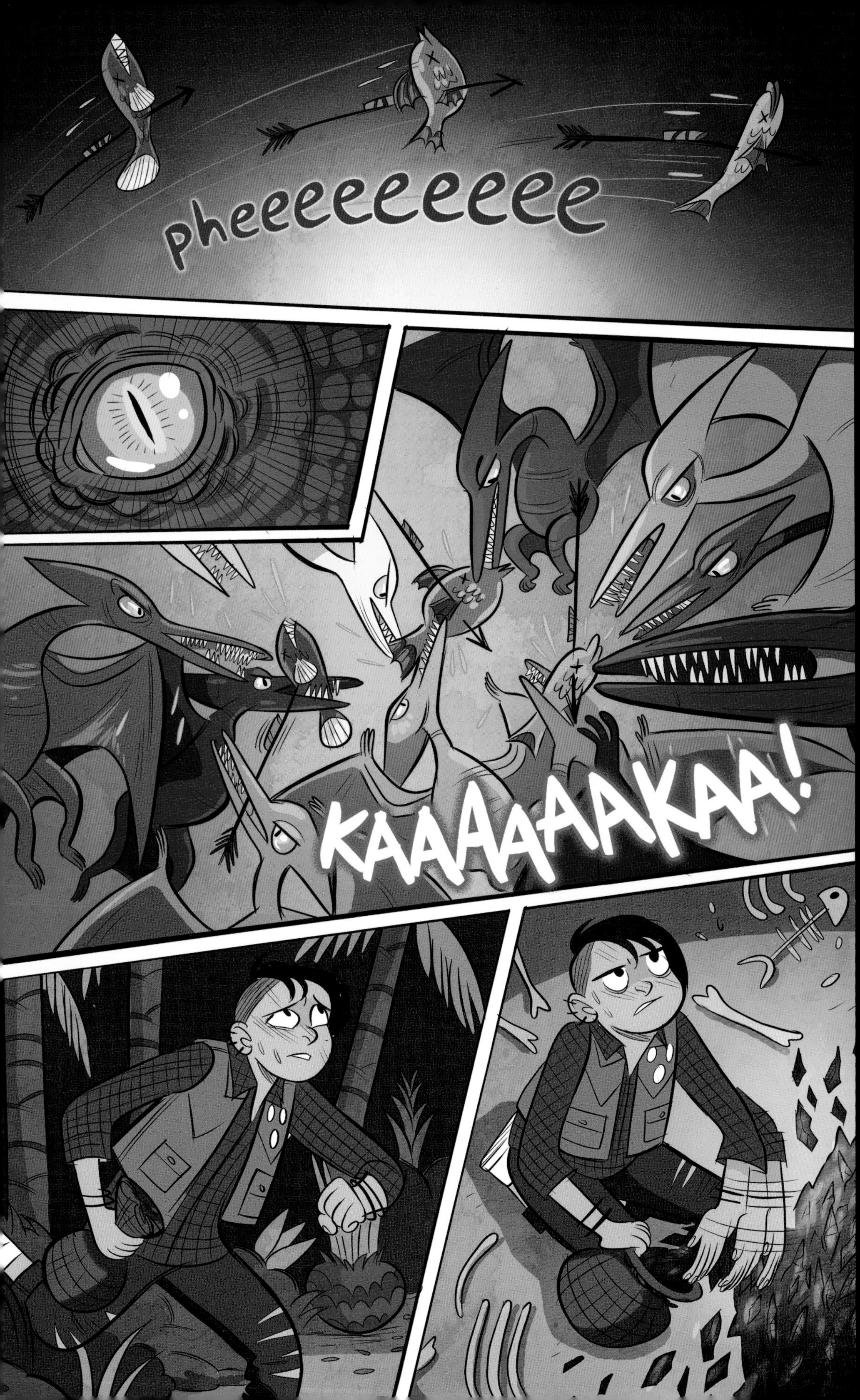
pheeeeeeeee
KAAAAAAKAA!

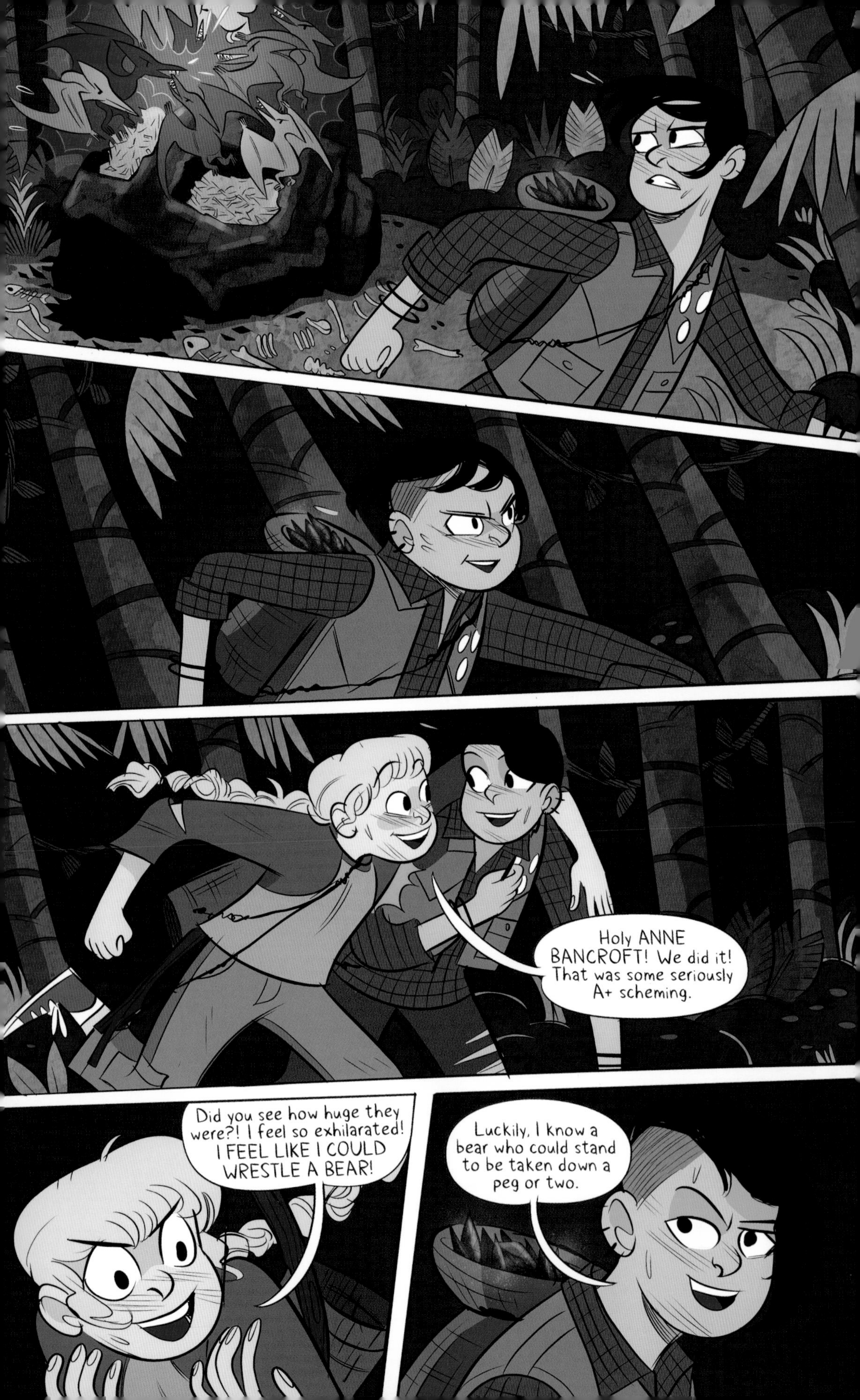
Holy ANNE BANCROFT! We did it! That was some seriously A+ scheming.
Did you see how huge they were?! I feel so exhilarated! I FEEL LIKE I COULD WRESTLE A BEAR!
Luckily, I know a bear who could stand to be taken down a peg or two.

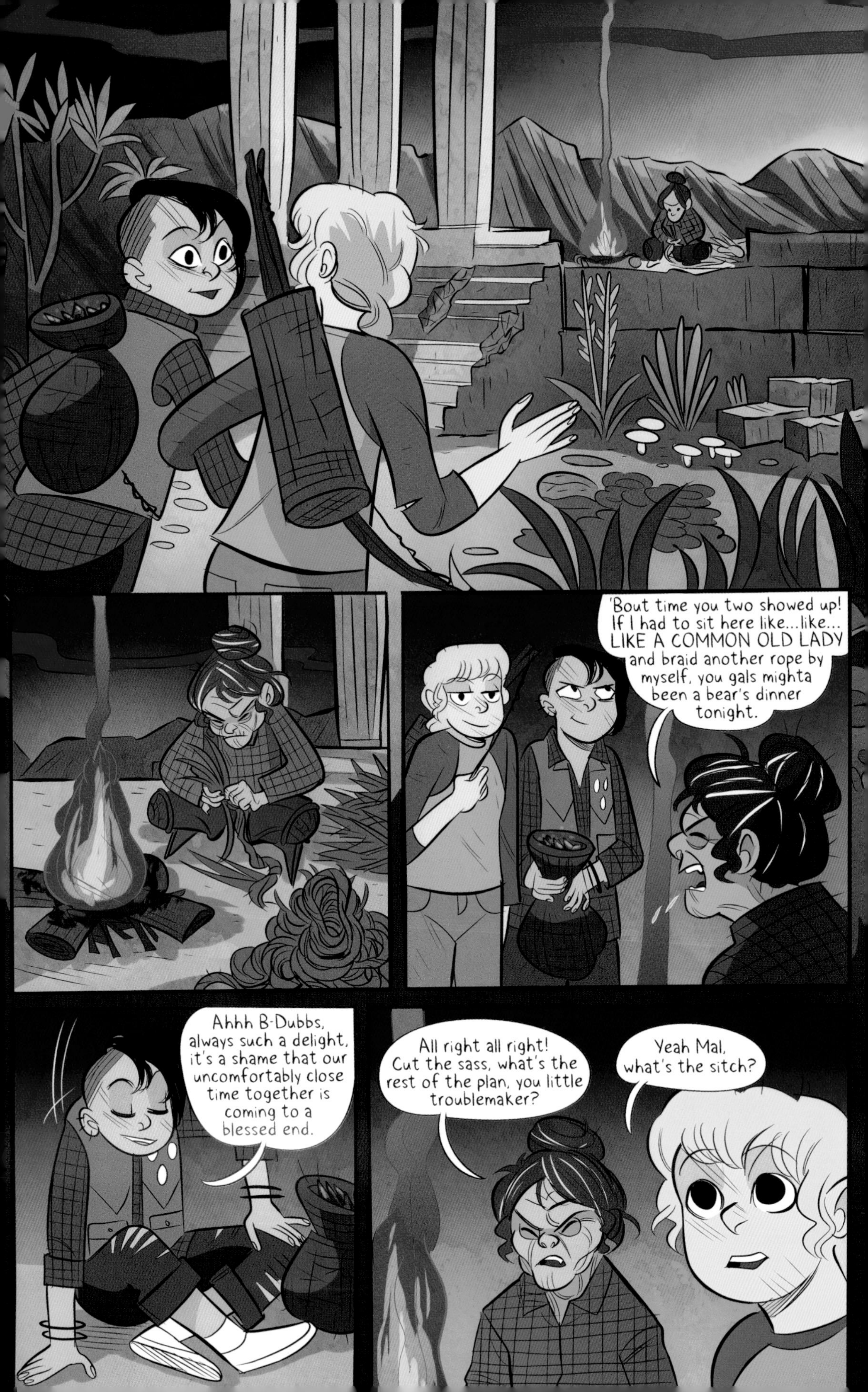
'Bout time you two showed up! If I had to sit here like...like... LIKE A COMMON OLD LADY and braid another rope by myself, you gals mighta been a bear's dinner tonight.
Ahhh B-Dubbs, always such a delight, it's a shame that our uncomfortably close time together is coming to a blessed end.
All right all right! Cut the sass, what's the rest of the plan, you little troublemaker?
Yeah Mal, what's the sitch?

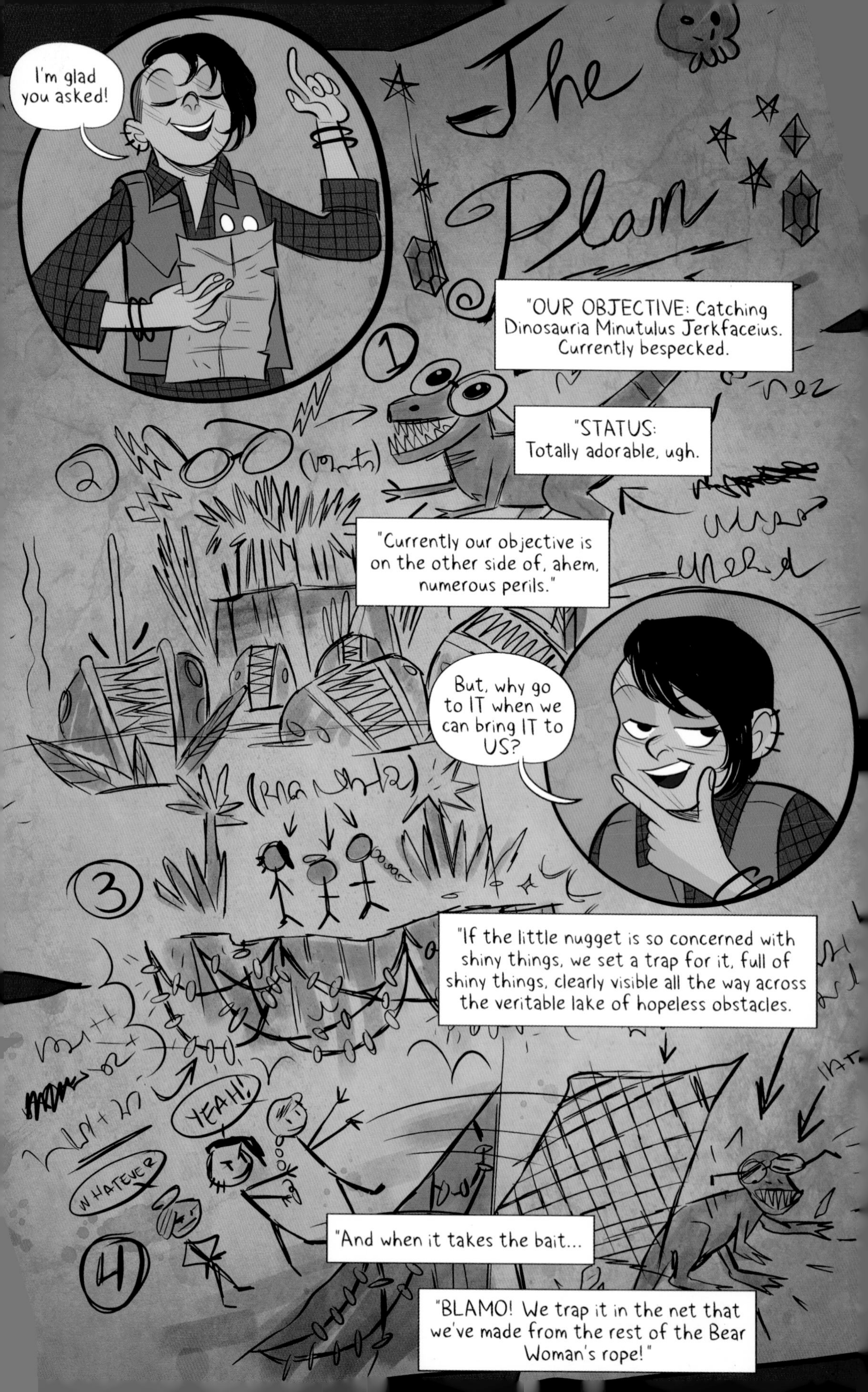
I'm glad you asked!
The Plan
"OUR OBJECTIVE: Catching Dinosauria Minutulus Jerkfaceius. Currently bespecked.
"STATUS: Totally adorable, ugh.
"Currently our objective is on the other side of, ahem, numerous perils."
But, why go to IT when we can bring IT to US?
"If the little nugget is so concerned with shiny things, we set a trap for it, full of shiny things, clearly visible all the way across the veritable lake of hopeless obstacles.
YEAH!
WHATEVER
"And when it takes the bait...
"BLAMO! We trap it in the net that we've made from the rest of the Bear Woman's rope!"

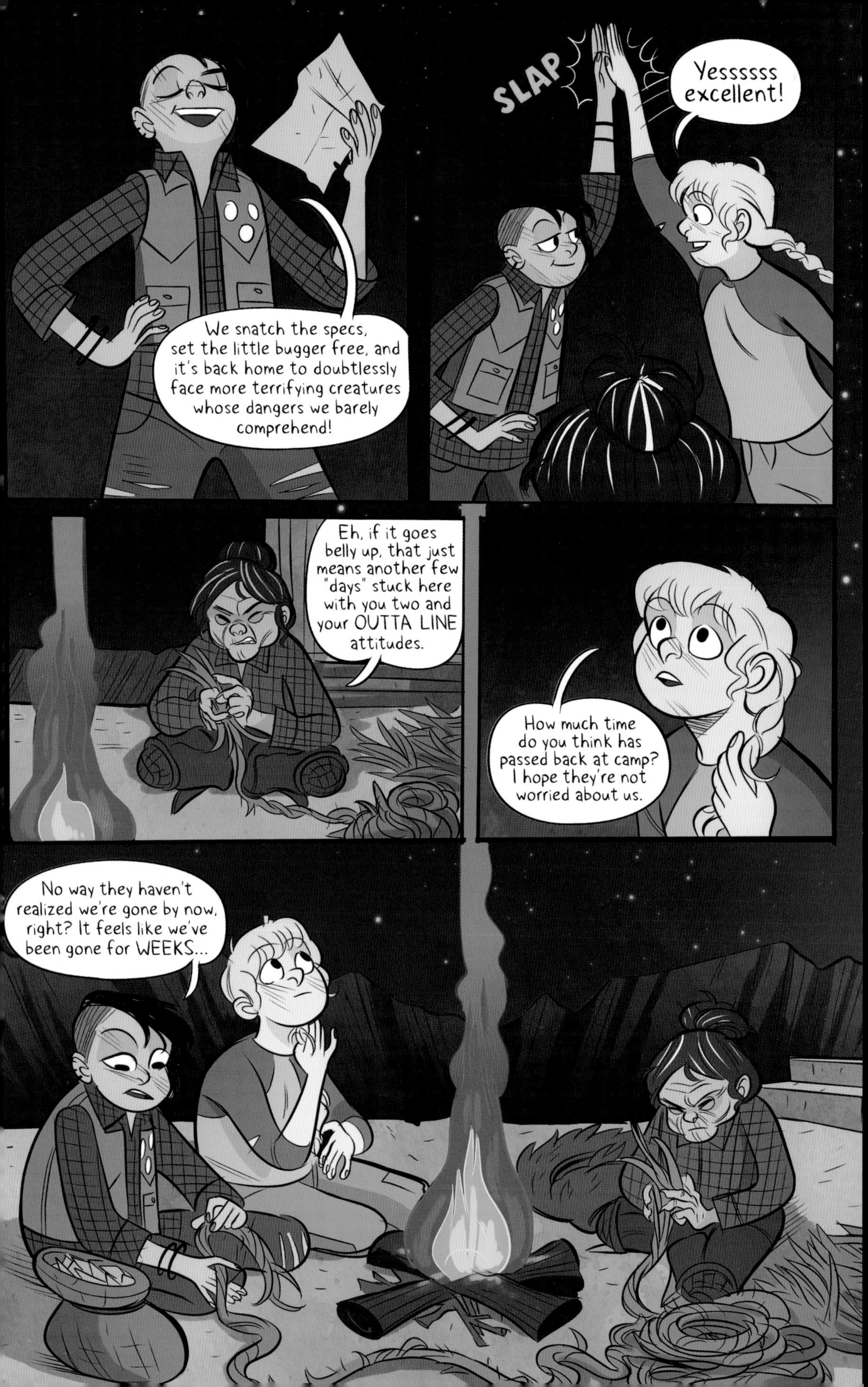
We snatch the specs, set the little bugger free, and it's back home to doubtlessly face more terrifying creatures whose dangers we barely comprehend!
SLAP
Yessssss excellent!
Eh, if it goes belly up, that just means another few "days" stuck here with you two and your OUTTA LINE attitudes.
How much time do you think has passed back at camp? I hope they're not worried about us.
No way they haven't realized we're gone by now, right? It feels like we've been gone for WEEKS...

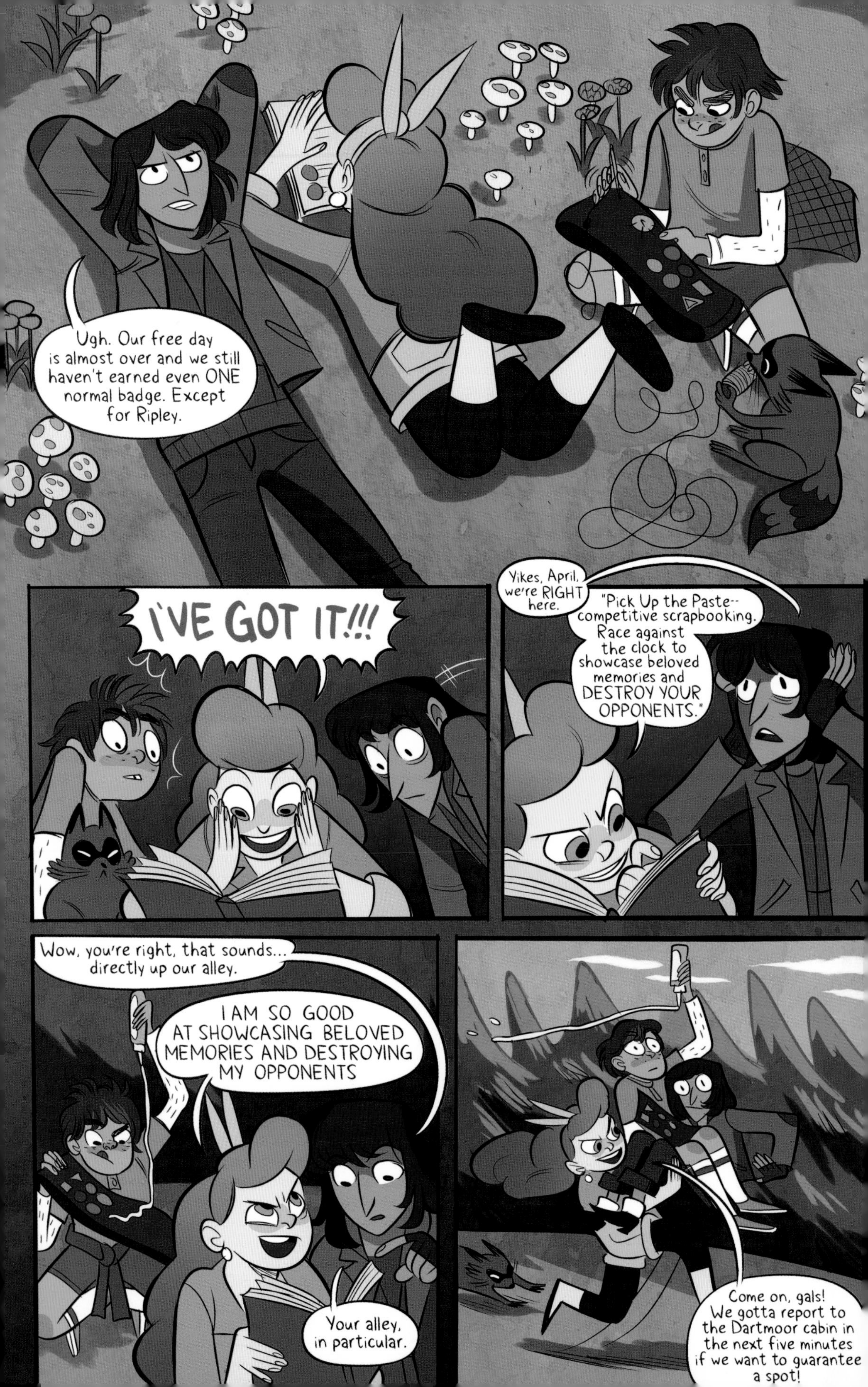
Ugh. Our free day is almost over and we still haven't earned even ONE normal badge. Except for Ripley.
I'VE GOT IT!!!
Yikes, April, we're RIGHT here.
"Pick Up the Paste-- competitive scrapbooking. Race against the clock to showcase beloved memories and DESTROY YOUR OPPONENTS."
Wow, you're right, that sounds... directly up our alley.
I AM SO GOOD AT SHOWCASING BELOVED MEMORIES AND DESTROYING MY OPPONENTS
Your alley, in particular.
Come on, gals! We gotta report to the Dartmoor cabin in the next five minutes if we want to guarantee a spot!

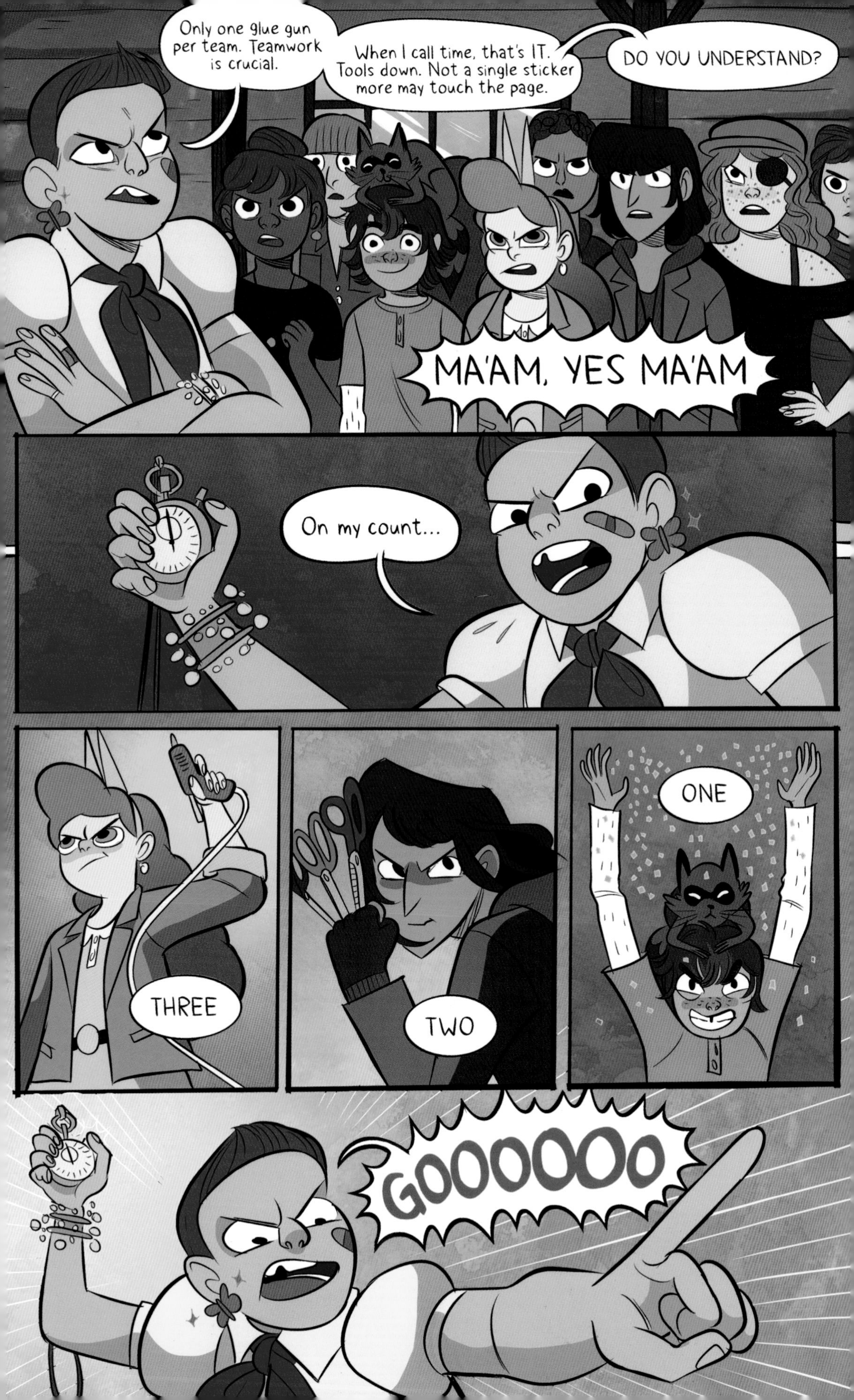
Only one glue gun per team. Teamwork is crucial.
When I call time, that's IT. Tools down. Not a single sticker more may touch the page.
DO YOU UNDERSTAND?
MA'AM, YES MA'AM
On my count...
THREE
TWO
ONE
GOOOOOO

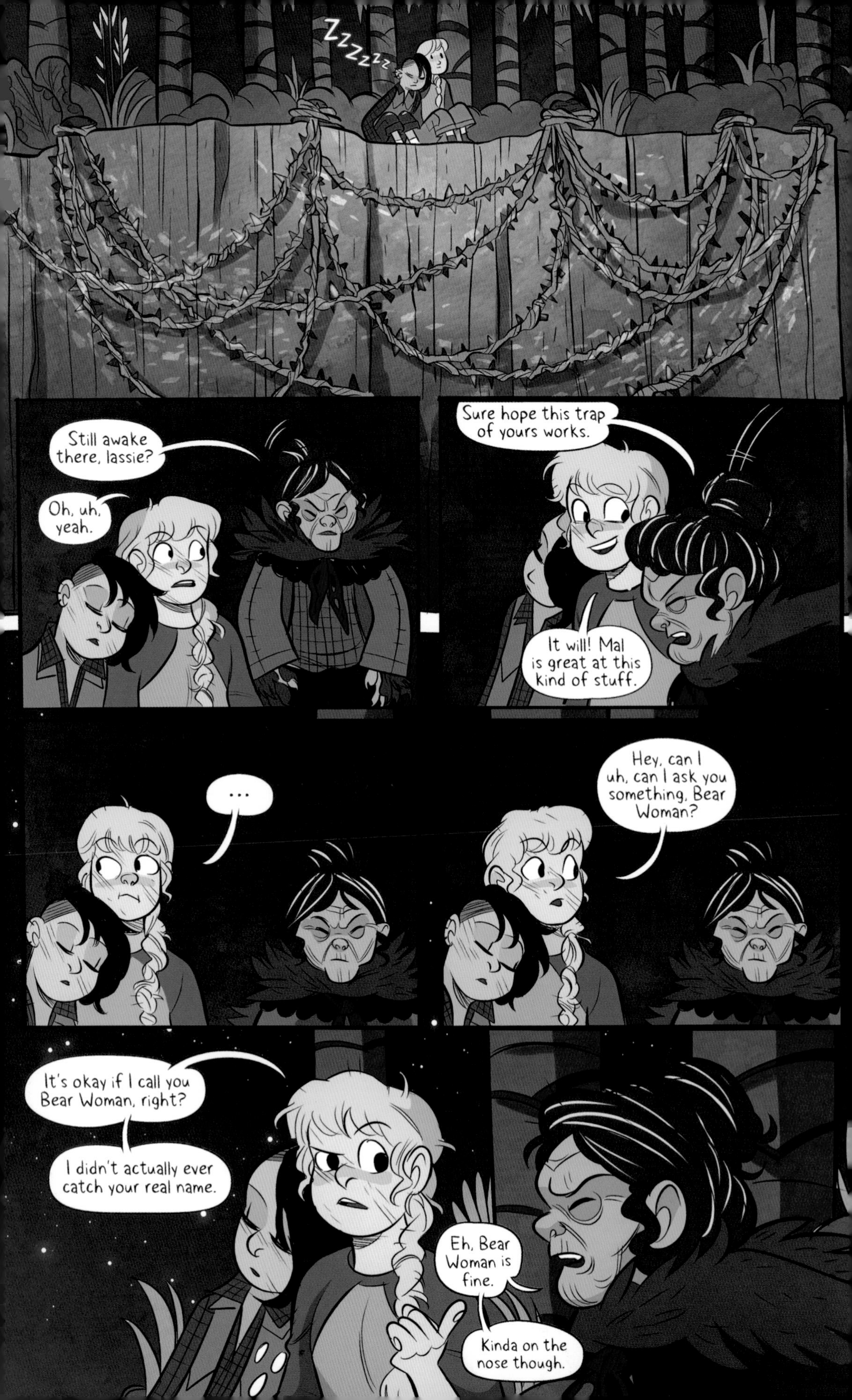
ZZZZZZ
Still awake there, lassie?
Oh, uh, yeah.
Sure hope this trap of yours works.
It will! Mal is great at this kind of stuff.
...
Hey, can I uh, can I ask you something, Bear Woman?
It's okay if I call you Bear Woman, right?
I didn't actually ever catch your real name.
Eh, Bear Woman is fine.
Kinda on the nose though.

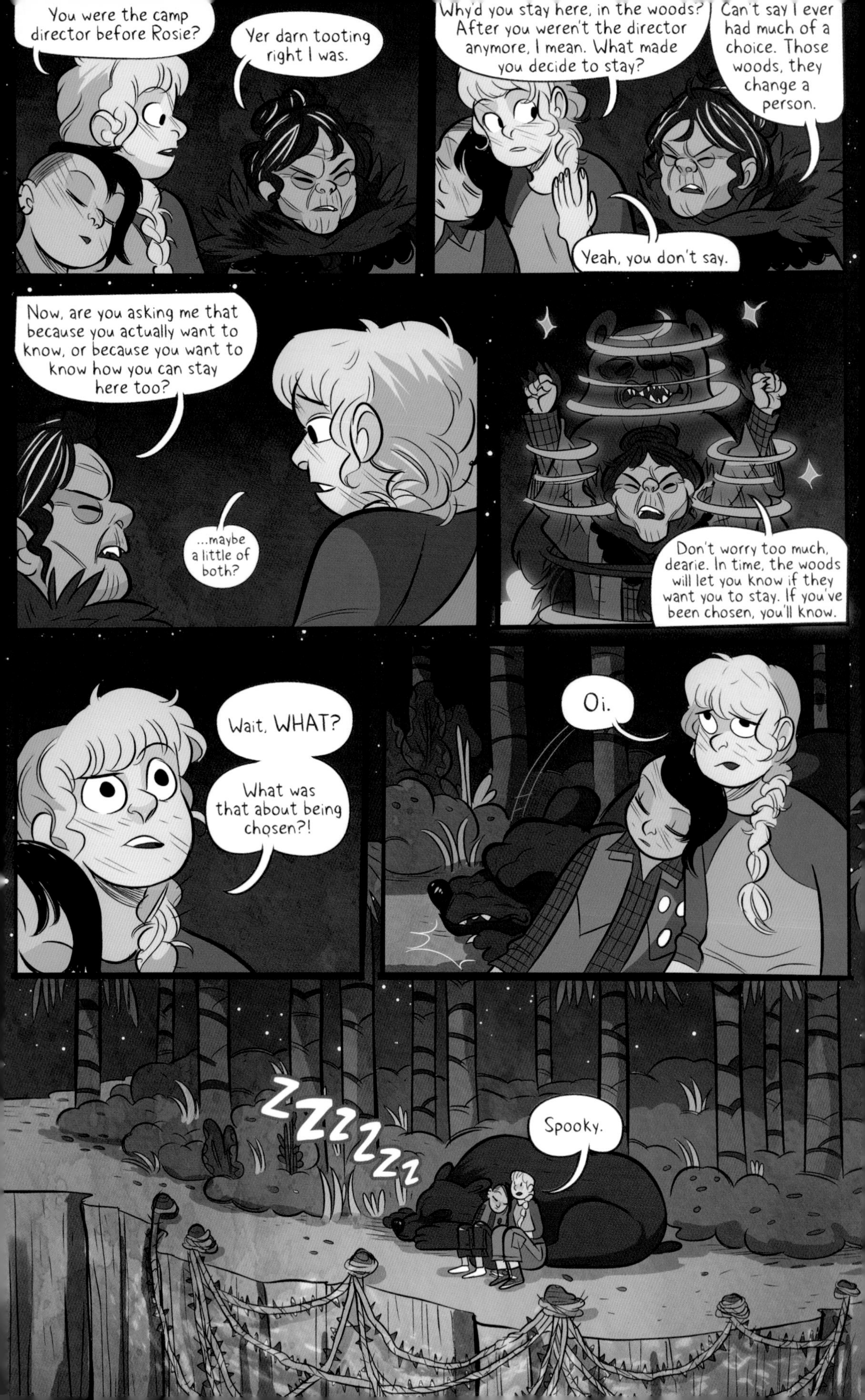
You were the camp director before Rosie?
Yer darn tooting right I was.
Why'd you stay here, in the woods? After you weren't the director anymore, I mean. What made you decide to stay?
Can't say I ever had much of a choice. Those woods, they change a person.
Yeah, you don't say.
Now, are you asking me that because you actually want to know, or because you want to know how you can stay here too?
...maybe a little of both?
Don't worry too much, dearie. In time, the woods will let you know if they want you to stay. If you've been chosen, you'll know.
Wait, WHAT?
What was that about being chosen?!
Oi.
ZZZZZZZ
Spooky.

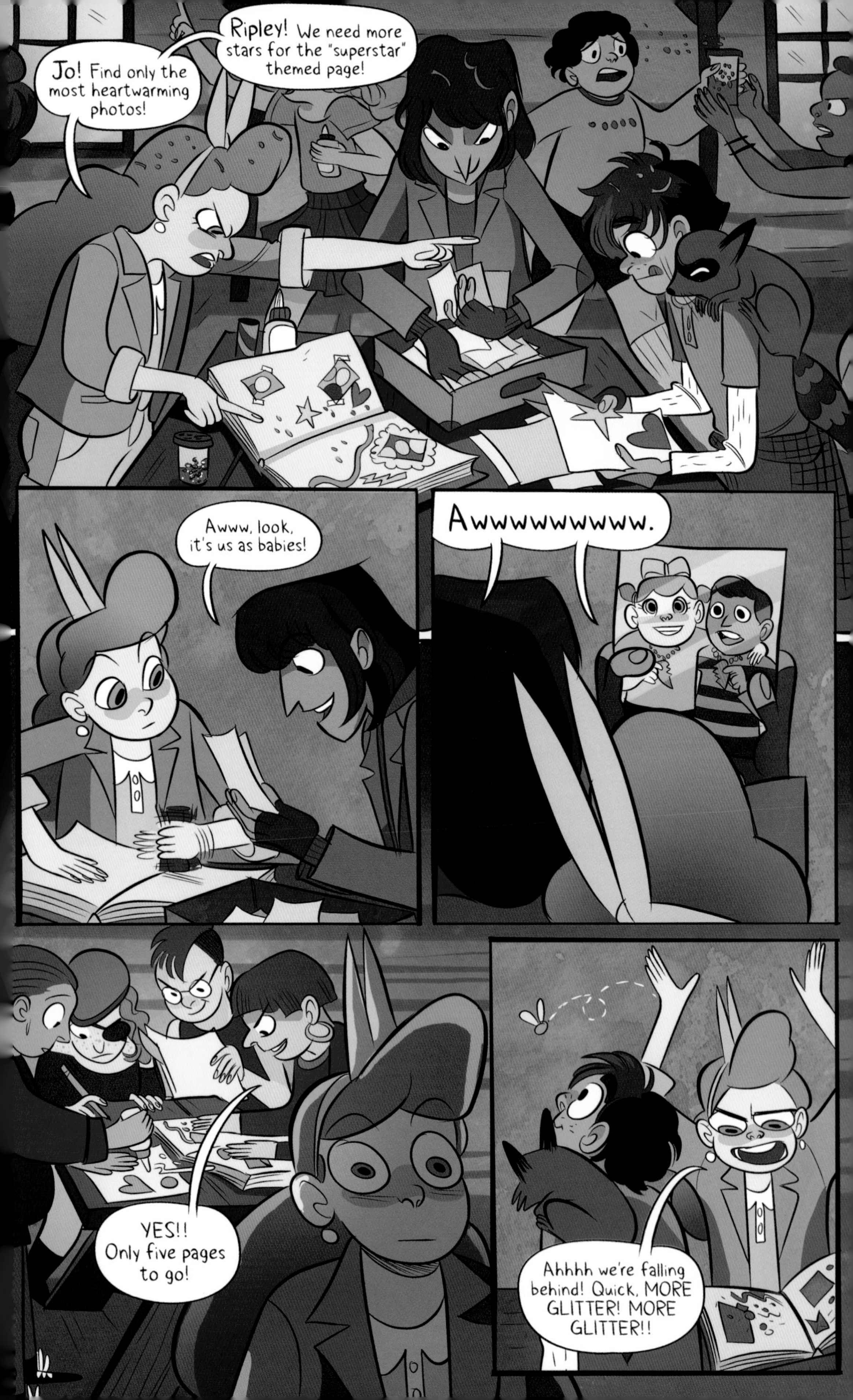

Jo! Find only the most heartwarming photos!
Ripley! We need more stars for the "superstar" themed page!
Awww, look, it's us as babies!
Awwwwwwwww.
YES!! Only five pages to go!
Ahhhh we're falling behind! Quick, MORE GLITTER! MORE GLITTER!!

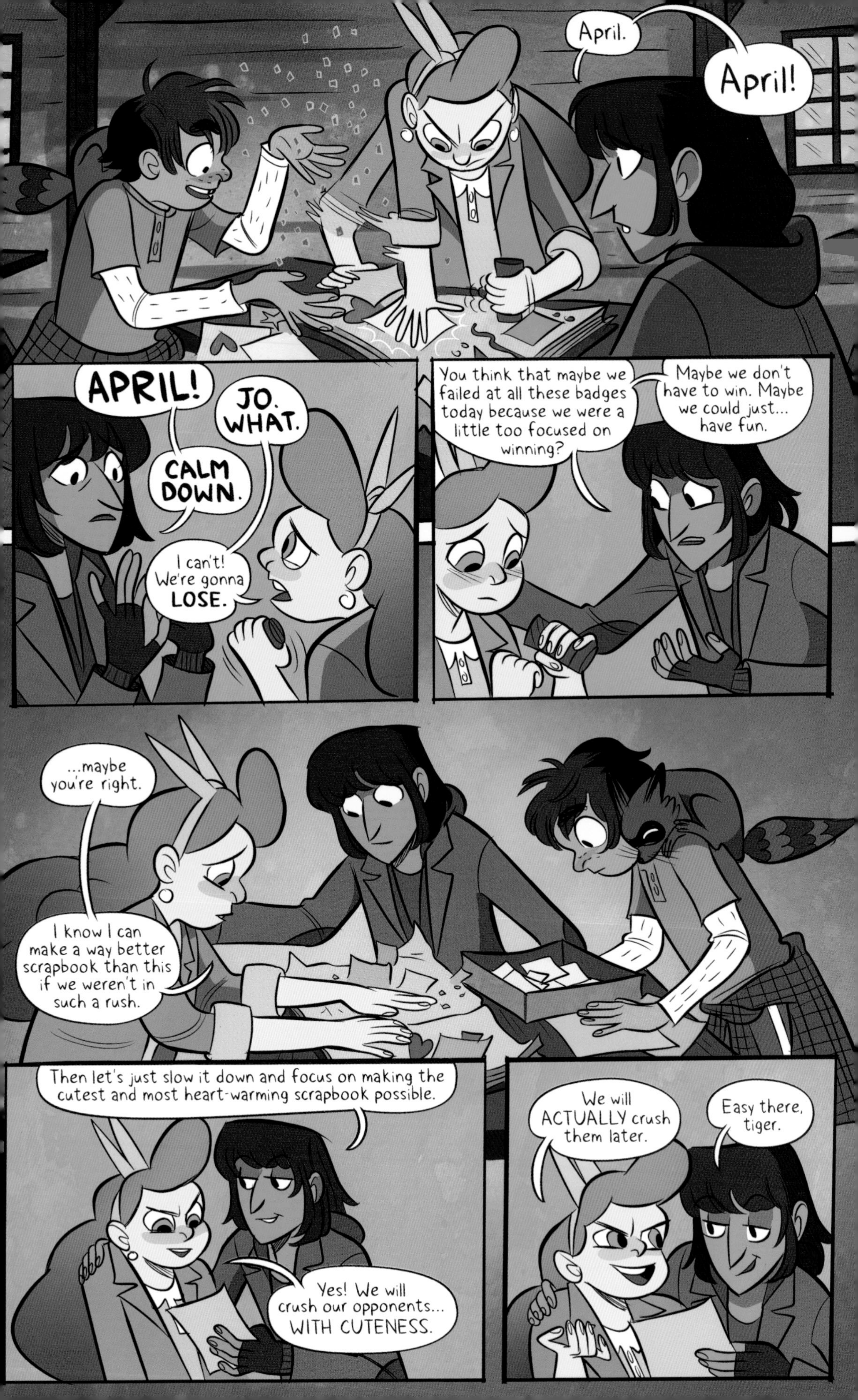
April.
April!
APRIL!
CALM DOWN.
JO. WHAT.
I can't! We're gonna LOSE.
You think that maybe we failed at all these badges today because we were a little too focused on winning?
Maybe we don't have to win. Maybe we could just... have fun.
...maybe you're right.
I know I can make a way better scrapbook than this if we weren't in such a rush.
Then let's just slow it down and focus on making the cutest and most heart-warming scrapbook possible.
Yes! We will crush our opponents... WITH CUTENESS.
We will ACTUALLY crush them later.
Easy there, tiger.

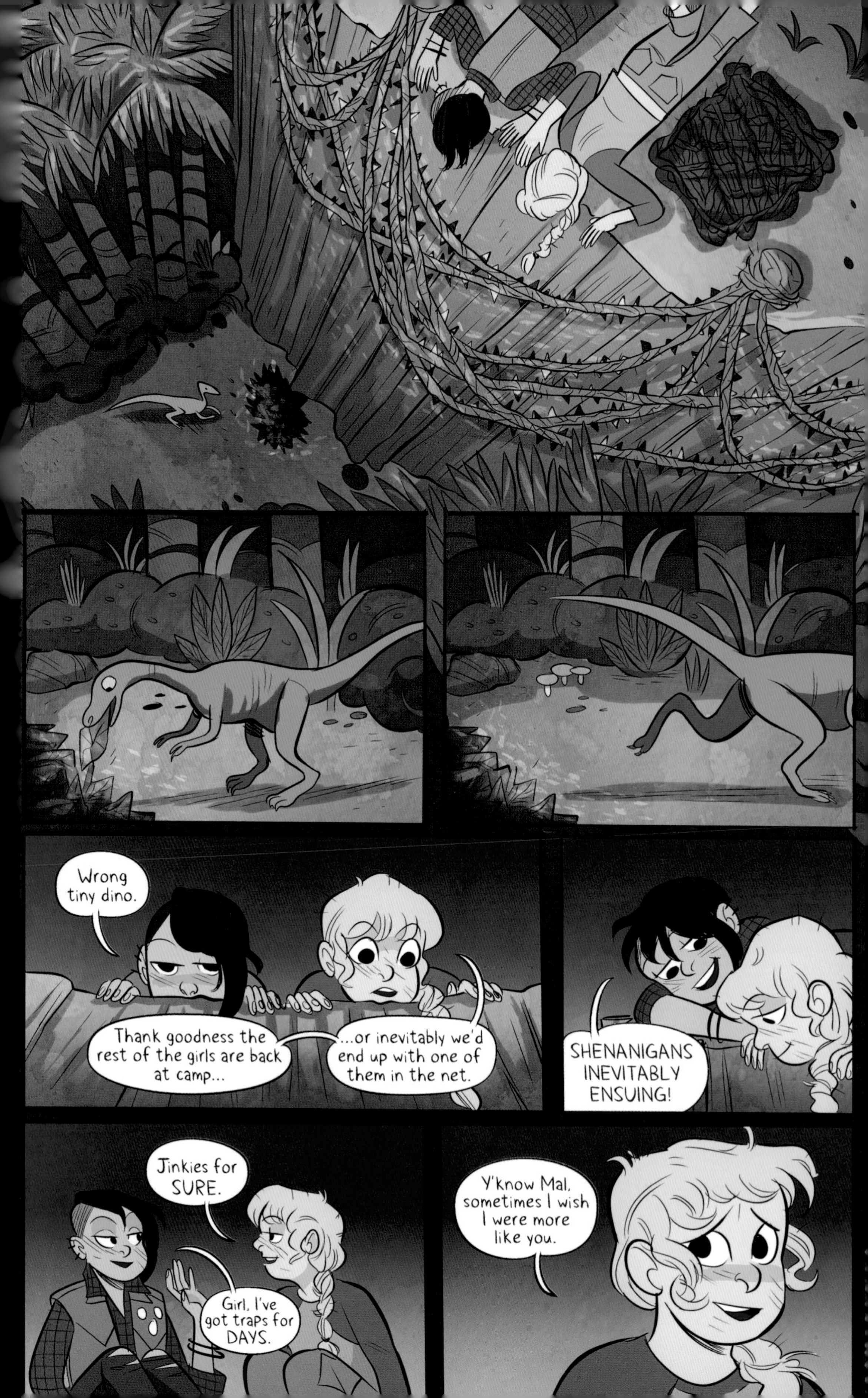
Wrong tiny dino.
Thank goodness the rest of the girls are back at camp...
...or inevitably we'd end up with one of them in the net.
SHENANIGANS INEVITABLY ENSUING!
Jinkies for SURE.
Girl, I've got traps for DAYS.
Y'know Mal, sometimes I wish I were more like you.

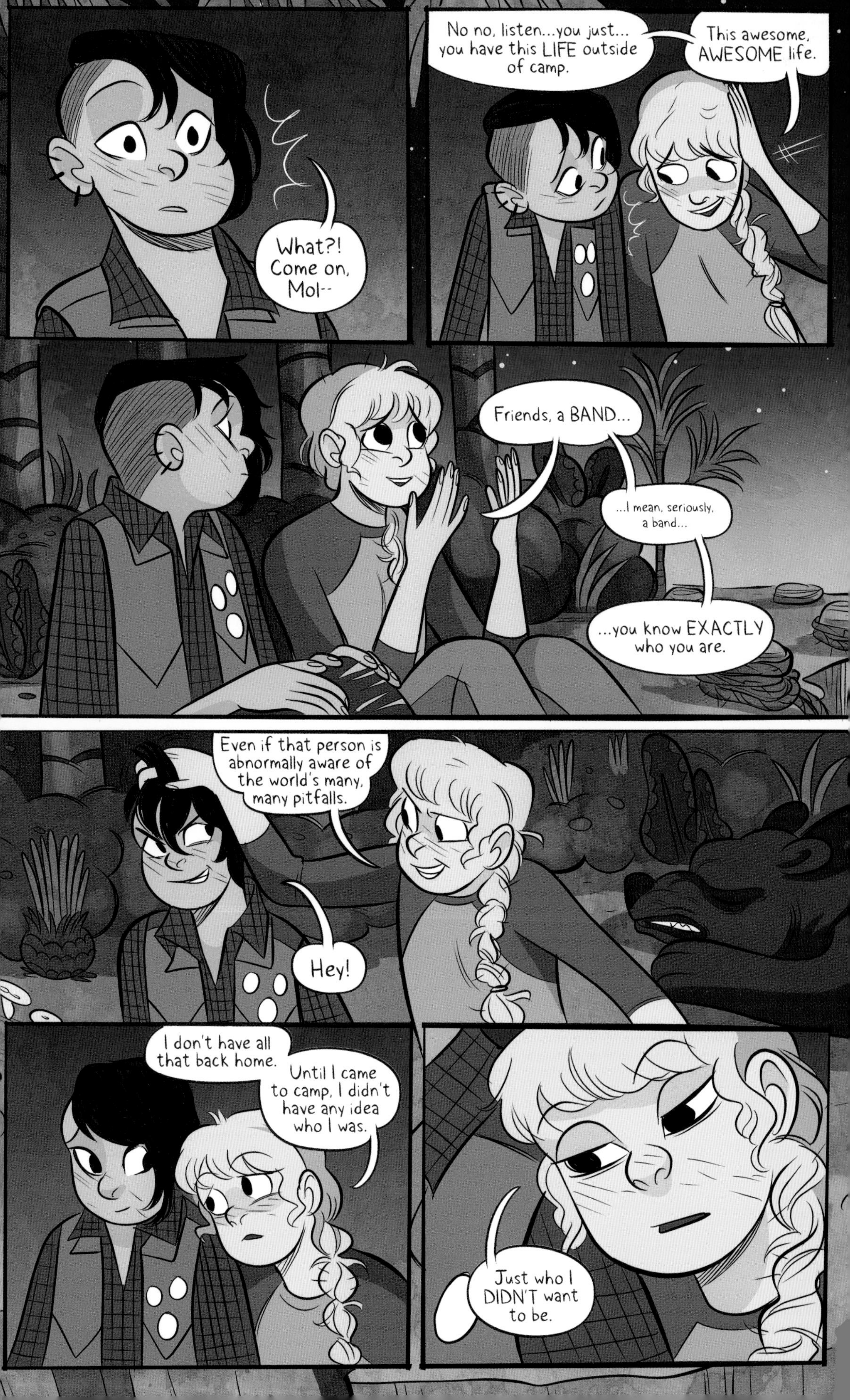
What?! Come on, Mol--
No no, listen...you just... you have this LIFE outside of camp.
This awesome, AWESOME life.
Friends, a BAND...
...I mean, seriously, a band...
...you know EXACTLY who you are.
Even if that person is abnormally aware of the world's many, many pitfalls.
Hey!
I don't have all that back home.
Until I came to camp, I didn't have any idea who I was.
Just who I DIDN'T want to be.

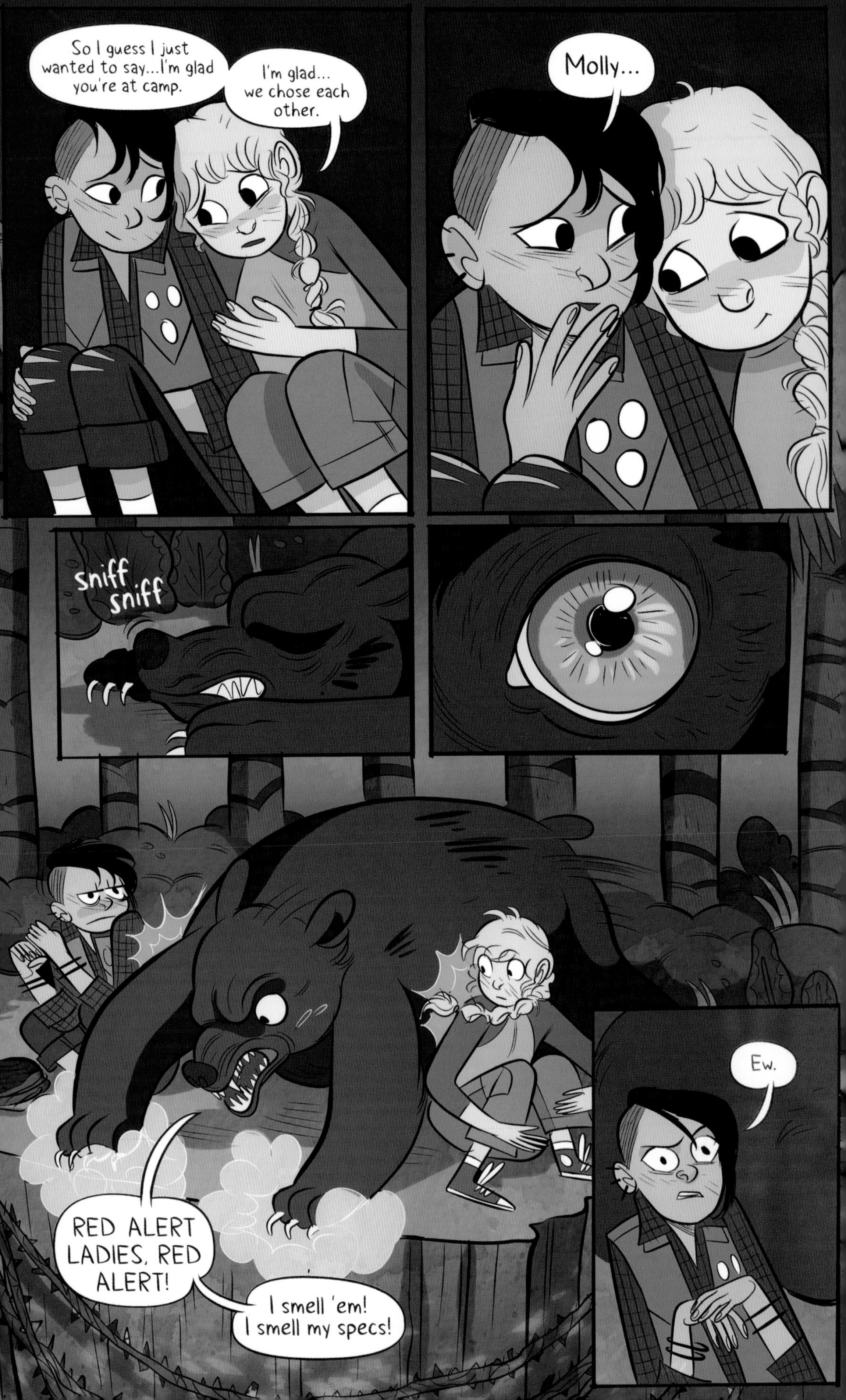
So I guess I just wanted to say...I'm glad you're at camp.
I'm glad... we chose each other.
Molly...
sniff sniff
Ew.
RED ALERT LADIES, RED ALERT!
I smell 'em! I smell my specs!

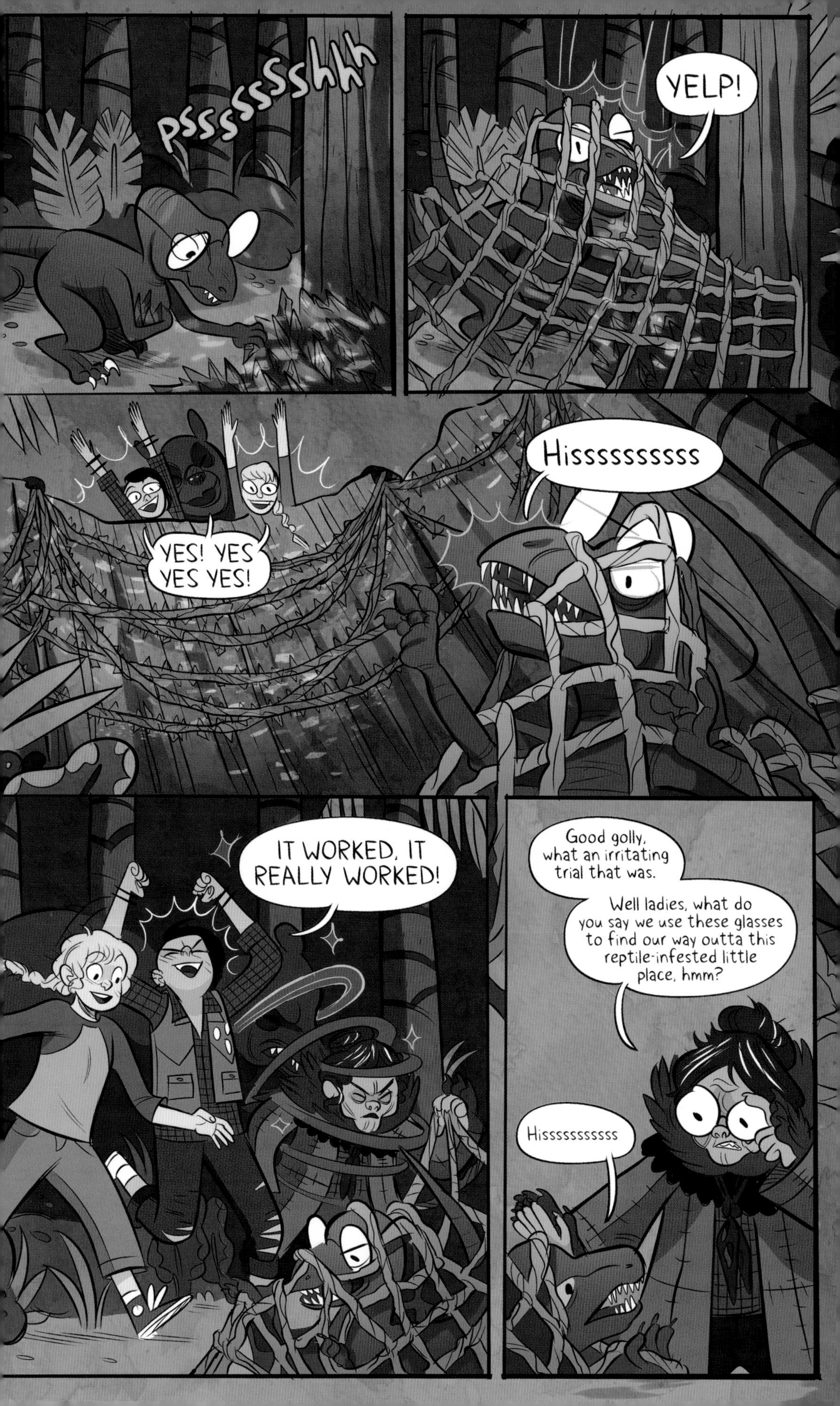
PSSSSSSShhh
YELP!
YES! YES YES YES!
Hissssssssss
IT WORKED, IT REALLY WORKED!
Good golly, what an irritating trial that was.
Well ladies, what do you say we use these glasses to find our way outta this reptile-infested little place, hmm?
Hissssssssssss

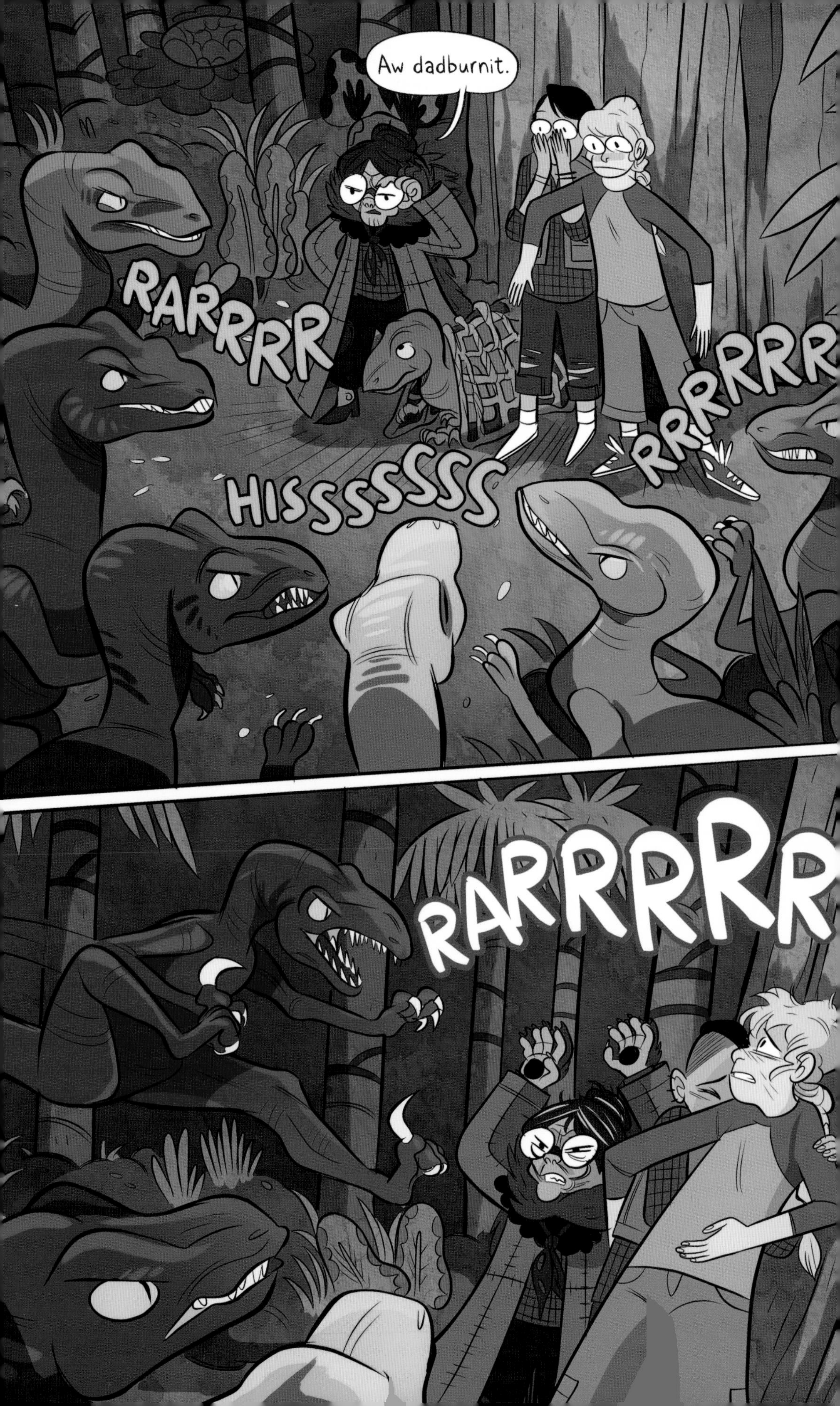
Aw dadburnit.
RARRRR
RRRRRRR
HISSSSSS
RARRRRR

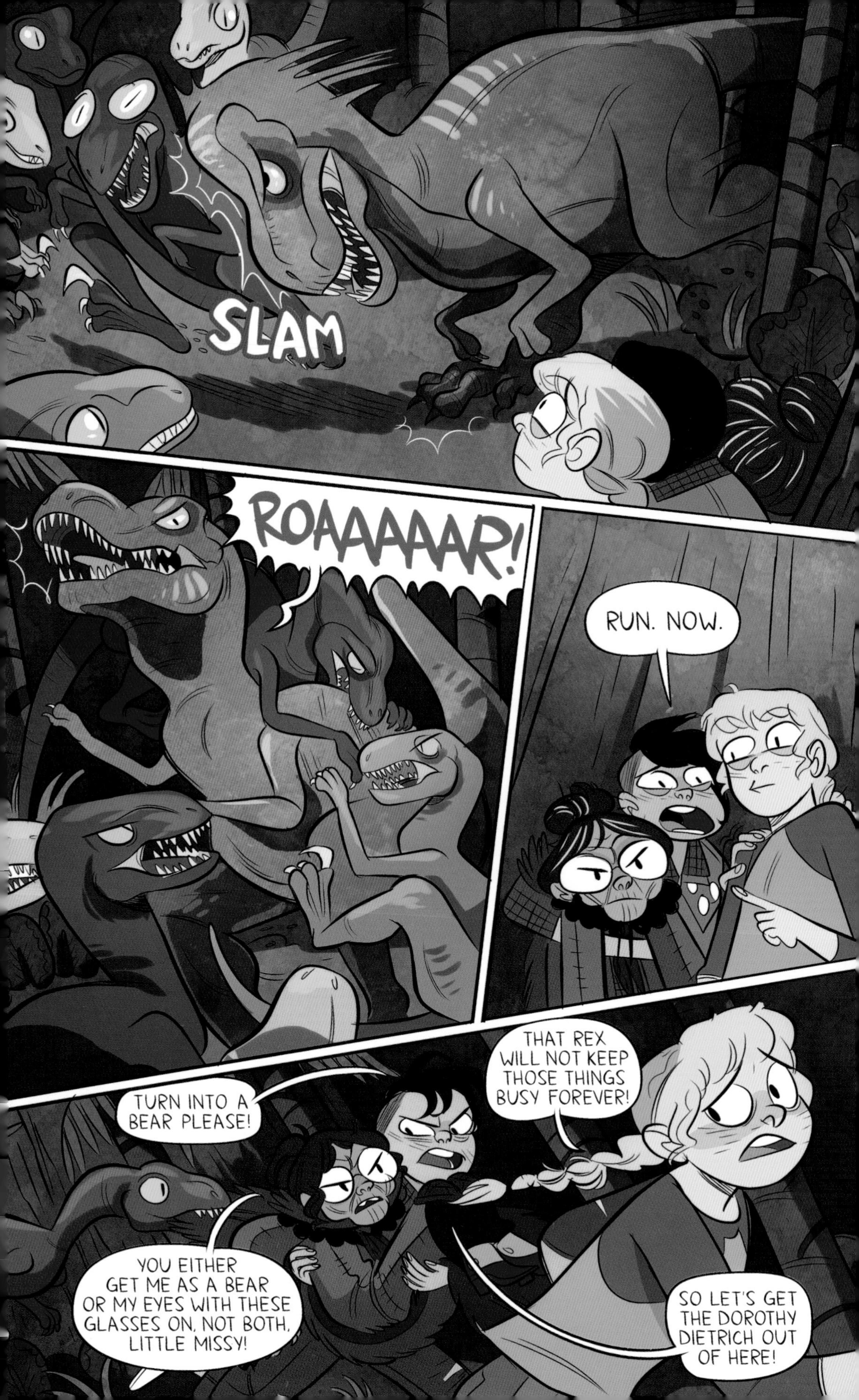
SLAM
ROAAAAAR!
RUN. NOW.
TURN INTO A BEAR PLEASE!
THAT REX WILL NOT KEEP THOSE THINGS BUSY FOREVER!
YOU EITHER GET ME AS A BEAR OR MY EYES WITH THESE GLASSES ON, NOT BOTH, LITTLE MISSY!
SO LET'S GET THE DOROTHY DIETRICH OUT OF HERE!

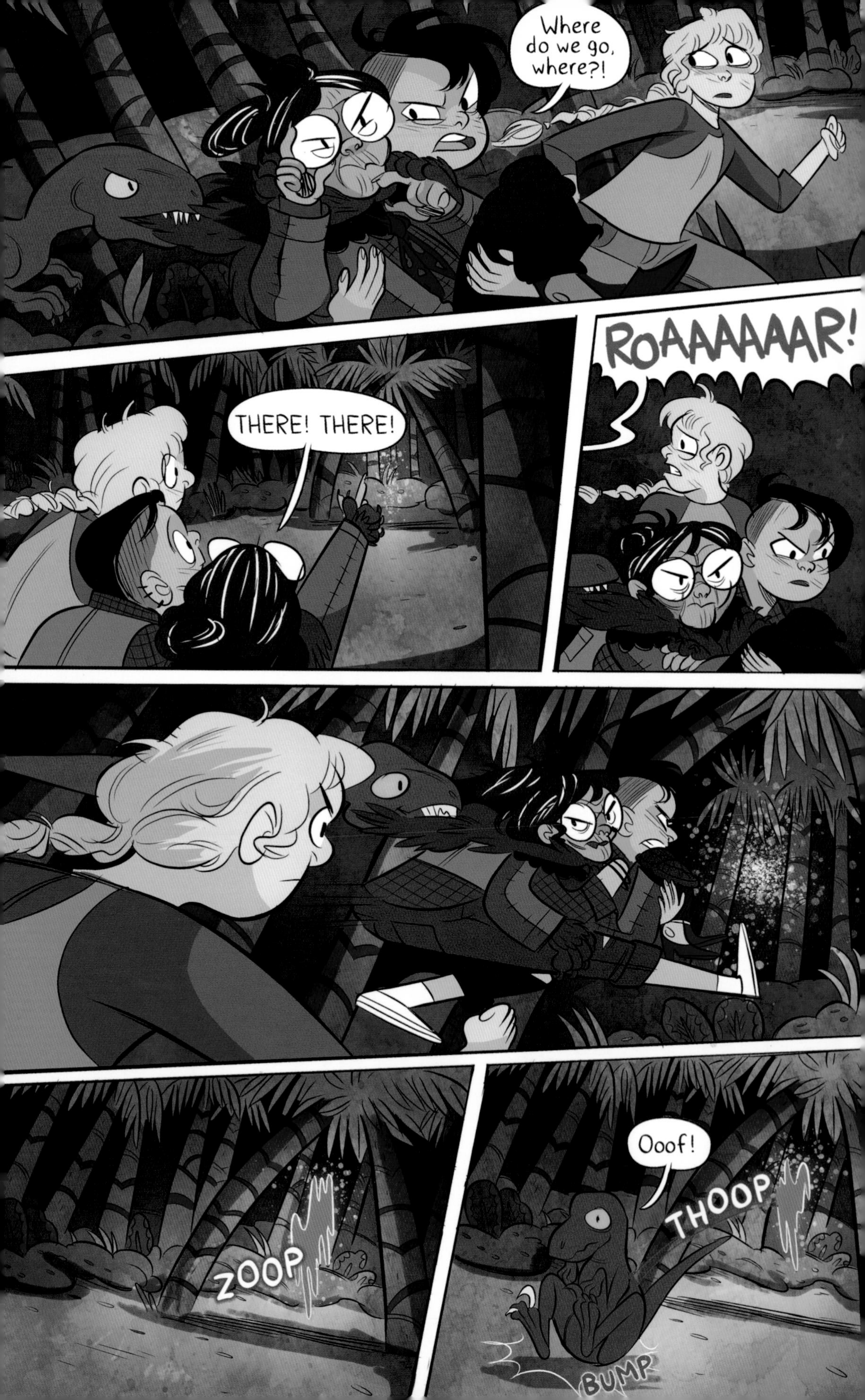
Where do we go, where?!
THERE! THERE!
ROAAAAAAR!
ZOOP
Ooof!
THOOP
BUMP

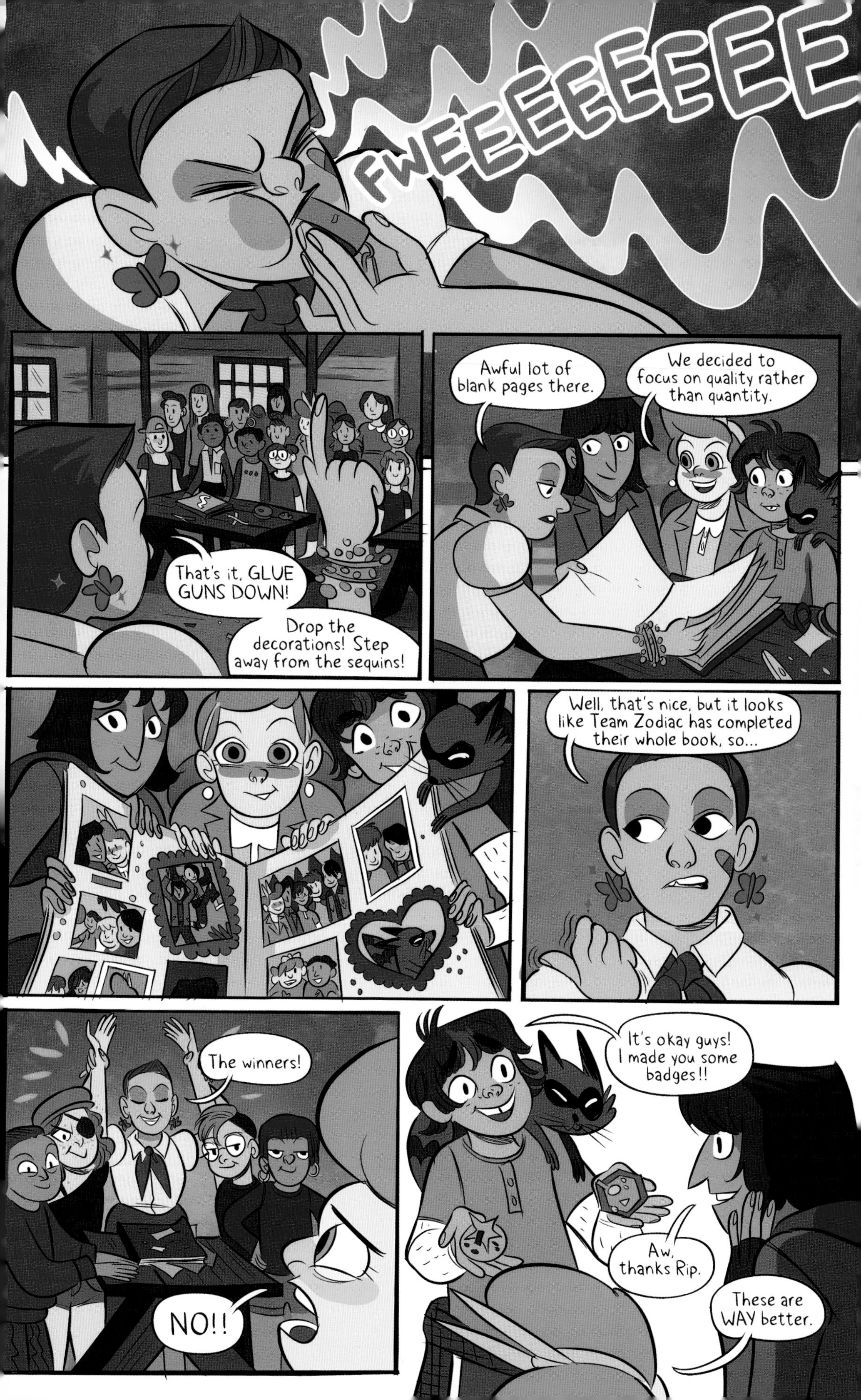
FWEEEEEEEEE
That's it, GLUE GUNS DOWN!
Drop the decorations! Step away from the sequins!
Awful lot of blank pages there.
We decided to focus on quality rather than quantity.
Well, that's nice, but it looks like Team Zodiac has completed their whole book, so...
The winners!
NO!!
It's okay guys! I made you some badges!!
Aw, thanks Rip.
These are WAY better.

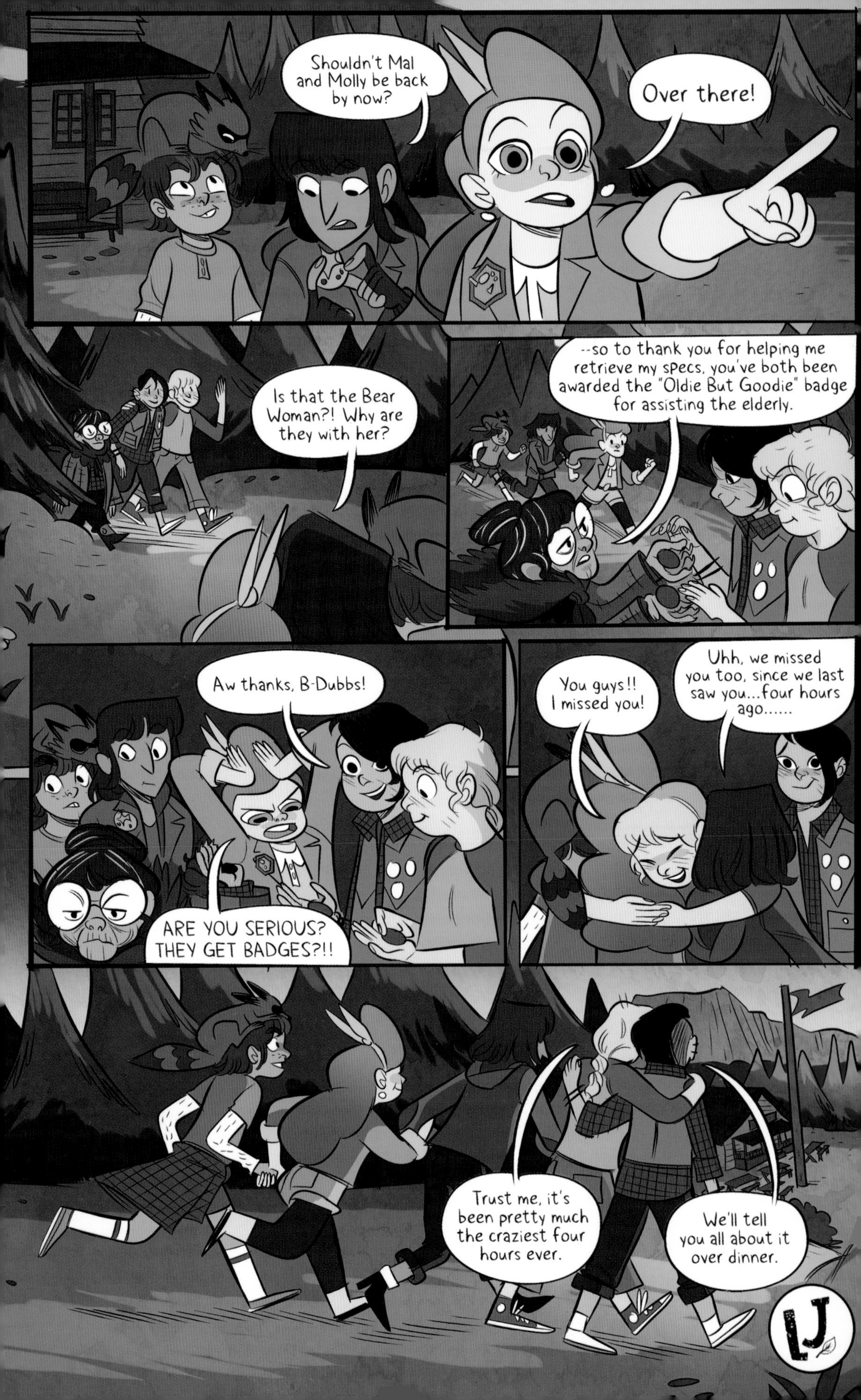
Shouldn't Mal and Molly be back by now?
Over there!
Is that the Bear Woman?! Why are they with her?
--so to thank you for helping me retrieve my specs, you've both been awarded the "Oldie But Goodie" badge for assisting the elderly.
Aw thanks, B-Dubbs!
ARE YOU SERIOUS? THEY GET BADGES?!!
You guys!! I missed you!
Uhh, we missed you too, since we last saw you...four hours ago......
Trust me, it's been pretty much the craziest four hours ever.
We'll tell you all about it over dinner.

will co

The

It helps

appearan

dress fo

Further

Lumber

to have

part in

Thiskw

Hardc

have

them

HOLY ANNE BANCROFT!

out grows her uniform or
ster Lumberjane.
signia she has
her
her

The
yellow, short sl
emb
the w
choose
slacks,
made o
out-of-do
green bere
the colla
Shoes ma
heels, roun   ings or
socks should   with the shoes or wi
the uniform. Ne   es, bracelets, or other jewelry do
belong with a Lumberjane uniform.

IT'S A TRAP!

HOW TO WEAR

To look well in a unifo
uniform be kept in ge
pressed. See that the skir
height and build, that the
that your shoes and stock
uniform, that you watch your p   The unifor
with dignity and grace. If the beret is   oors,   helps to cre
be sure that your hair is neat and kept in place with an   in a group.
insonspicuous clip or ribbon. When you wear a   active life th
Lumberjane uniform you are identified as a member of   another bond
this organization and you should be doubly careful to   future, and pr
conduct yourself in a way that will show everyone that   in order to b
courtesy and thoughtfullness are part of being a   Lumberjane pr
Lumberjane. People are likely to judge a whole nation by   Penniquiqul Thi   re Lady
the selfishness of a few individuals, to criticize a whole Types, but m   es will wish to have one. They
family because of the misconduct of one member, and to   can either bu   uniform, or make it themselves from
feel unkindly toward and organization because of the   materials available at the trading post.

MORE GLITTER!

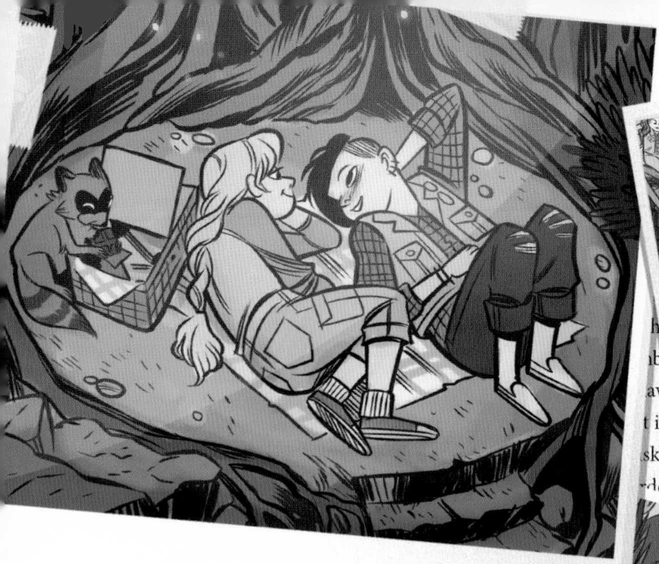

QUIET TIME TOGETHER IN THE WOODS

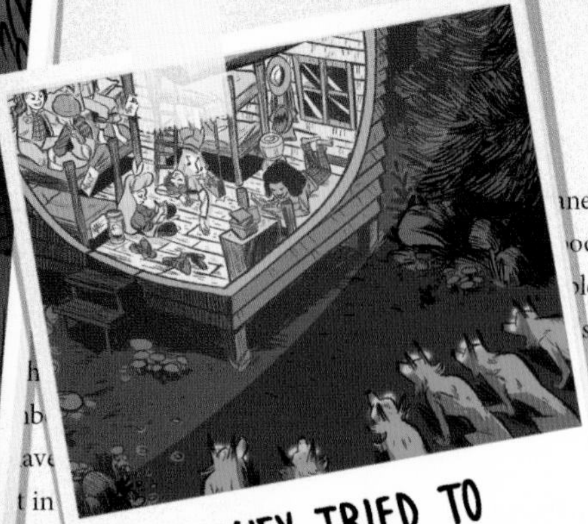

THEY TRIED TO OUT FOX US

...ne.
...od
...le
...s.
...h
...ab
...ave
...t in
...skwi
...dcor
...n, or make it
...lable at the trading post.

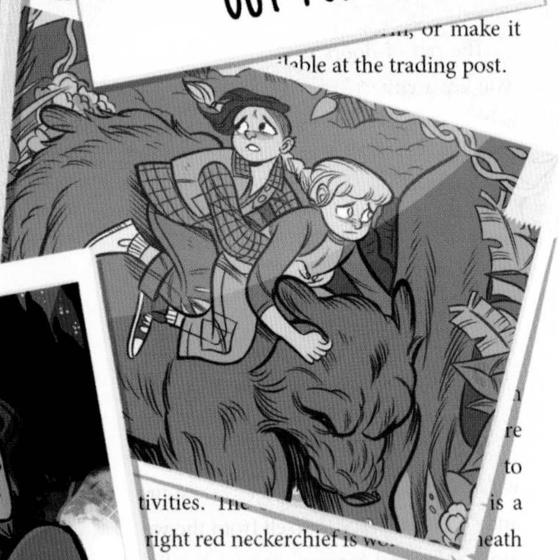

The Lumberjane uniform sh...
meeting...

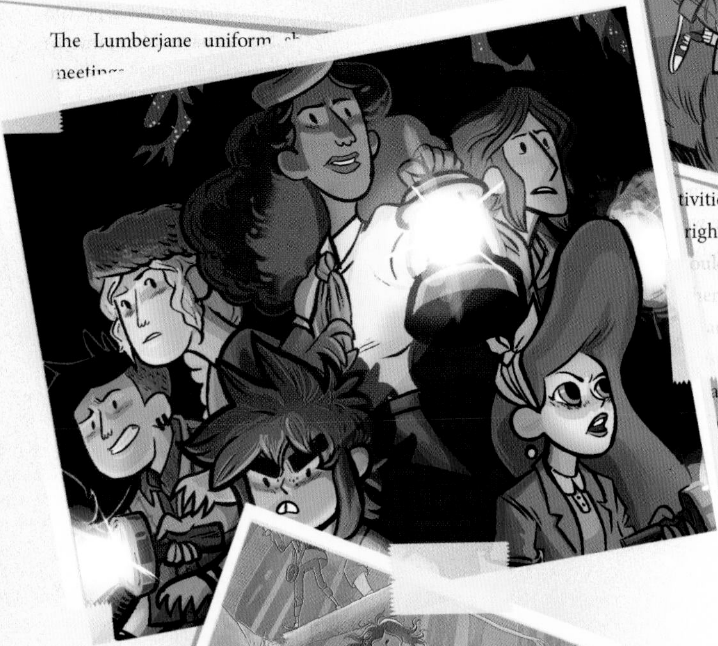

...tivities. The ... is a
...right red neckerchief is wo... neath
...ould be tied in a simple friendship knot.
...lack or brown and should have flat
...a straight inner line. Stockings or
...nd in color with the shoes or with
...aces, bracelets, or other jewelry do not
...erjane uniform.

...WEAR THE UNIFORM

...form demans first of all that the
...ood condition—clean and well
...t is the right length for your own
...e belt is adjusted to your waist,
...kings are in keeping with the
...our posture and carry yourself
...dignity and grace. If the beret is removed indoors, ...e sure that your hair is neat and kept in place with an insonspicuous clip or ribbon. When you wear a Lumberjane uniform you are identified as a member of this organization and you should be doubly careful to conduct yourself in a way that will show everyone that courtesy and thoughtfullness are part of being a Lumberjane. People are likely to judge a whole nation by the selfishness of a few individuals, to criticize a whole family because of the misconduct of one member, and to feel unkindly toward and organization because of the

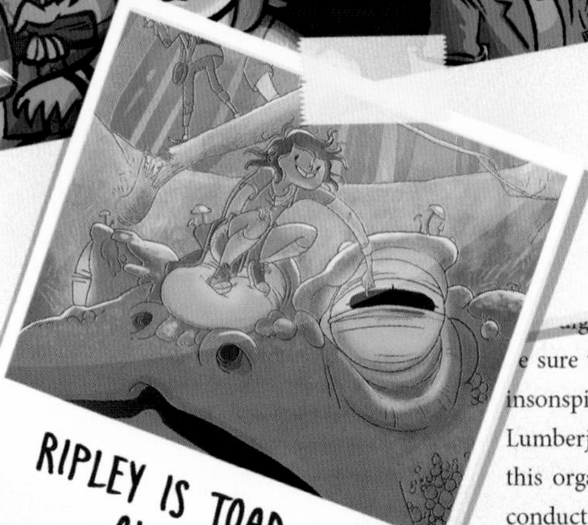

RIPLEY IS TOAD-ALLY AWESOME!

The
helps
in a g...
active
another
future.
in or...
Lumberjane p...
Penniquiqul Thistle Cru... ...y
Types, but most Lumberjanes wi... ...ey
can either buy the uniform, or make it them... ...rom
materials available at the trading post.

COVER GALLERY

Lumberjanes "Out-of-Doors" Program Field

GRUNGEON MASTER BADGE

"Put a pin in it."

There can only be one. Not really, but one day there might be a class where that is the case and it's important to remain vigilant as the lessons taught at this camp adapt and evolve with the times. At camp there will be many obstacles and challenges that the Lumberjanes will face as a team and just as many that they will face on their own. Grunge does not represent the ultimate movement within rock'n roll as every Lumberjane will learn, it is however, it was a great movement of music. Grunge was the last sort of unifying force that brought together a generation and it brought together a variety of people and creatures from any gender, age, or race. It was passionate, exciting, and those are just some of the qualities that we feel it is important for a Lumberjane to understand.

In the practice for the *Grungeon Master* badge, a Lumberjane understand what it means to go underground,

the importance of finding something that will separate her from her peers but will at the same time offer unifying aspect that will show her fellow scouts that while every member of this camp is unique and different, we are also all united in our differences. She will bring out the best of everyone she works with and will strive to bring out the best in herself as well.

To obtain the *Grungeon Master* badge, the Lumberjanes must display their knowledge in the art of plaid. They must be able to look at their challenge and understand where to place a pin and a patch. They must be able to understand what they are capable of and how their actions will affect those around them. This badge is meant to both unify the camp and help each scout show off their uniqueness and their independence. Every creature in this plane must enjoy what makes them different, embrace what separates them from the

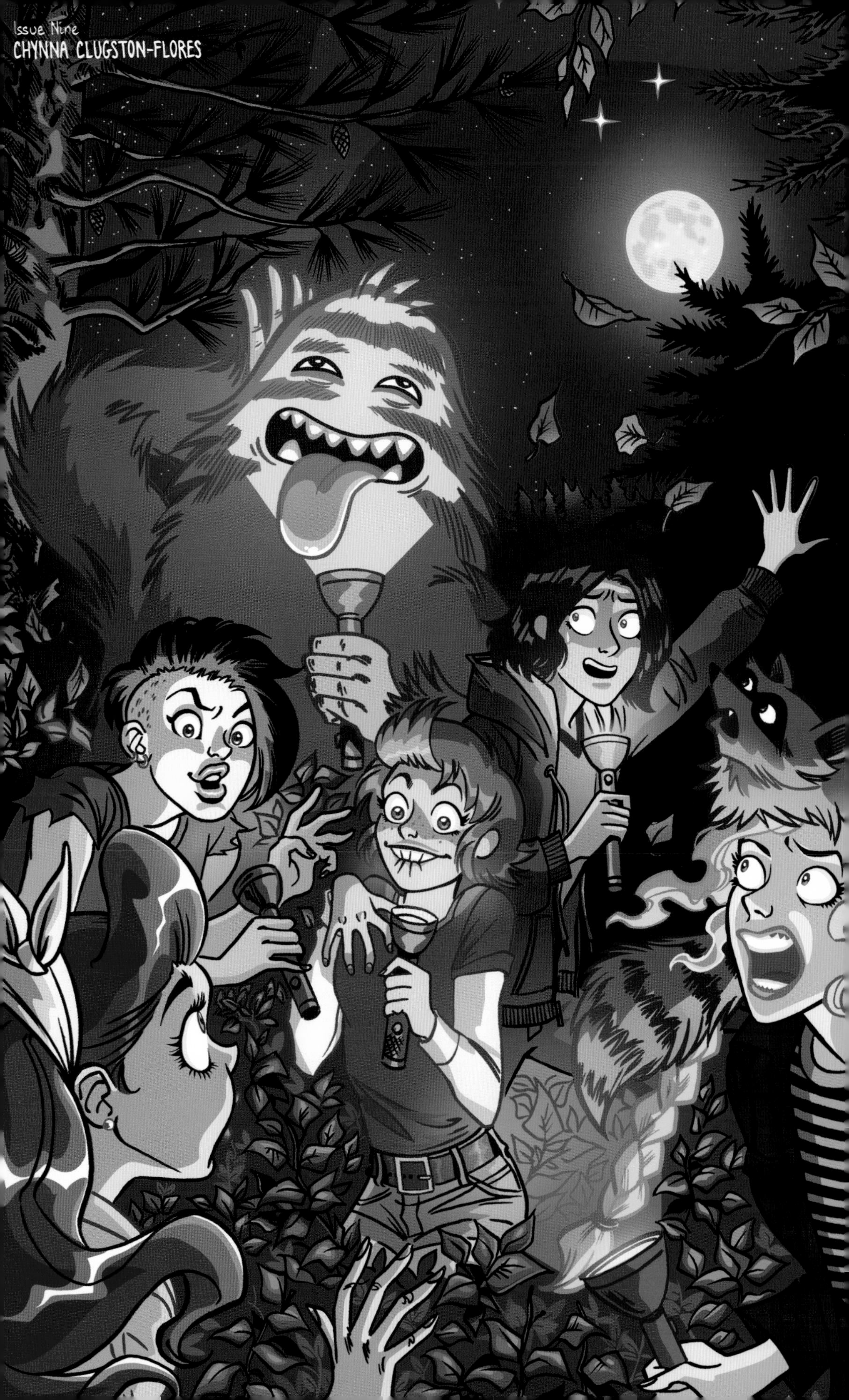

Issue Nine
CHYNNA CLUGSTON-FLORES

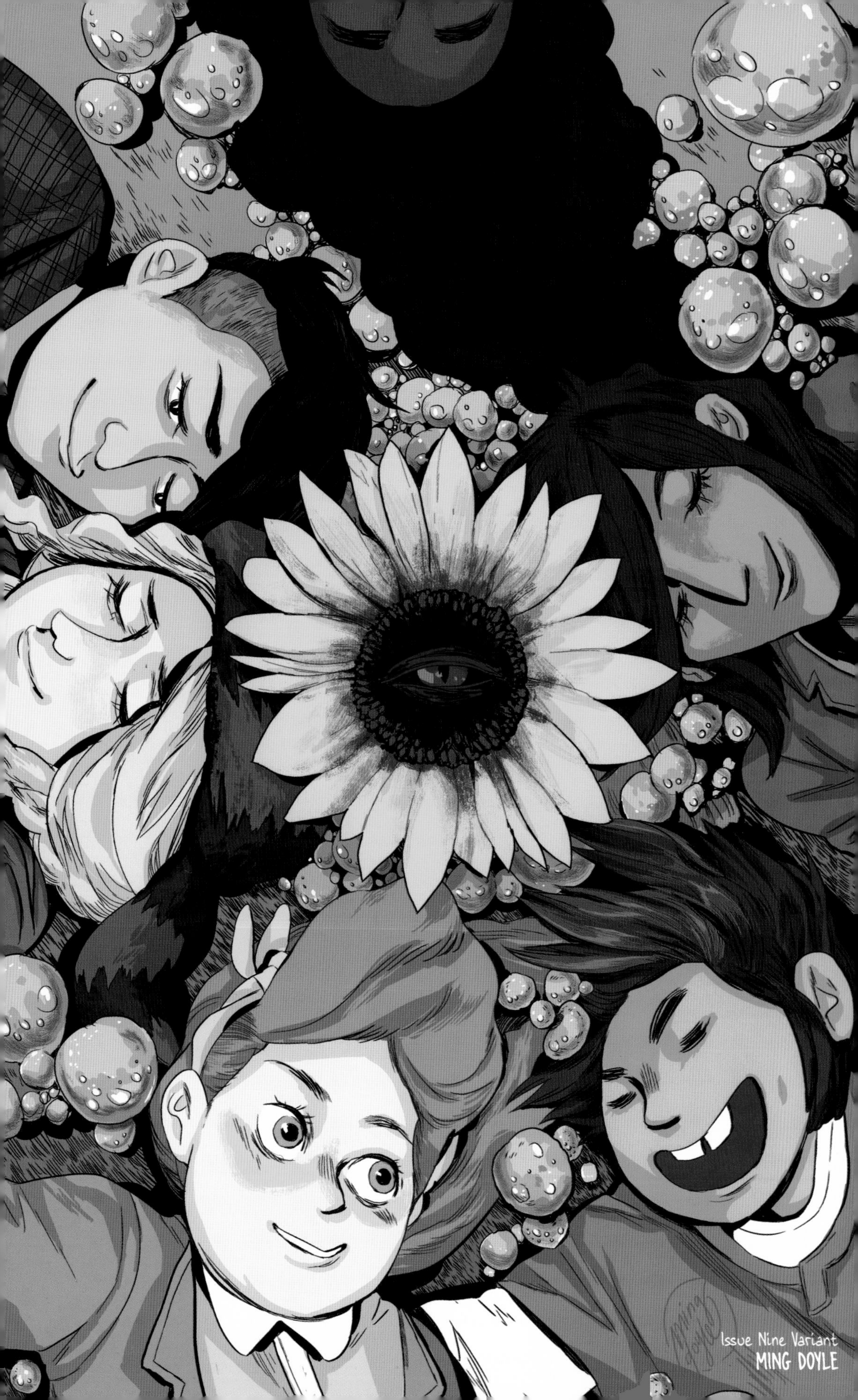
Issue Nine Variant
MING DOYLE

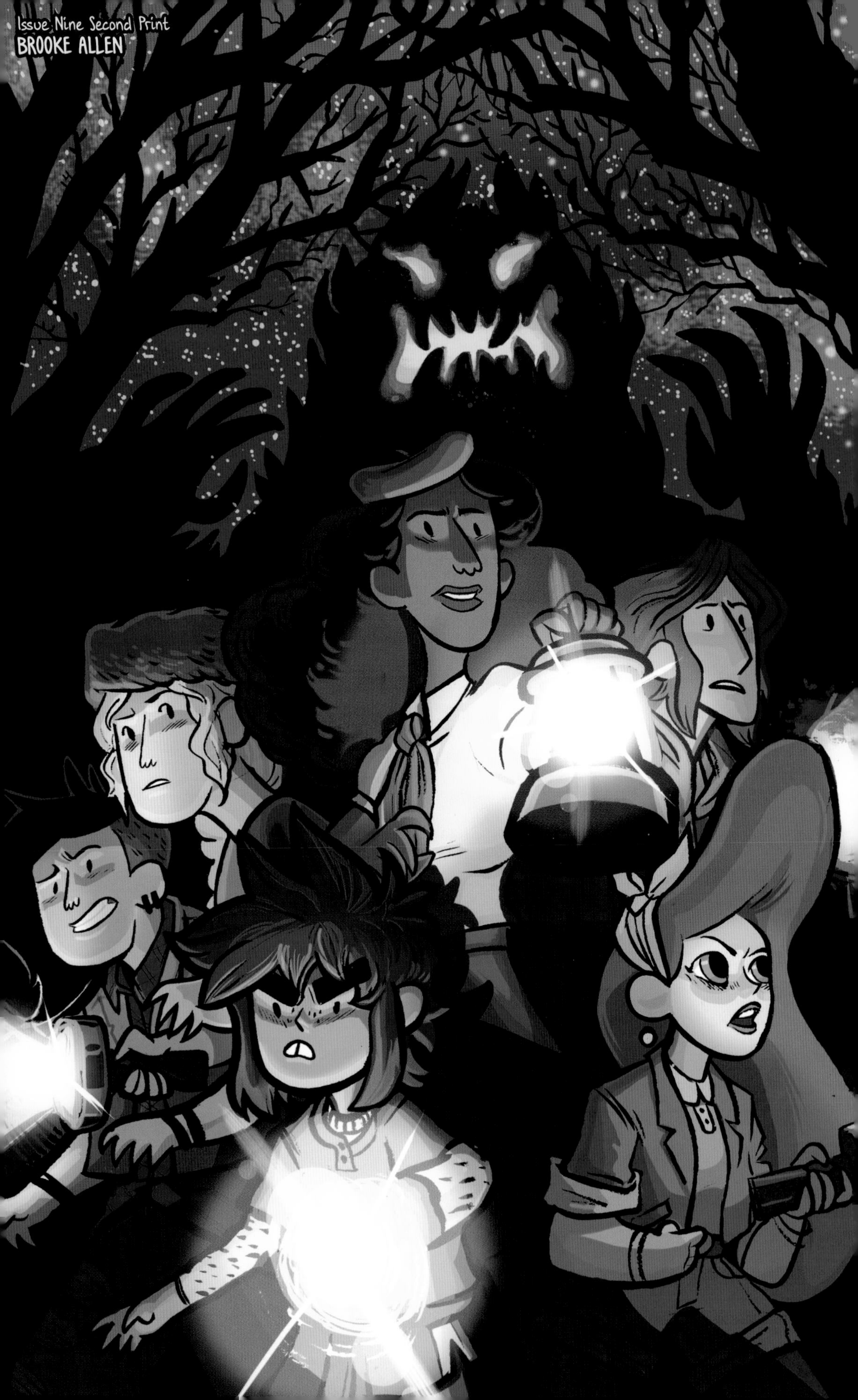

Issue Nine Second Print
BROOKE ALLEN

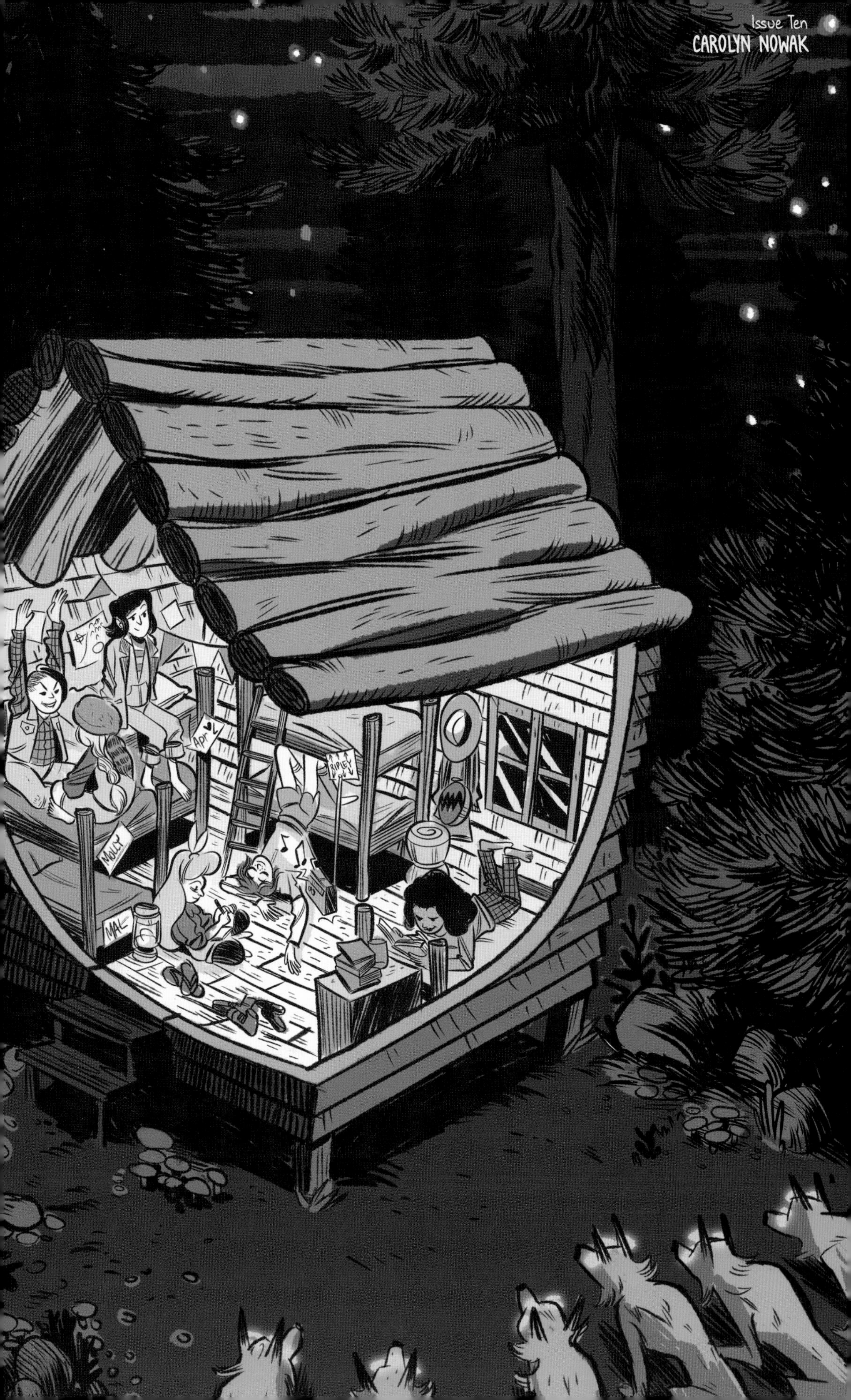
Issue Ten
CAROLYN NOWAK
Apr
RIPLEY
MOLLY
MAL

Issue Ten Variant
KAT LEYH

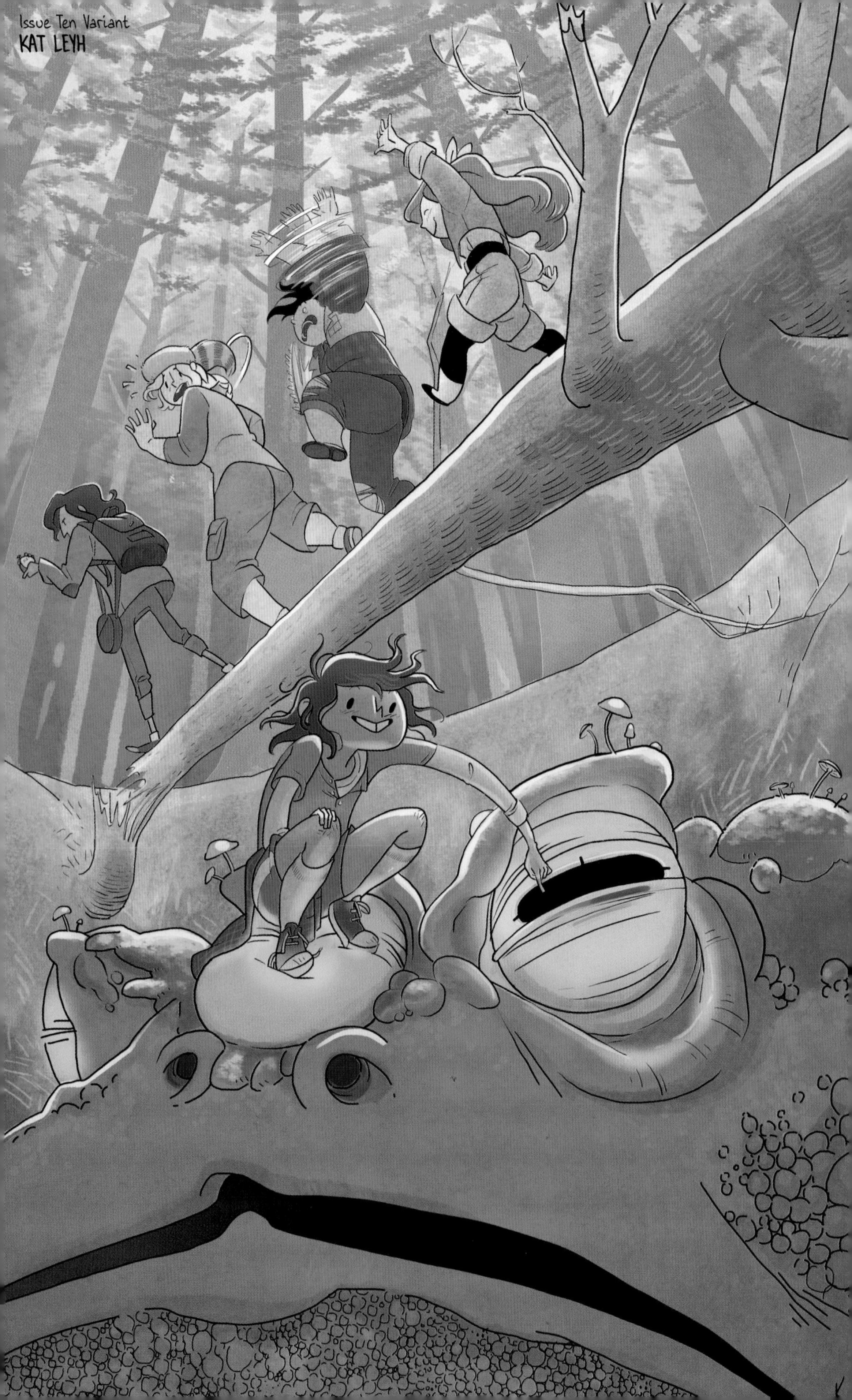

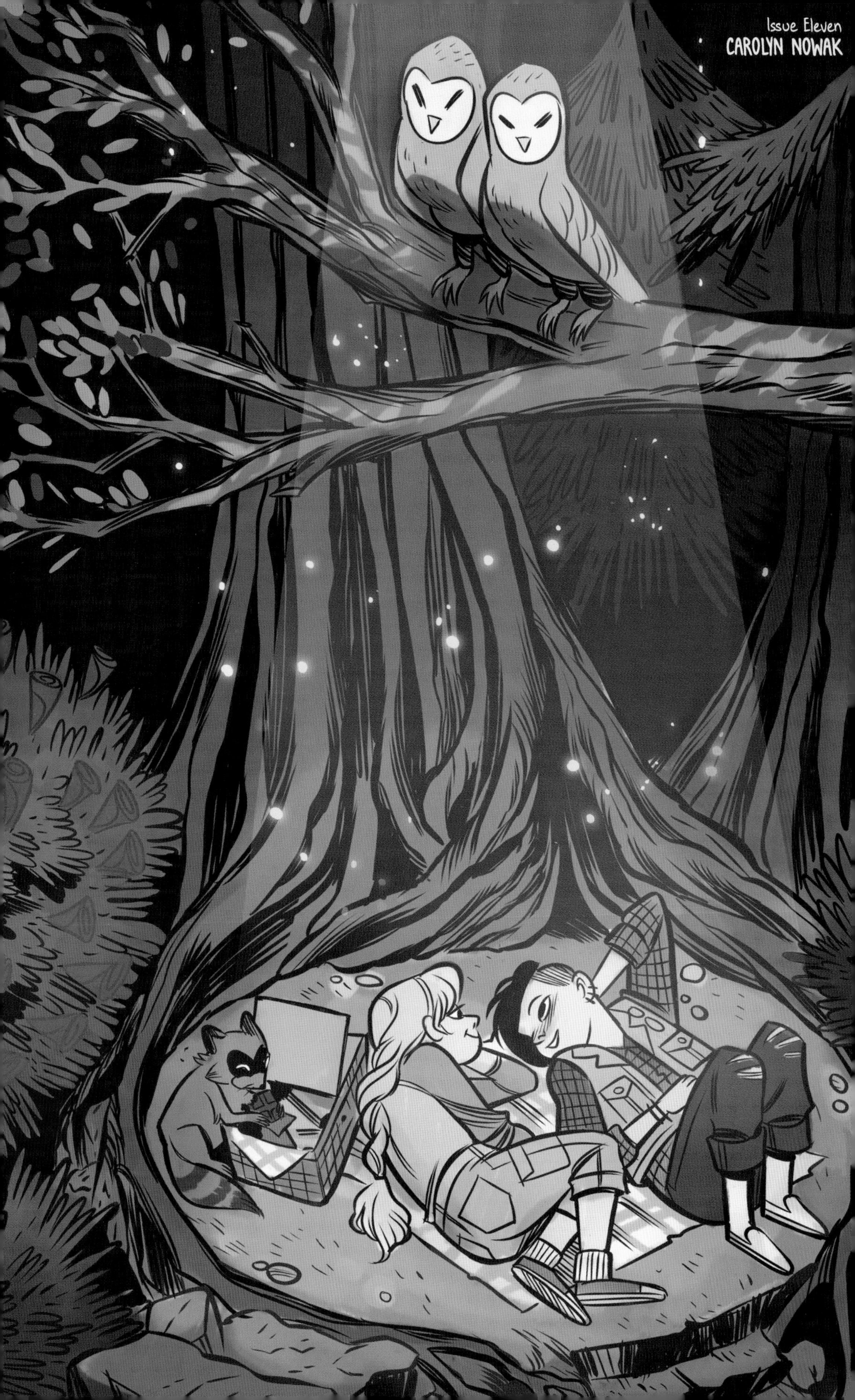
Issue Eleven
CAROLYN NOWAK

Issue Eleven Variant
EMILY HU

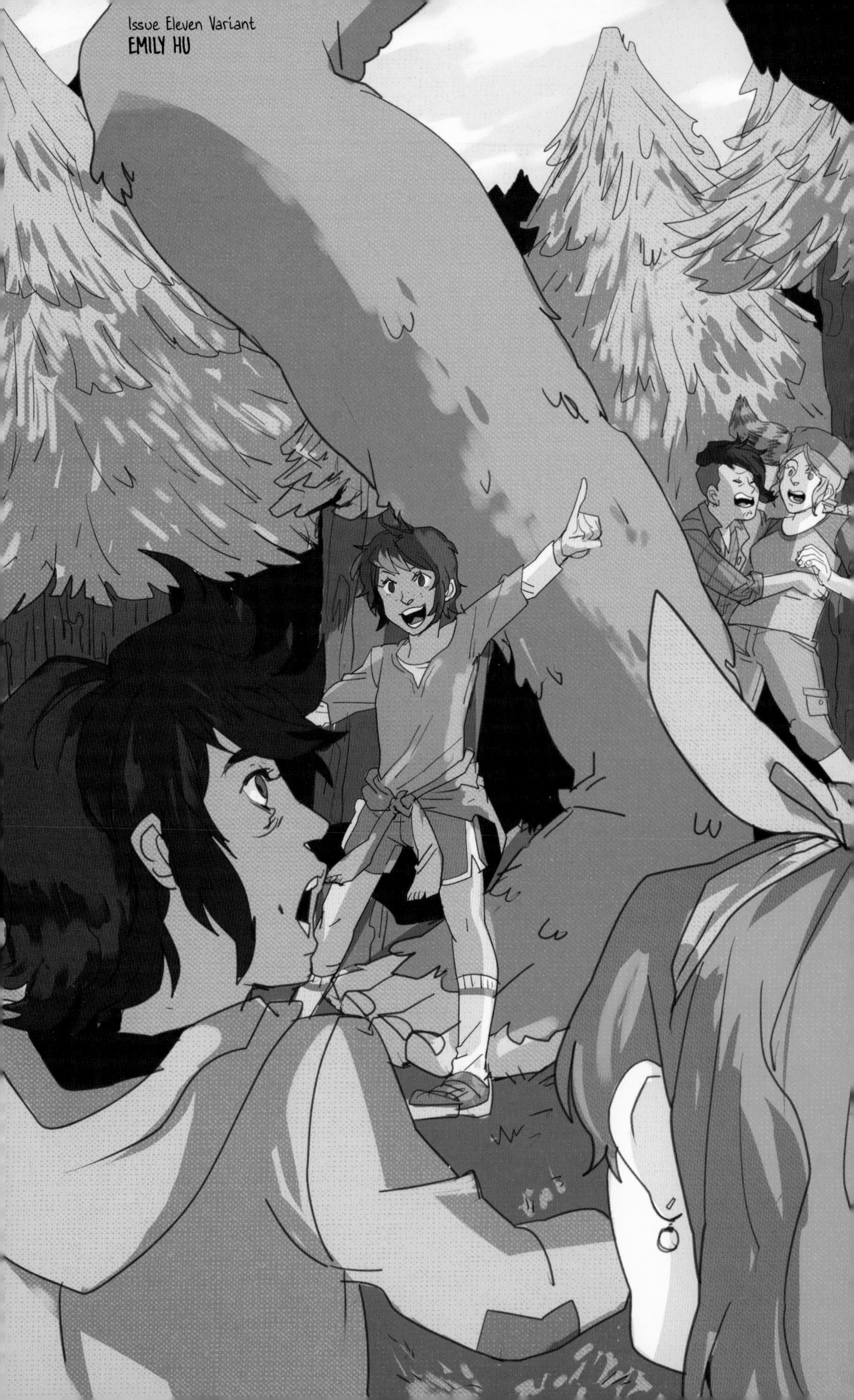

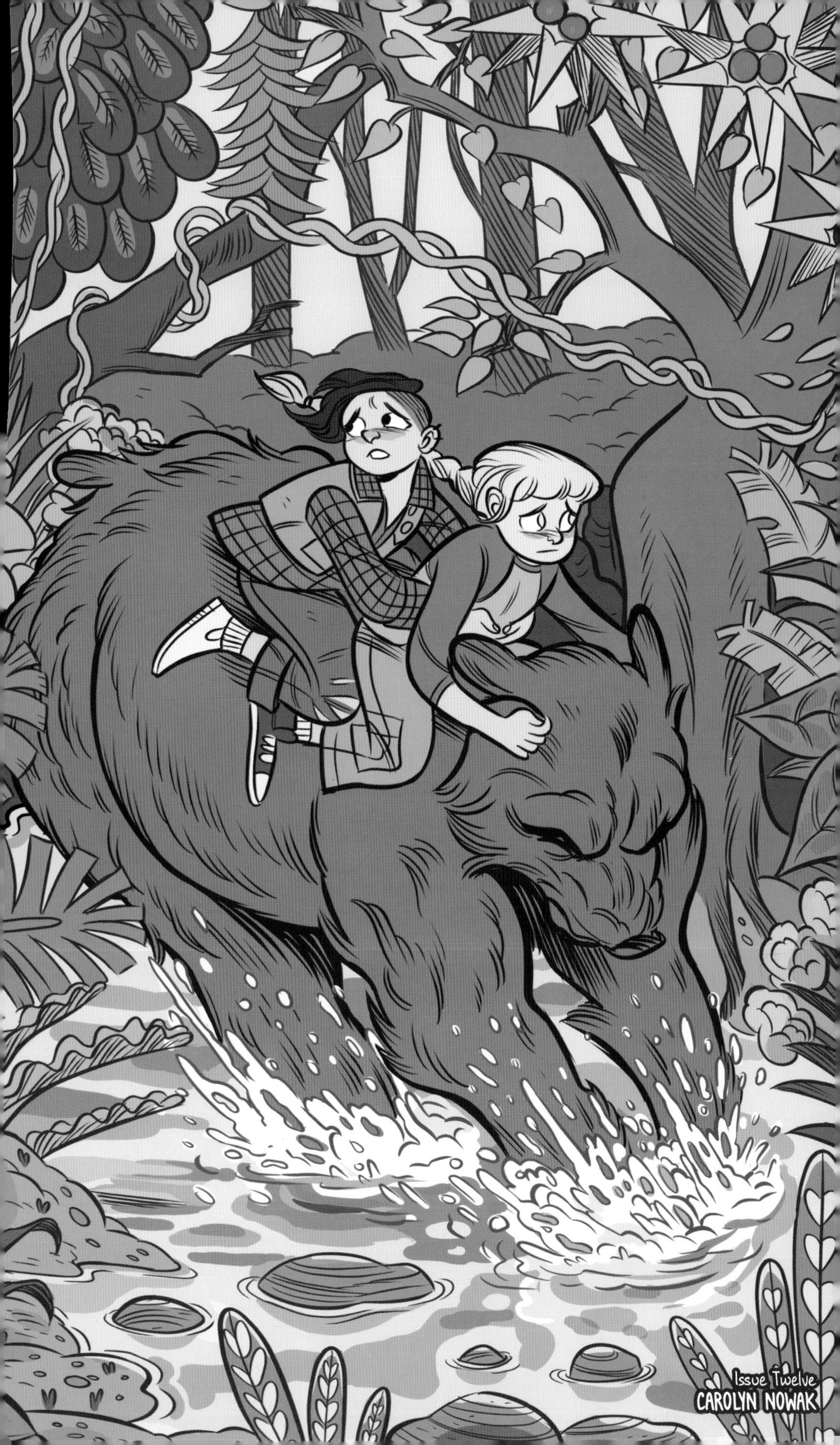

Issue Twelve
CAROLYN NOWAK

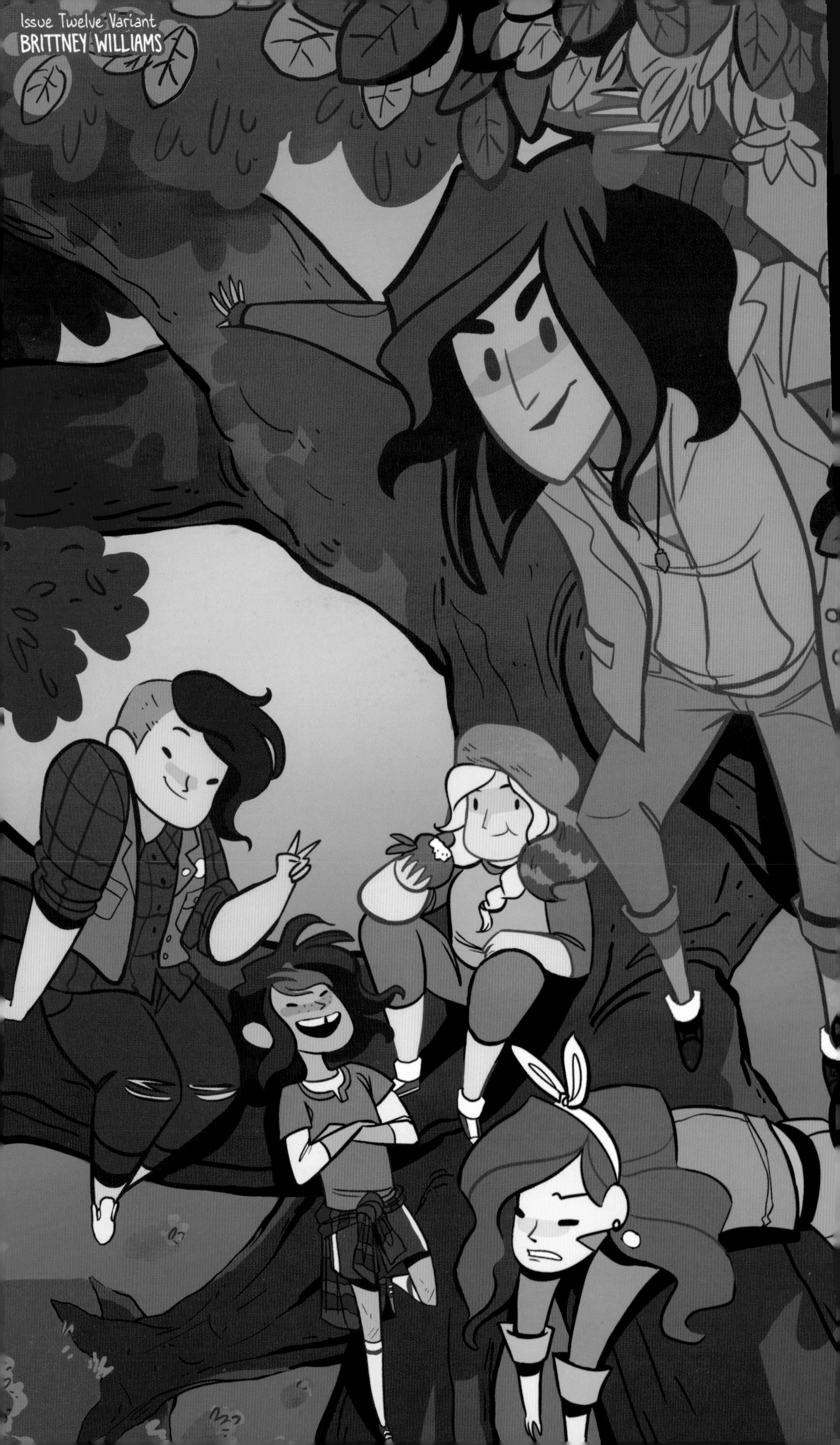
Issue Twelve Variant
BRITTNEY WILLIAMS